Thoughts on Life And the Absolute Power of Thought

Thoughts on Life And the Absolute Power of Thought

By Michael L. Urias

Self-Published with help from
MIDNIGHT EXPRESS BOOKS

Thoughts on Life And the Absolute Power of Thought

Copyright © 2013 by Michael L. Urias

ISBN-13: 978-0692396926 (Midnight Express Books)

ISBN-10: 0692396926

All rights reserved. No part of this book may be reproduced or transmitted in any form or by any means without written permission of the author.

Self-Published with help from
MIDNIGHT EXPRESS BOOKS
POBox 69
Berryville AR 72616
(870) 210-3772
MEBooks1@yahoo.com

Thoughts on Life And the Absolute Power of Thought

By Michael L. Urias

This book is dedicated to:

Leanor Urias

Camile Urias

Geralean Brown

&

Erica Urias

The reality in this book is so, so powerful that you might just overdose on it. One thing is for certain though; you will be extremely intoxicated with enlightenment, motivation, determination, inspiration, and knowledge when you're done reading this book.

This book is in remembrance of one great and true patriot who died in his endeavors to wake people up and expose them to the truth . . . Ex-Navel Officer and author of the astonishing book, "Behold a Pale Horse."

-William Cooper

1946 to 2001

I was dirt poor, and broke, one day and I was crying, because I didn't even have any shoes to put on my feet, and then I looked up and saw a man who had no feet.

--George Noorey

Coast to Coast, AM

Talk Radio Personality

PREFACE...

Now the reality and truth in this book is unabridged and completely uncut and I'm going to give it to you raw meaning not cooked up, sauced, or tampered with in any kind of way, straight raw just the way it is. And the following except you are about to read was first published in the Liberator which was a preeminent abolitionist newspaper started by William Lloyd Garrison on January 1, 1831 and what he said in that excerpt is just how I feel about what I wrote in this book:

I will be as harsh as truth, and as uncompromising as justice. On this subject, I do not wish to think, to speak, to write with moderation. No, no! Tell a man whose house is on fire to give a moderate alarm, tell him to moderately rescue his wife from the hands of the ravisher, tell the mother to gradually extricate her baby from the fate into which it has fallen but urge me not to use moderation in a cause like the present!! I am in earnest – I will not equivocate – I will not excuse, I will not retreat a single word or inch and I will be heard...

--William Lloyd Garrison

1805-1879

1. Now in this first thought I want to introduce, and acquaint you, with a phrase that you are going to be running across quite frequently in this book. And this phrase is one of the main themes and subjects of this book. So therefore when you run across this phrase I want you to fully and thoroughly understand, and know, what this phrase means and stands for. This phrase is: Those who clandestinely control the U.S. government. Now for you to be able to fully understand who those who clandestinely control the U.S. government are, what they do, and what they stand for I must give you at least a concise history on them. And yes I said them, because they are a group of people and they go by many names that have been operating in the world for the last 200 or so years. Now this group that I'm talking about like I said goes by many different names they have been called the secret government, the international bankers, the global elite, the shadow government, the intrepid omnipotent hidden hand, and the money magicians because they virtually own or control all of the world's finances. But I could go on forever with the names that have been ascribed to them I simply call them: Those who clandestinely control the U.S. government. Now in this book you are going to learn how those who clandestinely control the U.S. government have actually ran, and controlled the world from behind the scenes for the last 200 or so years. And these are not just my views but I'll be naming myriad other authors from various eras and times who have written whole books and dissertations on how those who clandestinely control the U.S. government have not only surreptitiously controlled America but the whole world for the last 200 or so years. Now I know that to the average person, I know that this sounds outrageous or completely impossible. But please bear with me, and believe me it's not, and the truth of what's been going on and really goes on in the world has been suppressed away from the masses of people is both a reality and a shock. Now this reality that I speak of is that damn near every major global negative event and some events that were really negative in intent, but were made to look plausibly positive on the surface (like the creation of our Federal Reserve system) were engineered and created by those who clandestinely control the U.S. government. Now the events that I speak of are events such as World War I, the 1917 Russian Revolution, World War II, and

the creation of Hitler, political assassinations such as the JFK assassination, and myriad other wars, violent revolutions, conflicts, intrigues, and terrorist attacks, that those who clandestinely control the U.S. governments have made and or caused to happen for their own benefit. Now like I said before this might sound crazy, outrageous, or impossible that any one group could have such unequivocal power. But like I said please bear with me and believe me, it's true. And the preponderance of evidence when looked at from an objective point of view decisively substantiates this. Now I know you're going to ask how or by what means any group or organization can wield such unequivocal and absolute power over the world. And I'm going to answer that. . . and the answer is that those who clandestinely control the U.S. government surreptitiously control from the top down all aspects of politics, religion, commerce, industry, academics, banking, the media, insurance, mining, and even the illicit drug trade. Now this labyrinth control did not just start it has been going on here in America for at least the last 150 years. And in this book in subsequent thoughts I will explain how this interlinking of power allows those who clandestinely control the U.S. government to actually and literally control America from behind the scenes. Now when you read thoughts like thought #460 which tells the story of how those who clandestinely control the U.S. government created, and own, and control the Federal Reserve System, which is the system that creates and controls our money here in America. And you read though #410 which tells how those who clandestinely control the U.S. government control and own all the major banks in America. And thought #408 which tells you how those who clandestinely control the U.S. government control nations, and governments, through money, and aid, and thought #406 which tells how those who clandestinely control the U.S. government run their organization and get and recruit members, and thought #405 which tells how those who clandestinely control the U.S. government caused 9-11-2001 terrorist attacks on our nation, and how they use wars, and conflicts to their own advantage. And thought #404 which tells how those who clandestinely control the U.S. government have been surreptitiously infecting America with cancer since the 1960's under what they call population control. And thought #412 which tells how those who clandestinely control the U.S. government have been since the late 1940's suppressing the truth about UFO's, aliens, and the underground cities where these aliens live. And thought #436 which tells of all the groups, cliques, organizations, and secret societies both overt, and covert that are controlled by those who clandestinely control the U.S. government. Then you will begin to understand how those who clandestinely control the U.S. government exert their power over American and the world. Now the thoughts I just named are but just a few, a fraction of the many thoughts that you are going to be coming across in this book that speak on those who clandestinely control the U.S. government. And which thoughts will be mixed in myriad other extremely uplifting, enlightening, and informing thoughts on life, nature, and the universe.

2. It's been said that governments control their people by making the people think they control the government.

3. Our government is no longer by the people, for the people, and from the people. Today our government is by the elite, and from the elite.

–Henry A. Wallace

4. The level of blindness and ignorance here in America has now reached the level of insanity.

–Ruddy D. J. Botty

5. The man who never looks into a newspaper is better informed that he who reads them, because he who knows nothing is nearer the truth that he whose mind is filled with falsehoods and errors.

–Thomas Jefferson

6. I know of no better way for the state to keep its people under control than a perpetual state of war.

–Joseph Stalin, 1879 to 1953. Former Soviet Dictator

Thoughts on Life And the Absolute Power of Thought

7. I have been a school teacher in our public schools for 12 years using history books, which I was later to learn blatantly distorted many important facts. I bumbled along reading the daily newspapers and magazines and listening to the news on T.V. and radio, not realizing more important political news is distorted and believing the problems I and the other average Americans were experiencing just happened.

  – Acclaimed Author and Writer, Len Martin

8. Always remember that people's thinking more times than not always fail them, because of its shallowness. People often mistake breath for depth, believing that with a quick scrutiny they can become familiar with any subject. Always remember that concerning education and learning there is no better education or learning than practical learning and/or education.

9. Reality, as Simon Moon said, "Is thermoplastic, not thermosetting. It is not quite silly-putty, as Mr. Paul Krassner once claimed, but is much closer to silly-putty than we generally realize."

  -- The Illuminatus Trilogy – 1975

10. Every man who gets anywhere does so because he first formally resolves to progress in the world and then has enough stick-to-itiveness to transform his resolution into reality. – excerpt from an article in Forbes Magazine, January 7th, 1922

11. Always remember and this is very real that one of the meanings of faith is: even if you don't know, have no answer, you will eventually know and have the answer. And if you believe that in the depths of your soul faith will absolutely, immutably, and without any question work for you. And I speak from personal experience . . . it worked for me. And those of you old enough who have experienced faith know exactly what I'm talking about here.

12. Always remember that as long as you are in this material physical world you are always going to experience and go through misunderstandings, arguments, debates, and

disagreements with other people, it's absolutely inevitable, but the thing to know and understand is that getting into it with people is rudimentary to the world. And it's not the end of the world when you get into it with somebody as long as you and the other person or persons don't get carried away with it and remain somewhat level headed it's nothing but something that happens, always will happen and passes. It will be alright. But all I'm trying to convey here is that getting into it with people is both inevitable and an immutable part of life. The only thing is how you deal with it when it happens.

13. Let me say something for those of you who don't think or doubt that God is omnificent and omnipotent. And that's that God in all his omniscience already gave you everything and anything that you could ever want, and how you might ask. Well, through your God given innate ability to create virtually anything and everything that you may ever want via and through your thoughts. And this is one of the great secrets. And also part of the Arcanum . . . believe that! This book was meant to disclose and impart some of the Arcanum to the average everyday person.

14. All men who have turned out worth anything have had the chief hand in their education.

–Sir alter Scott

15. Always remember that most of the things that we go through, we ourselves, for the most part, put ourselves through whatever we're going through. Why because of how and what we think . . . our thoughts. Because they do manifest. So please believe what I'm about to say, if you change your thoughts, and your thinking, you'll change a whole lot for yourself both inwardly and outwardly.

16. Always remember that people always have, and always will, play many types of games in their actions and interactions with other people. And lest you forget people have many facades that they portray.

17. Now in the next thought I'm going to give you an analogy and I want you to be totally objective as you read it. It goes as follows:

18. What would you think of a man who kept an arsenal in his home? And not only that, was collecting this arsenal at an enormous financial sacrifice to himself. What would you say if this man so frightened his neighbors that they in turn were collecting weapons to protect themselves from him? What if this man spent ten times as much money on his expensive weapons as he did on the education of his children? What if one of his children criticized his strange endeavors and he called that child a traitor, a bum and disowned him? And he took another child who obeyed and listened to him faithfully and armed that child and sent him into the neighborhood to attack the neighbors? For unfounded, and unjustifiable reasons. Just because they wouldn't listen to his dictates. And what would you say if this man had an inordinate voracious need to spy on his family and all the neighbors, and was secretly collecting dossiers on all of them? And not only that, but had an inherent propensity to control his family and all who he came in contact with? What would you say if this same man introduced poisons into the water that the people on his block and his neighbors drank? And what if this man is not only feuding with the people on his block, but involves himself in the quarrels of others in distant parts of the city and even the state? Such a man would clearly be a paranoid schizophrenic . . . with homicidal and even suicidal tendencies. Now this man is what the U.S. government has now become. And if this man would legally be labeled clinically insane. Why is the U.S. government not now labeled clinically insane?

19. A whole spectrum of crimes are committed every day. Crimes of the heart, corporate crimes, legal crimes, political crimes, and genocidal crimes.

–Woody Allen

20. Always remember that opportunity lies in everything that you see if you're creative. And how much opportunity lies there just depends on how creative you are.

21. Always remember that the entire world loves a winner and has no time for a loser. And remember that a quitter never wins and a winner never quits.

22. Always remember that anything acquired without effort and/or without cost is going to be, more times than not, unappreciated.

23. Always remember that in life everybody has a chance, and this is regardless of cultural, racial, economic, political social, or environmental, background to be great, wealthy, successful, or whatever they wish to be. Just as long as, and this is the key, that they believe in the debts of their soul that they can be. But also remember that you won't be the first nor the last to be great, wealthy, or successful. Because there has been myriad great, wealthy, and successful people before you and there will be myriad great, wealthy and successful people after you.

24. Always remember that here in America the majority of the poor, not all of the poor, but the vast majority of the poor, are poor because they want to be poor. And do you know what the coldest and saddest part of that is, it's that they didn't even consciously know that they choose and want to be poor. And that is for the simple fact that they're not doing anything about being poor or in poverty. Because the first step to achieving, attaining, acquiring or doing anything, is believing. One must first before anything else believe that he or she can do, or have whatever he or she wants. And then once he or she really believes in the depths of his or her soul then everything else will flow from there. Now back to the point at hand, the vast majority of the poor are poor or in poverty because they just simply believe that they can't be wealthy or do better for themselves . . . point blank, and for that reason they are poor or in poverty and will stay that way. And for those who want to blame the hand that they were dealt for their situation or circumstances I beg to differ they need to read the story of Helen Keller.

25. Always remember that knowledge of what is possible is the beginning of happiness and all things are possible if you believe they are.

26. Always remember that problems, hurt, and pain, are an immutable part of life. It's just how you perceive them and react to them that matters. If you perceive and react to them positively then you will grow, gain, learn, and become stronger through them. But if you perceive them negatively then they will without a doubt most definitely take you down. And when I say that they will take you down I mean they will take you down emotionally, physically, financially, spiritually, and in many other conceivable myriad ways.

27. Always remember that the more you realize that you don't know about life and the world is really the wiser and smarter you're getting.

28. Always remember that there are many people whose every waking hour is filled with something to do, but nonetheless, they still feel that their lives are pointless and meaningless. Why, well, that's simple, because they are not in tune with themselves and are stuck in what's known as extro vertism. Sad, but yet again . . . so true.

29. I like to call this book the book of life. Why? Because if you read it, understand it, and take heed to it, it will open up your eyes to unabridged truth and will set you free from the prison of lies, deception, ignorance, manipulation, and craftiness that now holds you prisoner. And I'm going to say this, it's one thing to be physically in prison . . . okay! You know that you're locked up, but to be mentally in a prison, and have no idea whatsoever that you're locked up is the coldest of them all . . . and has no equal. And that's just what this book sets out to do, and that's to set you mentally free. And how does it go about doing that by giving you unabridged truth. And therefore, enabling you to be mentally free so you can live the life that you were meant to live. That's why I like to call this book the book of life, and I guarantee you one thing that after you read this book you'll never forget it.

30. Now in this thought here I just want to concisely say, and you'll learn that this is so true once you start to read, and learn, and free yourself from that mental prison. And that's that so much knowledge has been systematically suppressed that it is really and literally beyond believe. It is impossible to try and sit here and explain and tell you how much knowledge has been systematically suppressed by those who clandestinely control the U.S. government and their predecessors. I mean it's like this, and this is the best way I can possibly put it to you. And this is no lie. . . if you had one hundred books and each book held one hundred thousand pages, you still could not list all the knowledge in virtually all areas and things that has been suppressed, and hid away from you . . . the masses of people. But I will tell you one thing, suppressed knowledge is starting to leak out, and the truth of the knowledge is starting to set people free from their mental prisons. And my god, that's a beautiful thing. This book and the books this book makes reference to are but one drop of an ocean of knowledge that has been suppressed and hid away from you . . . the masses of people. And I'll say this in closing, this thought, if you stay getting your knowledge and information from just the mainstream, I guarantee you, and absolutely assure you, that you will stay locked in a mental prison all of your days, because the mainstream in all its facets is unequivocally owned and controlled by those who clandestinely control the U.S. government.

31. Always remember that reality is real and one must stay in reality no matter how outrageous, surreal, unbelievable, or incredulous it is. Think about that, and it was once said that absolute truth, and absolute reality, are more times than not hidden from view by people's incredulousness.

32. Always remember that the world is a rough, sometimes cold, and dangerous place, so don't misunderstand it. (Please!)

33. Always remember that there is a whole lot of good in the world, you better believe it, but you also must understand that there is a lot of uncut and pure evil here in the world. And one doesn't necessarily overtake the other, as most believe. Because each one, good and evil, have their own constituents.

And are therefore supported in thought, deed, and action. And are therefore kept alive by their own individual constituencies. And this applies both here in the physical, as well as, in the supernatural realms. And remember that people have absolute free wills to support and/or do good or evil, wrong or right.

34. Always remember that you are capable of absolute evolvement, and absolute creativity. And you can without question have and create anything that you want via, and through your thoughts. And do you want to know the key to that? Well the key to that is meditation. You must meditate on whatever you want. And I don't care if it takes you a day, a month, or years to get what you want. As long as you keep meditating on it, I guarantee that you'll get it.

35. I have never been poor, only broke. Because being poor is a frame of mind. And being broke is only a temporary situation.

–Mike Todd

36. Remember self-esteem is the reputation that we have acquired with ourselves.

–Nathaniel Brandon

37. Always remember that the control that those who clandestinely control the U.S. government exert and exercise over the world and people is so intricate, so labyrinth, so profound, so wide-ranging, so sophisticated, and abstruse, and so camouflaged, that one would literally, and I mean this, literally have to be extremely knowledgeable and well advance in human nature, extremely proficient in all forms of deception and manipulation, and have at least a general understanding of how God and the universe really work. And I most definitely don't mean the general understanding that the churches and religions put out. And then one may began, and notice I said begin, to grasp and understand the control that those who clandestinely control the U.S. government have been and are exerting and exercising over the world . . . and the masses of people. And note that the prerequisites that I just named are absolutely imperative to understanding the control exerted by those who

clandestinely control the U.S. government. And without them, please understand that it is almost virtually impossible to understand or grasp the control that I speak of.

38. Always remember to do what you can do when you can do it. Or otherwise, you might lose . . . remember that!

39. Always remember that in this life and in this world that we live in there is absolutely nothing that is perfect. And when I say nothing, I mean absolutely nothing perfect. There's no perfect marriage, relationship, job, church, school, upbringing . . . nothing. And most definitely no perfect people. So please, remember that in this material and physical world that we live in, nothing is perfect . . . everything is going to have flaws, side-effects, and/or problems of some type or kind no matter what it is . . . and that most definitely includes people.

40. Always remember that no matter what you do. And I don't care what you do. You want to shine. And do it with force and energy. But at the very same time, you want to have style, class, and grace about yourself. And remember that nothing worth anything comes easy. Hard work in vast assortments is the only order of the day and if you aren't with that, then please don't kid yourself, because nine times out of ten there is no free lunch. For anything really worth anything, especially, if you're aiming for the top or to be great. Because let me tell you like this in this physical realm that we live in we must strive, push, and will everything that we want and/or desire into existence. Because if not, believe me we won't have nothing . . . please believe that. Because all that that you got to just let things flow and everything will be alright. And what's meant to happen is going to happen is straight bullshit, but a good number of people believe that. And you can't tell them anything else. So sad to say, but very true they just wait for something to fall from the sky in their lap which is the exception and not the rule. Because if what was meant was true or the rule. Now use common sense here don't you think the world after all these eons would already be fixed or right? Exactly! I think so too, and we all know the world is far from being right, or fixed. So therefore waiting on what's meant has got to be the exception or seriously lacking in something I just

don't know what. You feel me?! Because believe it or not in this realm (the physical) you have to do for you period. And I don't give a damn what nobody says – there is no and, ifs, or buts about it. And if you as an individual start to strive, push, and will what you want into your existence, then you will not only be taking yourself, but you will be taking your life to a higher and much more regenerated level. And if we as a collective would do that we would cause a shift in the mass consciousness for the good and or positive. Meaning we would cause the mass consciousness to reach a critical mass, in the form of humanity being taken to a much higher, enlightened, and regenerated level. But remember that it all starts with you as an individual and nobody else. And that's the key. You must resolve to live life in this physical realm to the fullest and this is without any exceptions. And you must not just say this. But you must mean this in the depths of your soul. And not just that, but you must put all, and any, necessary action or actions behind that. Like I said, hard work is the only order of the day if you want anything that's worth anything in this life. And let me say this as I bring this thought to a close and that's that you can do it if only you'll resolve to do it, and absolutely believe in the depths of your soul that you can do it. And I believe and know that you can do it if you'll only believe and resolve that you can do it. And that you will stop at nothing within reason short of death to achieve your goals. Praise the Lord. So let's go people, and I don't care how old you are. It's never too early or too late to start doing something especially for yourself. And remember this, doing is synonymous with living . . . so get up and start living, living for yourself if you haven't been.

41. Always remember that it was Sir George Wallace who made famous the slogan "that there is a not a dime's worth of difference between the democrat and republican parties." Many observers have noted that while the two parties use different rhetoric and aim their spiels at differing segments of the population. It seems to make little difference who actually wins the election. The reason for this is that while grass root democrats and republicans generally have greatly differing views on economy, political policies, and federal endeavors.

As you climb the sides of the political pyramid the two parties become more and more alike until at the very top they are . . . and actually become one.

42. Always remember that real and true happiness is deep, deep, within yourself. And only you can reach deep within yourself and excavate and bring out this real and true happiness that's innate, and dormant within you. And the only way you can do this is by getting in tune with yourself.

43. Always remember that in the real world, and in life, in a lot of instances and in a lot of situations, one has no choice but to be a victimizer or to become a victim. And this might not sound right, but nonetheless you better believe me it's true.

44. Always remember that we human beings have an absolute, total, and completely unabridged free will, and people really don't understand that, because that's a whole lot of unbridled power. And when that free will is misused meaning not used in harmony with God's laws and I'm not talking about some church's, or religion's laws, but I'm talking about God's true and real universal laws there are ramifications and those ramifications when we misuse our free will's are sin for you and the world. And this just goes to illustrate that man and not God or any other thing or entity brought sin into this world and continue to create sin in this world. And contrary to many churches and other religious dogma, for God to arbitrarily get rid of or put an end to sin would be for Him to abridge, and abate, our free will which He would never do. So it is on man to get rid of sin because it's his creature and not God's or anybody else's. And like I just told you a completely unbridled free will is a whole lot of power which is just what we got. And remember, through man's wrongful exercise of his free will sin was created so therefore it will be through man's exercise of his free will in a righteous way that sin will be eradicated. But nonetheless it will be through the use of man's own free will that sin will be eradicated. That's why I tell you, and been telling you to use your free will and choose to be positive in your thoughts, and actions so that you will be able to start to eradicate sin out of your life and the world. Because if we don't do it God isn't going to do it. Then nobody's going

to do it, and then we human beings will just be stuck indefinitely with sin. Primarily because of a lack of real and true knowledge of how God and the universe really work. And just so you know it's wrong and a sin for somebody to say or think that God created, or creates, or allows sin to exist. Because like I just told you sin is the ramification of the wrongful exercise of our free wills so therefore God has absolutely nothing to do with it, sin. And just keeping it real if you don't understand that then I don't know what to tell you.

45. Now, I'm going to briefly endeavor to explain why people in this world sometime's do what they do, meaning why they sometimes steal, manipulate, lie, cheat, and even kill well that's because this world is now, and has been for eons completely permeated with sin. So therefore this world is far from perfect, or right, and is in no way in harmony with God's universal laws right now. So out of necessity, and pure survival, people sometimes steal, manipulate, lie, cheat, and even kill. Now I'm not speaking for all people here, because some people do, and indulge, in the aftermentioned for no other reason than just because. But I'm speaking on people who out of pure necessity and survival sometimes indulge in the aftermentioned. Now my personal opinion about that is, well, me knowing, and having profound experience in the real and practical world is that there really not wrong. Now don't get me wrong, I'm not condoning and promoting the aftermentioned in no kind of way. But I live in reality and in the real world. So all I can say is be no fool and know where you're at and understand that the world is permeated with sin, but that doesn't negate you from doing your part to get it right.

46. Always remember that everybody is not crafty, sneaky, and manipulative in the same way. But people are crafty, sneaky, and manipulative each in their own unique and individual way. So don't think that just because a person is not crafty, sneaky, and manipulative in one way that he or she cannot be or is not crafty, sneaky, and manipulative in other ways, or in their own ways.

47. Always remember you'll be amazed at what you'll be able to do once you start to break down and get rid of your mental blocks and barriers that consist of myriad "I can'ts," "I just don't have the time," "I don't know how," and "I'm scared," and replace them with I can, I know I can, I will and I'll find or make time, point blank. And you need to ponder on these extremely positive thoughts, meaning thinking them over and over again in your head and saying them to yourself under your breath . . . "I can, I will, I know I can, I'm going to do this and succeed at it." And you'll be amazed at what you'll be able to achieve, accomplish, and attain once you start to break down all those mental blocks and barriers that you have put in your mind either consciously or unconsciously over the years.

48. Always remember that failing, making mistakes, messing up, fucking up, missing the point, not being perfect, and basically just falling flat on your face are all natural. And believe it or not are all just as natural as falling down when you were learning how to walk. And the reason that I'm saying this is because I know from experience that there are people out there who are under the delusion. And believe me that is just what it is a delusion that they can never ever make a mistake that they must be perfect in every way imaginable, which is just crazy, unreal, and straight delusional. Now you must remember that the human mind is not infallible meaning that it is capable of and can make mistakes and errors. And if you think otherwise you are truly delusional. Now let me tell you this the greatest minds, and the most accomplished and successful people to have walked the face of this earth have all made mistakes, fucked up, missed the point, and have basically just fallen flat on their face. And not just once, but innumerable times . . . believe that. But do you know the difference between them and the pseudo-perfectionist is their attitude, and how they looked at things. Meaning whey they failed, or messed up, or completely fucked up, they knew that it was nowhere near the end of the world. They kept a positive attitude, knew that failing, and messing up, is completely natural. And most important of all they learned from their failure or mess up, so that they would not make that same mistake again. And that's the most important thing of all that I can impart here to you. And that's to learn from your failures, and mistakes. Because

like I said making mistakes, and fucking up, is completely natural. And if you think otherwise, you're crazy.

49. Always remember that you will always end up where your thoughts and beliefs take you.

50. Always remember that whatever happens here in this world good or bad, happy or sad, life goes on, and you'll only be here for a very short transitory period of time. Then you'll inevitably move on to a much better, and grander place in the hereafter . . . But please don't take this statement out of context to lead you, or get you to believing that what happens here doesn't matter because you best believe me it does.

51. It was once said that in life you either adapt, evolve, compete, or die.

52. Always remember that the greatest undeveloped natural resource in the world is the human intellect.

53. Always remember that life is nothing but perpetual evolvement, change is inevitable, and learning, and experiencing are nonceasing and infinite. And on a last note never think that you know so much about something that you can't be shocked or amazed.

54. Always remember that development in anything . . . the body, the mind, the intellect, is usually more times than not gradual, and slow, but nonetheless palpable and real.

55. Always remember that only a fool resists change, and therefore impedes his or her own evolvement and learning.

56. Always remember that the more mainstream news, T.V., media, publications or whatever that you take in the more that you will become conditioned to believe and accept things that are not only not true, but norms that are completely disadvantageous to you in more ways than one and are very, and highly advantageous to the controllers which are those who clandestinely control the U.S. government. And please don't let the profoundness, and truth, of this statement escape you.

57. Always remember that the world is not what it seems. And is most definitely nothing like what it's portrayed to be in the mainstream press, media, and publications, and the average person would be completely shocked and taken aback if they saw the world or knew how it really is. And if you don't believe me well let me give you just one example children are starving in third world countries, the mainstream press, media, and other publications portray that to be a sad unfortunate thing beyond all control of all human intervention. But hear me, and hear me well nothing could be farther from the truth. People not just children are starving in third world countries not by accident but by a coldly calculated plan, and design, which constitutes extremely disastrous and pernicious policies, and other stealth techniques administered by the International Monetary Fund, World Bank, and other world bodies that are surreptitiously controlled by those who clandestinely control the U.S. government. And this is just one example of myriad.

58. Always remember that anything and yes I said anything done gradually is seldom if ever noticed.

59. Always remember that patience is an extremity pivotal asset and virtue in life. The key is to attain nice, meaningful, and worthwhile things slowly.

60. Always remember that if a person does not read a person will be stupid.

61. Always remember that if a woman does not have anybody to take care of but herself then she is only half a woman.

62. Always remember that when the body and mind are brought to peak condition, that person is than very capable of achieving the extraordinary.

63. If you have the desire to be the very best that you can possibly be as a person in all ways and aspects then this book is a must read for you.

64. Always remember that when aiming for success to base your thinking on where you want to go and not on where you've been or where you're at.

65. Always remember that the real and the truth in life are always more times than not kept hid.

66. Always remember that money isn't everything all of the time. I mean it might be when you're young but when you get older things tend to change. Check this study out when researchers questioned two thousand people over the age of fifty-five, they found that those with poor health and few friends were more likely to be depressed even if they were wealthy.

67. Always remember that life is nothing but a never ending and constantly ongoing process of learning, thinking, and doing, and if you fall short of out of this process and order, you will not be in line and in tune with the secular laws that govern the never ending constantly ongoing process of life. And therefore, your life will suffer accordingly. So always, but always stay learning, thinking, and doing. And therefore you'll stay in tune with life.

68. Always remember that a person who has never went through or suffered real burdens or real adversity is nine times out of ten a weak person, because going through and suffering burdens and adversity is what makes one strong.

69. Always remember that in life sometimes the unbelievable happens and it could be for the good or the bad. But you best believe it, the unbelievable does happen. Remember that.

70. Always remember, and this is so real. And as you go through life and age, you'll appreciate how real, and true this is. And that's the lies, craftiness, deception, and manipulation are now so prevalent in the world that it's really a damn shame. They have stealthily permeated almost everything that we know, hear, and see.

71. Always remember that the weak will always succumb to the strong. Now I'm not saying that it should be like this, but you can bet your last dollar that that's the way it is in the real world.

72. Now I just want to say this about negativity and this applies to everyone. There are no exceptions, sometimes in life things will happen, circumstances and situations will come about that will drive us unabatedly, and involuntarily into an abject or despondent state. Now we know that these are two negative states of being. And you know that I always tell you that when negative thoughts come to you for you to immediately without delay change the thought, resist the thought, or somehow get rid of the thought. But in every single instance that's not practical. And I know that because I speak from experience and to say otherwise would be not true and impractical. So what I'm telling you here is in them instances when abject, and/or despondent, thoughts and feelings unabatedly, and involuntary over take you and at that time you just cannot and absolutely can do nothing but succumb involuntary for whatever reason or reason to them. Don't feel bad, and I reiterate, don't feel bad . . . don't beat yourself up . . . don't think you're a loser, and can't fight the good fight. You've only been knocked down or maybe out, but the thing is to get back up and fight. Now if you allow yourself to stay knocked down or out. Meaning you stay entertaining them abject and/or despondent thoughts or feelings on a constant or protracted basis then you're a loser. But to just go through a state of feeling abject or despondent for whatever reason for a time is nothing like I just told you. Things can happen . . . situations and circumstances can come about that can unabatedly and involuntary drive the best of us into abject and despondent states. And if anybody says otherwise they're lying. But also like I just said, we're only knocked down or out for a time. The thing is to get back up and fight. Meaning to get rid of, and/or shake off those abject and/or despondent thoughts and feelings. And go back to thinking positive, feeling good about yourself, believing in yourself and in your higher power, which is God. And go back to knowing. And notice I didn't say thinking but knowing in the depths of your heart and soul that it's going to be alright. And you should not stay in abject or despondent state longer than three to five days. And if it's something extremely grave the absolute tops is ten days. And these abject and despondent states should be pretty infrequent.

73. Always remember that the more that you like or love something the more you'll have tolerance with it or for it.

74. Always remember that just like God gave you breath the day that you were born he is going to take it away the day that you die. So remember that even dying is a natural, absolute, and immutable part of life.

75. Always remember that the power of faith and believing is so inordinately powerful that it will most definitely and literally make you or break you. It will make you rich or it will make you poor. Negative thoughts and beliefs will kill you. Just like positive thoughts and beliefs will enhance and enrich you and your life in myriad ways.

76. Always remember that no matter how big or how small a challenge is if you are to succeed you must believe and dwell in your own confidence. Because your belief and your confidence are the only ones that will protect you, shelter you, comfort you, strengthen you, and carry you all the way through whatever you're facing and/or going through because remember that as long as you live and have breath in your body you will have challenges in life . . . large and small and if you are to be a winner in life you must conquer and overcome your challenges and the only way to do that is to believe that you can and to dwell in your confidence. And I mean one must marinate in his or her own confidence and therefore stop marinating in fear, worry, I can't, and all the other adverse and negative thoughts, which will only bring you down, keep you down. And inevitably make you a straight loser in all areas of life.

77. Always remember that your beliefs and what you believe will determine how far and where you go in life.

78. Always remember that in this life we stand and always will be between two forces. And that's good and evil. And if we fail to cling to the good, then the evil will most definitely claim us for itself.

79. Always remember that one can be miserable no matter if he is rich or poor.

80. Did you know that a bowl of fresh cherries everyday is extremely healthful and inordinately good for you? Because cherries are rich in cancer fighting and age defying phytochemicals.

81. Did you know that the average human brain weights 2 ½ points . . . equivalent and the same amount as Merriam-Webster's collegiate Dictionary.

82. Did you know that smoking constricts your arteries and that people who smoke their hearts get 21 percent less blood than that of nonsmokers? And smokers' blood has extremely higher levels of vessel damaging free radicals.

83. Now in this thought I'm going to tell you how those who clandestinely control the U.S. government got and have undisputed control of all the outlets of public information without exception here in America. Well, this control over America's T.V., newspapers, media magazines, radio, and all other periodicals according to Congressman Oscar Callaway stared in 1915. He was in office at the time and placed the following comments into the official congressional record – in March 1915 the J.P. Morgan interests got together 12 men high up in the newspaper world and employed them to select the most influential newspapers in the united States and sufficient number of them to control generally the policy of the daily press of the United States. These 12 men worked the problem out by selecting 179 newspapers and then began an elimination process to retain only those necessary for purposes of controlling. They then found it was necessary to purchase control of 25 of the greatest papers. An editor was then furnished for each paper to properly supervise and edit information regarding the questions of preparedness, militarism, financial policies and other things of national and international nature considered vital to the interests of the purchasers . . . And just so you know this control of America's outlets of public information was started back in 1915 by Mr. J.P. Morgan who at the time was one of the executive

governing members of those who clandestinely controlled the U.S. government. And this control has been continued and is most definitely in de facto existence today.

84. Did you know that the media, newspapers, magazines, and most periodicals are designed and put out for one thing and for one thing only? And that's to keep the people believing and thinking in a certain way. And that is to keep the people believing and thinking in the way that those who control the outlets of public information want. Because the media, newspapers, magazines, and most periodically are nothing but tools. And tools that are used, and are being used to surreptitiously control the way the masses of people believe and think. And of all the outlets of public information, one of the most effective and efficient next to the T.V. that is in controlling the way people believe and think is the newspaper, especially if it's read constantly and on a regular and daily basis. It is the most effective and efficient of all the outlets of public information in controlling the way the masses of people believe and think. But now thanks to the internet that might be fading.

85. Always remember that the pressures and circumstances of real life are very able and capable of making you do things and become things you never thought in your wildest dreams you do or become. And if you're 30 years old or older then you know what I'm talking about.

86. You would be utterly surprised to learn how many people survive by lying and manipulating. From the homeless bum on the corner all the way on up to the rich and the super rich. It's all the same, these are the going on's of everyday real life.

87. Always remember that it's hard to grasp the real realities of life, as the ones set forth in this book. When your only reality is paying the bills, trying to get some money, and trying to make ends meet . . .

88. Always remember that in life we all have regrets, it's inevitable of things we did, and of things we should have done or not have done. But don't feel bad, because you best believe me

whether we admit it or not, we all got them. Because as we are experiencing life regrets and mistakes are a natural part of it. But the thing is to not hold on to them and release them . . .

89. Always remember that life without all the challenges, and struggles wouldn't be shit. It would be immensely boring . . . believe that.

90. Always remember the great thinkers and philosophers of old looked at all of life's challenges, struggles, and problems as puzzles and riddles of various degrees of complexity – and they took great delight in solving them. Because you best believe me that there is an answer and a solution to every challenge, struggle, and problem that life throws at you. You just have to believe, be positive, and willing to be a real player at the game called life. And stop letting life beat you down. And what I just said is not something that you do for a week, a month, or a year, but it's how you live your life . . . it's a way of life.

91. Always remember that things in there totality are now such, that one cannot trust 100%. Meaning that you never can really trust what's made of flesh (people) too much, because they're much too susceptible to too many whims, things, and influences, and besides that human beings have too many needs, wants, and desires, which makes them suffer from cupidity. Which in turn makes them prime targets for all sorts of venal.

92. Always remember that when you pray you must be serious, and pray to God, with all the earnestness that you possess. And then, and only then, will you be actually, and really praying.

93. Always remember that how small and limited is the human mind, even of the most learned.

94. Always remember the words of one of the most prominent journalist and editors of the 20th century. John Swinton, of the New York Time told his staff at his retirement dinner . . . and this is quote on quote verbatim:

"There is no such thing as a free press. You know it . . . and I know it. There is not one of you who would dare to write his honest opinions. The business of journalism is to destroy the truth, to lie outright, to pervert, to vilify, to fawn at the feet of mammon, and to sell oneself, his country, his race for his daily bread. We are the tools and vessels of very rich men who are behind the scenes. We are jumping jacks, they pull the strings; we dance. Out talents, our possibilities, and our lives are the property of these men. We are nothing but intellectual prostitutes.

95. Always remember that most of the time people don't find out the truth, or the real about people, things, and situations until it's too late, or they themselves are in a bad or unfavorable condition.

96. Always remember that it was once said by one of the greatest minds the world has ever known, Socrates, that if you want to shut down someone's mind so they stop thinking for themselves, and therefore delink their minds from its real and infinite potential then all you go to do is sell them some type of dogma. And once that dogma is assimilated by them that dogma, whatever it may be, will control their every thought and mind. And therefore who ever administers and controls the dogma will unequivocally control the mind. And for more on how the dogmas of myriad kinds have been used throughout the ages to control the masses of unsuspecting people . . . please read on.

97. Always remember that conquering oneself is one of life's ultimate and profound goals. Plato said it best when he said that the first and best victory is to conquer self. And to be conquered by self is of all the things the most shameful and vile. But sadly to say the majority of people today are really and actually conquered by self. Let me explain and give you a little insight on what self is. Self is your flesh and your flesh has an inherent propensity to sin by nature. Self only wants to indulge in pleasure, point blank . . . and that's it and that's all. Self doesn't want to exercise, because that hurts . . . and self isn't into that. Self only wants to feel good. And self only wants to indulge in whatever feels good whether it be eating,

drinking, getting high, watching T.V., laying around . . . whatever. And self loves being lazy and to procrastinate. And self doesn't know, understand, or recognize patience, because self is into instant gratification. And don't ever make the mistake of underestimating self, because what self wants nine times out of ten self gets. Because self is very powerful and is usually controlling its subjects 80% of the time. And self is very self-centered, egocentric, boastful, and extremely greedy. And last but not least, self cares nothing but about self. Self is a very cold thing. So remember once one conquers self and I mean really conquers self he or she has indeed conquered a great thing. And everything and anything else after that is conquerable to the one who has successfully conquered self. Because self is one of, if not the greatest thing that one can ever conquer. Some people have conquered kingdoms and nations, and have attained success in many areas of their life . . . and acquired great financial wealth. But yet and still, they have not conquered self, which is like I said . . . one of, if not, the greatest accomplishments of all. Because once one has really and actually conquered self he or she is well on his or her way to regeneration, and on a much higher plane than the average person who has not yet conquered self. And is still fighting and battling with self and is 8 out of 10 getting beat up by self. Because like I said previously, self is a very cold thing and cares nothing but about self. And if self is not sooner or later put in check self will ultimately destroy itself and its subjects.

98. Always remember that because the human mind always did and always will demand some type of intellectual explanation and expression. Those who clandestinely control the U.S. government and their affiliates have sowed the seeds of scholastic and intellectual confusion into America and the world. And therefore have caused to appear numerous orders of learning, which are convincingly plausible but are yet untrue.

99. Always remember that people compromise daily their integrity and spiritual values in the quest of power, wealth, pleasure and status. And that's sad, very sad, but it's very much true.

100. Always remember that one masters and overcomes the world by first mastering and overcoming the worldliness in his or herself.

101. Always remember that the entire universe is sustained by one immeasurable and indefinable God.

102. Always remember that each and every day that we live we are always constantly going to struggle to do what is right. So always remember that it's a never ending fight to do what is right.

103. Always remember that in life there's time for everything. So be patient and take your time.

104. Always remember that life is about feeling happy and good about yourself. And therefore doing whatever it is going to take for one to feel happy and good about oneself. Because for one to really and truly feel and be happy about his or her life and their selves is all that really matters in life. And I'm not just talking about one feeling physically happy. But one being at peace with oneself and really and truly being happy in the core depths of one's soul. And the only way for one to be able to do that is for one to be in tune with oneself.

105. Did you know that physical exercise causes your body to produce endorphins? The chemicals that dull pain and help produce what's known as exercise high. And strenuous weight training in particular raises your testosterone level, which will help improve your moods and help you deal with stress better. And according to Harvard Psychiatrist, John J. Ratey, M.D. and co-author of a book on psychological disorders called <u>Shadow Syndromes</u> strenuous physical exercise can raise your brain's level of antidepressant chemicals, such as dopamine, serotonin, and norrepinephrine, and that regular strenuous physical exercise such as weight training improves the flow of blood that carries oxygen and nutrients to the brain. And if you're exercising outdoors that sunlight has a positive effect on brain chemistry.

106. Always remember that in the end it's what you believe that's going to make you or break you. You either believe you can or you believe that you can't. And it's as simple as that. And that applies to everything in life without exception.

107. Always remember that a positive frame of mind is not holly jolly, I'm happy. From a scientific perspective it's energy in motion . . . it's moving forward in a positive and optimistic way or direction.

108. Always remember to say good things . . . live with peace in your heart . . . and keep forgiveness at hand.

109. Always remember that you'll never get any real knowledge out of any public library. And when I say real knowledge I mean knowledge like the knowledge that you're getting out of this book. And that's because all public libraries just like all public schools are financed and controlled in one way or the other by those who clandestinely control the U.S. government. And therefore all the public information in the public libraries is censored . . . you better believe it because you will not find anything on those who clandestinely control the U.S. government in a public library. Because those who clandestinely control the U.S. government try their best to keep real truth and real knowledge suppressed away from the masses of the people.

110. Always remember that love is whimsical and temperamental. It comes when it pleases and goes away without warning. But one must accept and enjoy it while it stays and remains. But one should spend no time worrying about its departure when it departs. Because worrying will never bring it back. But I can most definitely understand why one would worry, stress, and feel sick when love departs. Because to feel and experience real and genuine love is really inexplicable . . . it just feels so good to one's soul. It just makes one feel so good inside that just plain words cannot describe the feeling. Because real and genuine love brings about a state of mind closest to that of the spiritual that one may ever know or experience on this earthly plain. So like I said I can most definitely understand why 9 ½ out of 10 people worry, stress, and feel sick when real love

departs. Because it is only natural that once one has felt and experienced real genuine love one would want to keep it for all time. But love does depart, but it also comes back. And people need to forget and dismiss the thought that love only comes around once in a life time. Because that's a straight lie, because love comes and goes as it pleases and will more times than not come more than once in a life time. So people need to and should stop feeling resentful and cynical when love makes its departure. And remember; don't look for love, because if you do look for it you'll never find it. Because love is state of being not something you find somewhere like most people think.

111. Always remember that when things go right everybody wants to take credit, but when things go wrong nobody knows what happened.

112. Always remember to never let them see you sweat and to never lose your power and control, in whatever you do. Because if you do, you best believe me, people will try to take advantage.

113. Always remember that respect, if not given voluntarily, needs to be taken. And there are no ifs, ands, or buts about it.

114. Things are moving so fast nowadays that it's really scary.

115. There is a law ordained by god that few people know about. Well, most of God's real and true laws have been suppressed and hid away from you (the masses of people) for control reasons. So the controllers can control you. But this law that I'm speaking about in particular is the law ordained by god concerning the maintenance protection, and upkeep of the human body. Meaning that it is your job to feed, protect, and maintain your human body. And I say this to people everywhere, that if you let or allow anyone to hit you, abuse you, mistreat you, talk bad to you, or allow anything of the sort to happen to you, then you are in direct violation of one of God's laws. And you best believe me that you will pay the penalties, because like I said previously so much information and knowledge, has been suppressed and hid away from us that it's not even funny anymore. And all that in the Bible that says turn the other cheek; believe me, it's disinformation of the first

order. And I say that with the power of the universe behind me, because just the opposite is true.

116. In this thought here let me say a word or two on what's called or known as street smarts. Well, street smarts contrary to what you have been taught all your life are nothing but basic fundamentals of life, common sense, that have been systematically suppressed and hid away from mainstream society by those that clandestinely control the U.S. government and their predecessors. And why? So you (the masses of people) would be easier to control. That's why. And then through their control of the mainstream have made street smarts look like a bad thing. But I guarantee you one thing those that clandestinely control the U.S. government are taught street smarts in special schools here and abroad, and use them against you (the masses of the people) everyday, while at the same time encouraging you not to use them. So all I can say is . . . let's wake up people.

117. Now for a word on belief, because that's basically what a lot of this book is about, okay. When one believes one must really in the depths of his or her heart, and soul, really believe. And therefore make that belief a reality within his or her self. And then live that reality until it manifests into the tangible and physical realm. Now this might now happen overnight, but I guarantee you, and you best believe me, if you sincerely believe and hold fast to that belief it will materialize. See where people go wrong at is that they think if they believe, for something for a week, month, or a year, that it supposed to happen. And that's just not how it works. You can't rush the universe; you have to wait your turn. And just to be honest with you, from what I done seen and from my experience it takes anywhere from 3 to 5 years of constant believing and thought projection for any substantial thing to materialize. And in reality that's no time. Believe me because you got to understand you're dealing with the universe here and 3 to 5 years in our perception may seem like a long time. But in the whole of the universe that's absolutely nothing. But people don't understand that. And I'll say is this, desire is the fuel . . . how much desire you pump into your belief. Meaning how badly you desire it will determine how fast you get it. And remember that this is not an overnight

process. But believe me . . . it's real and it works. And remember believing and projecting the thoughts you want to create are not things that you do for a day, a week, a month, or a year. They are how you live. They are a way of life. Then and only then will they be effective. And like I've previously said you have to learn how to believe, how to create your own reality. You have to learn how to live that way. But once you do, believe me, it's a wonderful way of life. So as you read throughout this book and as I speak profusely about positivity, believing, and the power of thought. Remember this thought is key . . . it's very important, because what I'm speaking on is not an overnight process but a way of life. You are your thoughts . . . whatever they may be.

118. Remember there is so much more to our history than we are being told. And there is so much more happening on this planet today than most people could ever begin to believe.

119. Always remember that just because something is good right now doesn't mean that it's always going to stay good. Just like if something is bad right now, that doesn't mean that it's always going to stay bad.

120. Always remember that in moments of failure we often question everything including our faith. It isn't collective action that makes this nation prosperous and secure. It's the initiative and creativity of the individual.

--Mark Sandford

Governor of South Carolina

121. If you can dream it, you can do it . . .

--Walt Disney

1901-1955

122. Always remember that it's your experience and what you have learned that makes you who you are . . .

123. Always remember that in dealing with life and with what happens in life. I don't care if you're 100 years old, you still got a lot to learn . . .

124. One thing that makes it possible to be an optimist is if you have a contingency plan for when all hell breaks loose.

--Randy Pansch

In His National Best Seller "The Last Lecture"

125. Evidence that should have put many high government office holders behind bars for crimes with minimum sentences of 10 to 20 years – Not the community service given those convicted of lying to Congress – was heard by Senator John Kerry's committee in secret session and will never be revealed to the American people.

--Former DEA Agent and Bestselling Author, Michael Levine

126. Always remember that when it's all said and done and you're on your death bed and on your way out of here. It isn't really about how much success or money you have even though money is important because it keeps you comfortable. And success makes one happy, but what really is important, once it's all said and done and is indelibly lasting is how much of a positive difference you made in the lives of others. And all I can say to that is the more the better. And believe me that's what matters once it's over and the book is shut.

127. Always remember that life in a heartbeat can change for the good or for the bad. Think about that, ponder on that for a second and give it its due credit because it's real, very real.

128. Always remember that if you're up to it, and open for it, life has so many, many experiences and in so many different assortments, varieties, and forms, that its really ineffable. But the key is that you got to be up to it, and open for it . . . and not afraid of adverse or bad experiences, which a smart person only uses as stepping stones and learns from them.

129. How can one mentally evolve and develop his mind when one has no time to sit down and think. Because of work, family, and a whole long list of other exigencies of life.

130. Only the small secrets need to be protected, because the big ones are kept secret by the public's own incredulity.

--Marshal McCluhan

131. I may not have all the answers and I'm damn sure not the smartest, but you better believe one thing, I'm watching, paying attention, and thinking.

--Howard Hughes

1905 – 1976

132. Did you know that people are aging physically faster these days than they were in times past, because they stress and worry so much? Did you know that? And the very negative thoughts that people should not even so much as entertain the thoughts of having such thoughts, are worrying thoughts and stressing thoughts. Because worrying thoughts and stressing thoughts alone can be so detrimental, and pernicious to a person that they can sometimes not even be able to think or rationalize straight. And did you know that stressing and worrying can even make you, and have you physically sick? It can and will cause your physical body all different kinds of aches and pains. You can have headaches and all other kinds of aches constantly. And you will not even know why you are experiencing such aches and pains. And you will probably blame it on everything else except your constant worrying and stressing. And just so you know, such worrying and stressing can even escalate to all out depression, and even manic depression, and lead one to having all kinds of suicidal thoughts and tendencies.

133. Always remember that sometimes you just have to accept things the way that they are, or the way that they went. And just let them go. And when I say let them go, I mean just let'em go. Completely stop thinking about them in order for you to

keep your sanity and for them things to stop bothering you. Because life moves on and so should you.

134. Always remember that the uncut, and unabridged, raw truth is a lot of the time, and for a lot of people more than they can bear. And please believe the realness in that statement. You might want to re-read it.

135. To fully grasp all the profound truth in this book it's advisable that you read the book over and over and over again. Because reading this book only once I can almost guarantee you will not do you justice.

136. Always remember that anybody can read these thoughts, but if you don't heed them and put them into actual practice then they mean nothing.

137. It's been said, and this is very real in practice, that when the going gets rough, the tough get going.

--Gordan Graham

138. Many of our personal goals are stranded on a little island called maybe someday "I'll".

--Roger Van Orsch

139. Always remember that the realities of life will sometimes shock you to your soul, and beyond, in good ways, bad ways, and indifferent ways.

140. Always remember that pain is inevitable. But misery is an option. Meaning that it's up to you to choose or not to choose to be miserable.

141. In the province of the mind what one believes to be true either is the true or becomes true.

--John Lilly

142. Please understand that realness and truth of what I'm about to say, because it bears and has a direct impact on what you're

reading in this book. And that's that it's a known and provable fact that people automatically block out and lock out information that conflicts with what they already believe to be true. And this right here is the number one barrier and impediment to people learning, growing, and evolving. So please don't let this happen to you. The information in this book or anywhere else for that matter that does not coincide with what you already believe don't just dismiss it or block it out, rather consider it on its merits, and objectively check it out. And I guarantee you'll be absolutely astonished at the learning, growth, and evolving that you will do. (Wake up people) And don't impede or stagnate your own growth.

143. These thoughts contain living truths, if applied . . . believe that!

144. Always remember that the idea of having to wait for something always makes it somehow more exciting.

145. I know one thing if I don't know anything else . . . and I mean nothing else. And that's that we create our own reality via our thoughts.

146. Things we must deal with in life. Every person has been given a great deal of work to do . . . a heavy burden lies on us all. From the day of our birth until the day we go back to the Earth, the mother of us all. We are confused, and fearful, we all dread the loss of our independence, and our health, and this goes from the richest person in the world to the poorest person in rags, and living in poverty. And all through our lives we must deal with jealously, trouble, violence, death, famine, sickness, conflict, and the evil impulse that's in us all. And even when we go to bed, if we dream we might have a nightmare. And things like that disturb us. And in the end everything that comes from the Earth goes back to the Earth . . . just like all rivers and all waters flow back to the sea. And please don't take this thought in a negative light, because it just speaks on some of the things that we must all deal with in life.

147. Let me speak on guilt for one hot second . . . guilt is a natural human emotion, but when one gets stuck in it or indulges in it for a long or protracted state of time then it becomes a

hindrance and negative to one's life and spiritual progress. So therefore I tell you that if you got to go through it or experience it for whatever reason or reasons to go through it as fast as possible and be done with it and release the concept. And just because you did something that you were not supposed to do. No matter how great or small it's not the end of the world. Life moves on, and so should you. But not if you get stuck in guilt. And it can become a form of bondage. So let's grow up people and stop falling for the tricks of the controllers, who want people stuck in negativity, and putting out negativity by any and all means. And guilt can have you in an impasse in your life you never thought possible. And can have you stuck in a state of straight negativity and you won't even know it. So please people release them guilt concepts and move on because they're nothing but negativity.

148. Now this book right here, I, the author, really believe in the depths of my soul is going to be the book that wakes up the masses of people to the truth about those who clandestinely control the U.S. government and their odious activities. And I believe this book is going to start and set innumerable people off on a journey of infinite knowledge. And not only that, but this book is going to start a revolution against those who clandestinely control the U.S. government. Now I'm not being or trying to be pretentious here but this book is right now already a classic and will be remembered for all time after its published as the book that exposed and brought to light for the average everyday person those who clandestinely control the U.S. government. And I the author take great relish in the thought that untold millions will be able to credit this book with waking them up to unabridged truth.

--The Author

August 30, 2005

149. Did you know that in 1994 Congress passed a law to help the federal government make their eavesdropping on the United States legal? Not that it matters to the federal government or that the federal government cares that eavesdropping on people without a court order is illegal or is supposed to be illegal. But

it was just a law to make eavesdropping on the masses of people for no reason officially legal. And the law was the 1994 (CALEA Act) communications assistance to law enforcement act, which made and forced all phone companies and telecommunication companies in the United States and those outside of the United States that want to do business in the United States to install special wire tap devices compatible with those of the federal government directly into their systems so to provide to law enforcement agencies and the federal government direct eavesdropping access to the phone, and telecommunication companies customer's communications. And do you know what the coldest thing about this, well, is the coldest thing about this is that not the government or the phone and telecommunications companies tell or let you the people know what they did.

150. Always remember that everything, and when I say everything, I mean absolutely everything in life and this is without exception that happens to you or that you go through. How you go through it and how it will affect you depends on your attitude and what mind set you take to it.

151. Always remember that people are losers in life for two reasons. One, they lack knowledge and or real education. And two, they don't believe they can attain or achieve.

152. Your good name and reputation depend more on what you conceal than what you reveal. People of power, however, are undone not by the mistakes they make, but by the way they deal with them. Because once the truth is revealed, events will snowball out of your control.

--Robert Greene

In His National Bestseller "The 48 Laws of Power"

153. I would rather betray the whole world than let the world betray me.

--General Ts'ao Ts'ao

154. Your public actions are like artworks. They must have visual appeal. And they must create belief – a belief in you.

--The Great statesman, Lawyer, Financier, and Vice President

Charles G. Dawes, 1865-1951

155. Words like freedom, options, and choice, evoke a power of possibility far beyond the reality of the benefits they entail. When examined closely, the choices we have – in the marketplace, in elections, in our jobs – tend to have noticeable limitations: they are often a matter of choice simply between A & B with the rest of the alphabet out of the picture. Yet as long as the faintest mirage of choice flickers on, we rarely focus on the missing options. We choose to believe that the game is fair, and that we have our freedom. We prefer not to think too much about the depths of our liberty to choose. This unwillingness to probe the smallness of our choice stems from the fact that too much freedom creates a kind of anxiety. The phrase unlimited options sounds infinitely promising, but unlimited options would actually paralyze us and cloud our ability to choose. Our limited range of choices comforts us. This supplies the clever and cunning with enormous opportunities for deception. For people who are choosing between alternatives find it hard to believe they are being manipulated or deceived. They cannot see that you are allowing them a small amount of free will in exchange for a much more powerful imposition of your own will.

--Robert Green

In his national bestseller, "The 48 Laws of Power"

156. Necessity if what impels people to take action and once the necessity if gone, most of the time, only rot and decay are left.

--Niccolo Machiavailli

1469-1527

157. We have met the enemy, and the enemy is within our gates.

--Former Rapper

2-Pac

158. I recently told a friend that he needed to go read my book (Thoughts on Life) over and over again so that he would know it frontwards, sideway, up and down, and even know it with his eyes closed. And then, only then, I told him that I would able to guarantee him success in whatever his endeavors may be. And guess what? He did do as I said. And I kid you not; he came back to me with pure sincerity in his eyes and said you know this has got to be one of the most important books on the planet at this time.

--The Author

159. Since thought attracts, you have brought to you the experiences of your thoughts.

--the Handbook for the New Paradigm

160. The people are abandoned by their government and so must fend for themselves within situations of less and less available necessities, and more and more regulations. And unfortunately government of the people, by the people leads to tyranny in quick succession through many small steps.

--the Handbook for the New Paradigm

161. There exists a shadowy government with its own air force, its own navy. Its own fundraising mechanism and the ability to pursue its own ideas of the national interest free from all checks and balances, and free from law itself.

--Senator Daniel K. Inouye

162. It has been said that those who clandestinely control the U.S. government would rather cause thermonuclear war and kill half or damn near all the people on the planet before they would

allow the people to find out the truth via the mainstream (because people believe the mainstream) about the power of consciousness and thought. Because once the people find and figure out the truth about the power of consciousness and thought, the game is over for them. Believe that! Because the power of consciousness and thought is completely and totally absolute and it supersedes religion, and all those other ideologies, dogmas, and tenets, that have been inculcated in the people since birth. And once the people find out and understand that they are totally free and that nothing, and I mean nothing, not God or anything else is controlling them or making things happen to them, good or bad. Because they are sovereign free agents with a free will that is absolute and will not be infringed upon, not by God or anyone else. Then the people will understand their real power and understand they either consciously or unconsciously via their thoughts are creating their reality. And not only that, but they will understand that their thoughts once focused and concentrated (and this is what those who clandestinely control the U.S. government don't want you to know) can over take and/or create anything . . . and believe me, I mean anything in this material physical world. And the key to this is for people to completely and totally program and inculcate themselves to their core with the belief that their thoughts are supreme and can over take and/or create anything and this is without exception in the material physical world. And I must say amen to that.

163. Now in this thought here I just want to briefly speak on how you the masses of people can overthrow those who clandestinely control the U.S. government, and you best believe me that there's only one way, and I want to disclose that to you. But first you got to understand that their execrate plan for American, and the world, as a whole has been in motion and in the making for centuries. Second, you got to understand that they own and control damn near everything. From banking, politics, business, the intelligence agencies, police, the military industrial complexes, education, and the media. And I don't have time or room here to detail their extremely labyrinth web of ownership and control. But if you would like to read on that I recommend a great and highly acclaimed book . . . it's called: "The Truth Shall Set You Free", by David Icke. But the point

is that those who clandestinely control the U.S. government own and control damn near everything. Third, you must understand that those who clandestinely control the U.S. government have in their possession technology at least, and this is at minimum 50-75 years in advance of us regular people, and of mainstream society, meaning that the technology they got right now, we mainstream society won't see for another 50-75 years. And this is not even to mention all the advanced esoteric and Arcanum knowledge of life, nature, and the universe that they possess. So now that you understand what you and I, and the rest of the masses of people are up against. I'm going to tell you how we as a collective (because that's the only way that it's going to work) can overthrow those who clandestinely control the U.S. government. And that's by us collectively putting out positive thought energy. It might sound crazy, but let me explain. Alright, you know that thoughts are real and that they exist in a live state in their own world known as the astral plane or the mass-consciousness. Now in thought #380 when I concisely explain to you how the universe is set up. I explain that... And that when you think and/or put out negative energy that it not only comes back to you. But that it compounds and adds to the rest of the negative thoughts and/or energy that's being put out on the planet. Now that's just what those who clandestinely control the U.S. government and their superiors the negative forces of the universe want is for the masses of people to constantly and incessantly think negative and therefore, put out negative energy. But what I'm here to tell you, like I've belabored you throughout this whole book is that it doesn't have to be that way. If we the masses of people collectively think positive and put out positive energy we can eradicate and overtake the negative energy. Therefore leaving the negative forces with nothing to feed on. Put another way, you already know that thoughts are real and that they exist in their own world called the astral plane or the mass-consciousness. Now if we the masses of people can fill the astral plane or mass-consciousness with positive thoughts, and not just any kind of positive thought, but positive thoughts directed at removing and eradicating from power those that clandestinely control the U.S. government. Then we the masses of people can literally think these idiots out of existence. And those that clandestinely control the U.S. government at the upper echelons know this. Why do you think they use their power, money, influence, and advance technology to keep wars, conflicts, famine, calamities, upheavals, unrest, terrorist attacks, and so called natural disasters happening all around the world? So the masses of people will stay thinking and putting out negative thoughts and energy, i.e. being fearful, worried, scared, and to be thinking pessimistic bad, and negative thoughts. And therefore assuring that those that clandestinely control the U.S. government stay in power. So basically they need your consent to stay in power and as long as you think negative energy you're giving it to them. So all I'm saying is that we as a collective, all we have to do is think positive. That is put out positive energy and we can remove and overthrow those who clandestinely control the U.S. government because we can't beat them in no other kind of way. That's the only way we can do it. And let me briefly speak on prayer for those of you thinking about prayer. Because there is a phenomenal power in prayer and I'm with it, support it, and encourage it a 150%. It's our telephone to God. It will strengthen you, sustain you, and carry you through the darkest and trying of times that you could imagine. But you must understand how God works. It's like this, we all have free wills, and even those that clandestinely control the U.S. government are God's creatures and have free wills. And God will never impose upon the free wills of His creatures. No matter how evil or malevolent they may be, they are still his creatures, and contrary to what you have been taught or told God loves all of his creatures and creation, good or evil, very much. And this just goes to say that god will not by any arbitrary act of His power stop those that clandestinely control the U.S. government. And therefore, impose on their free wills. That will never happen. It just doesn't work that way. When people do wrong they will have to pay for it. So don't think that those that clandestinely control the U.S. government are getting away with anything. Because they're most definitely not. Because every single human being will have to account for what they did or didn't do. That's what the universal law of compensation is for. And I just said this for the people who might say why doesn't God help us? Why doesn't God get us out of this and remove those that clandestinely control the U.S. government from power? No, but I'll tell you what God will do. He'll strengthen you when you pray to Him. And not only that, but God will spread the word about those that clandestinely control the U.S. government and people will begin to wake up to the truth of who really runs the U.S. government, America, and the world. And when the truth starts to spread and the masses of people really start to wake up to what's really going on than those that clandestinely control the U.S. government will have a real problem. And on thinking positive, all I'm asking you to do is to ceaselessly put out positive energy by thinking positive. And it's this simple. I want you to think not how fucked up the world is, but to constantly think how you would rather like the world to be. And with your life the same thing. Don't think about what's wrong with your life, but instead ceaselessly think about how you would rather want your life to be. And with that you're putting forth positive energy. And how much desire you put into it will determine how potent it is. And if we do this on a collective scale I guarantee you we will have massive results. And on a last note, even if we all just pray to god for people to think positive, we will have massive results. Because once the positive thoughts reach a certain or critical point in the mass-consciousness, then the whole mass-conscious will be dominated and overtaken with positive thought. And when that happens our whole world would be unequivocally full of positiveness. And even those who want to think negative and put out negative thoughts and energy will not be able to. Now isn't that a beautiful thing? But it's just the opposite of what's going on now. So tell a friend, and remember positive thinking is not something you do for a week, a month, or a year. But it's a way of life. And when you're going through things and just trying to make it from day to day, and you need help just pray and ask . . . all help is available, if you would just ask. Because God has innumerable flocks and flocks of spirits just waiting to help you, if you but ask. And remember when you pray and ask for help stay strictly in the positive. Be explicit and a 100% sincere. And remember, thinking you're a victim in any way, shape or form, is negative. So don't do it.

164. Always remember that for the ultimate empowerment just ask God to fill your soul with His divine love. Now that's the ultimate empowerment one can get and/or receive . . . period.

165. Always remember that the really and truly unbelievable dose happen and occur all the time. And that's for the good and/or the bad. It's just what do you believe will happen to you, is probably what will happen to you . . . whether good or bad, but just understand and know that the truly unbelievable is more common than you think or may know.

166. The masses have never thirsted after truth. They demand illusions and cannot do without them. They constantly give what is unreal precedence over what is real. They are strongly influenced by what is untrue as by what is true – they have an evident tendency not to distinguish between the two.

--Sigmund Freud

1856-1939

Works on Sigmund Freud Vol. #18

167. Always remember that you must believe in extreme positivity, and power, and then just will them into your life.

168. Always remember that it is up to you to do what you do, and to do whatever you got to do to get where you want to be.

169. It has been said that most people tell lies and hide their true feelings because complete and total free, and honest expression is a social impossibility.

170. The truth is often avoided because it is ugly and unpleasant. Never appeal to truth and reality unless you are prepared for the anger that comes from disenchantment. Life is so harsh and distressing that people who can manufacture romance or conjure up fantasy are like oasis in the desert: everyone flocks to them. There is great power in tapping into the fantasies of the masses.

-- Robert Greene

In His National Bestseller "The 48 Laws of Power"

171. The previous thought can be most prominently applied to those who clandestinely control the U.S. government and all their infinite trickery.

172. For a long time I have not said what I believe, nor do I ever believe what I say, and if indeed sometimes I do happen to tell the truth, I hide it among so many lies that it is hard to find.

--Niccolo Machiavailli

In A Letter to Francessco Guicciardini, May 17, 1521

173. I believe in the power of desire backed by faith because I have seen this power lift men from lowly beginnings to places of power and wealth. I have seen it rob the grave of its victims. I have seen it sever as a medium by which men staged a comeback after having been defeated in a hundred different ways.

--Napolean Hill

Author of the all time Bestselling book: "Think and Grow Rich"

174. Always remember that it is not from the benevolence of the butcher, the baker, the brewer, or the candle stick maker, that we expect our dinner, but from their regard to their own interest.

175. Now I just want to say something in regard to the power of thought, and that's that the controllers of this world which are those that clandestinely control the U.S. government are themselves completely and totally infused with the power of thought to a degree that's just ineffable. And that's how they do what they do. They are masters and are completely proficient at using thought to create what they want. And that's how they do what they do. And I can't make it any simpler than that. And that power, the power of thought, which they the controllers have been using for eons to control the world I'm trying to give and convey it to you. Because you best believe me it's there for

the taking. It's just they, the controllers don't want you to know that.

176. I will not believe a thing, because any man says it. Not even if it be the reputed word of God. I will only believe it when to me it is true.

-Buddha

177. Always remember that good fortune is not good to the ignorant or the foolish. And by the same token is evil fortune evil to the wise and truly enlightened. Because the ignorant and the foolish are incapable of benefitting from that which is good. Why? Because the ignorant and foolish see, and feel, but don't understand. And conversely, the wise are incapable of being injured or affected by evil, because real truth and real understanding renders all things bad or good usable. And the same bad or evil fortune is rendered imperious against the wise and truly enlightened.

178. Always remember that the substance of faith is not formality and custom but sincerity and truth.

179. Always remember that whoever chooses to escape the responsibilities of life exhausts himself in his efforts to dodge the inevitable.

180. Always remember that nobody is ever ready for a thing until he or she really and actually believes that they can have it and/or acquire it.

181. Always remember that nine times out of ten excuses are only for the weak or incompetent.

182. Don't ever let society tame you or contain you.

--Eunice Kennedy

Sister of JFK, as quoted by Maria Shriver

183. The worth of money is not in its possession but in its use.

--Fables, Aesop, 6th Century B. C.

184. Always remember to never hold on to or be so stuck in your tenets or beliefs that even in the face of compelling and irrefutable evidence you don't change. Because that means that your mind is absolutely closed and you're basically stuck on stupid. And I don't care what your beliefs or tenets are concerning God, life, nature, or the whole universe. No one living in the 3rd dimension and I can't stress this enough, knows enough about God, life, nature, or the whole universe to make, or have absolute tenets or beliefs about them. No . . . I'm sorry and I don't care what you've been taught or conditioned to believe to the contrary. Because in real reality it just isn't so. There's only one constant in the universe . . . and that's change. And it applies to everything. And most definitely to your beliefs. And I really don't understand why people don't understand that. There are certain truths, notions, concepts, and principals that the human mind and I don't care how developed can never in this 3rd dimension understand or even begin to conceive. People act like if they change their beliefs their whole life is just going to collapse. People need to grow up.

185. To be a brilliant exploiter one's reputation and status must be firmly established or you will be accused of deception.

--Financier Daniel Drew

1797 to 1879

186. Always remember that in life your decisions are only, and can only be as good as your information.

187. Always remember that all the thoughts, ideas, and attitudes of mere man, for the most part are just that . . . nothing but of mere man. And in all reality & actually really have nothing to do with the big picture as God ordained it or with real spirituality. Please understand that . . . think.

188. Always remember society is in a state of constant flux, but there is something that does not change: the vast majority of people conform to whatever is normal for the time. They play

the role allotted to them. Conformity is constant because humans are social creatures who are always imitating one another.

189. Always remember that the role you were given in life is not the role you have to accept. You can always live out a role of your own creation.

190. Always remember that love, money, and health, assuming that you got freedom make life good and worth living . . . and without any one life won't be too good or too much worth living. And the thing is all you need is a little of each one. Because love will give you joy and happiness, and money will enable you to do what you want. And of course you must be healthy to enjoy anything. Like for example some people who live in poverty have a whole lot of love in their household, but little to no money. So therefore, life isn't too good. Then you got people with enormous amounts of money but no one to love or receive love from, and again, life isn't too good. Then you got people with a whole lot of love and a whole lot of money, but for one reason or another their health isn't no good. Then again, life isn't too good. So remember in the physical world you need love, money and health to make life good and/or worth living, because a lot of people don't understand the principles of living in the physical world. They get it mixed up with all kinds of dogmas.

191. Did you know that one of the most often and most over looked joys and therapeutic activities in life is the simple act of playing or listening to your favorite CD or song over and over and over again? And if not your favorite CD or song then one you really, really, really like. Why? Because it's a proven fact and even quantum physics has begun to substantiate by a preponderance of irrefutable evidence that it's pivotal for one to be happy and feel good. Because when you're happy and feeling good you're not only putting out positive energy and thoughts but you're lifting your vibratory rate to higher levels, which not only strengthens your immune system but causes you to produce numerous life sustaining, enhancing, and age retardant hormones, such as (for example to name one of the many . . . human growth hormone [HGH].). And for more on this you

might want to read: "The Only Answer to Cancer," by Leonard Cladwell (or Coldwell). And this is why I say that there is something in this book for everybody from age 9 to 90, meaning that if you're from age 9 to 39, this book will most assuredly give you meaning and insight, and direction for your life. And if you're at age 40 or in your forties this book will teach you and please hear me and hear me – well, because more people, and this is according to demographics, are 40 or in their forties today than ever before. This book will teach you how to be made all the way new spiritually, physically, and mentally . . . basically new at forty. And if you're 50 or in your 50's, this book will teach you how to completely rejuvenate. And if you're 60 or in your 60's, this book will teach you how to live and feel like you're 45. And if you're 70 or in your 70's, this book will teach you how to live and feel like you're 55. And if you're 80 or in your 80's this book will teach you how to live and feel like you're 65. And if you're 90 or in your 90's, then this book will be like an elixir to you and your life. And everything I just said from this book, giving meaning, insight, and direction to one's life. To new at forty, to rejuvenation, and everything else I said is completely interchangeable and absolutely applicable to anyone at any age. Because just to be 100% honest with you and to break it all the way down for you it's what you believe more than anything else that keeps you going, young, healthy, and happy.

192. Always remember to always drive carefully, because it's not only cars that can be recalled by their maker.

193. Always remember that it was once said that once extreme luck or success find their way to you, you had better lookout. Why? Because the people to fear the most are those closest to you and those in your own circle. And again, why? Because envy and jealousy know no bounds, especially among family, friends, and lovers.

194. It has been said with few exceptions that the two best times in life are childhood and those times when you are in love.

195. Always remember that life is delicate. And be under no illusions, because anything can happen to anybody at any time.

196. There is no religion higher than the truth.

> --The Theosophist Society

197. If you become rigid and stuck in your views, you become trapped by your beliefs you are no longer empowered, because you are no longer free.

> --Dr. Bruce Goldberg
>
> Author & Hypnotherapist

198. Always remember that our current culture addiction to reality T.V., pop singers, athletes, film stars, and celebrities may give us a fleeting moment of entertainment and a quick distraction from the stress of daily life. But they cannot and will not give us the true enlightenment, which we all so dearly crave.

199. Always remember that not even a completely and totally innocent new born baby fresh out of the vulva is assured life and survival in this world if it were not for the doctors and other humans attending to it at the time of birth. Because if not it would surely die. And I just said that to say that don't never think that you're assured anything in this life unless you get up and get it and do it for yourself. And for all those who say that they just put stuff in God's hands and leave it there and are waiting for God to make something happen for them. Well you'll just be waiting. And I'm not saying that prayer doesn't work because it does. You can be most definitely helped by it, but at the same time you must do for you and nothing else, because it like this and this is what most people don't know . . . God in all His knowingness already gave you all the innate and physical power that you will ever need to get and or do whatever you so wish or desire . . . period. And that's how great God is. So remember the example of the new born baby you are assured nothing in this life unless you get up, get it, and/or do it yourself. Because you got the power.

200. All truth passes through three states. First, it is ridiculed. Second, it is violently opposed. And third, it is accepted as being self-evident.

--Schopenhauer

201. The conscious and intelligent manipulation of the organized habits and opinions of the masses must be done by experts. The public relations mavens better known as the propagandists . . . they are the invisible rulers who control the destinies of millions.

--Public Relations:

Edward L. Bernays

And the American Scene.

Published by Faxon Books,

1951

202. Any man who tries to be good all the time is bound to come ruin among the great number who are not good.

--Nicco Machiavelli

1469-1527

203. Of all the disorders of the soul, envy, and jealousy are the only ones no one confesses too –

--Plutarch

46-120 A.D.

204. Do you want to hear about justice in America? Well check this out, Salvatore (Sammy the Bull) Gravano was excused and the key word here was excused for 19 murders in exchange for his testimony against former mob boss John Gotti. And now for those of you who do not know compensating anybody in any kind of way, form, or fashion for testimony is a federal offense and a straight violation of Title 18 USC 201 (c) (2) and if you

don't believe me then check it out for yourself. But hey, that's justice here in America. And if you want to read more about all kinds of travesties of justice committed by the CIA, FBI, DEA, Justice Department, and virtually all levels of government then you must get the book: "Drugging America," by Rodney Stich.

205. Always remember that it was once said that only the paranoid survive. Why? Because you got to really be crazy, out of your mind, and a zip damn fool to think that people are not talking behind your back, probably plotting and scheming on you and hoping for your downfall. And only god knows what else. And this applies to everyday people, but really applies to you if you're engaged in politics, financial dealings, or other business where people might have something to gain. And as a rule of thumb the greater the stakes the more it would apply. So remember don't be no fool only the paranoid survive.

206. Always remember that life is delicate, and temporary. And therefore, should be greatly appreciated.

207. Let me reveal and expose a couple of profound truths to you. And that's one no matter what kind of facade one may present to the world we are all just human, meaning that we all have real problems, fears and insecurities. But that's just natural; it's only human to experience the aftermentioned. But the thing is to not let the aftermentioned control you or to get stuck in the aftermentioned or become dominated or subservient to the aftermentioned. But to experience, go through, and always keep the aftermentioned at bay. And two, that's that we all without exception have secret agendas and thoughts that we will never expose or reveal to any living soul. And if you say no . . . you're lying to yourself right now. Because like I said, we are all only human. And you may have an impeccable and immaculate façade. But remember it's just a facade.

208. Those who manipulate the unseen mechanism of society constitute an invisible government that is the true ruling power of our country. We are governed our minds molded, our tastes formed, our ideas suggested. In almost every act of our lives whether in the sphere of politics or business, in our social conduct, or our ethical thinking. We are dominated by the

relatively small number of persons who understand the mental processes and social patterns of the masses. It is they who pull the wires that control the public mind.

--Ed Bernays

In His Revelatory Book:

Propaganda, 1928

209. Always remember that the game is rigged. We are being sold out by leaders more beholden to certain interests, and corporations than to their constituents. We cannot expect very much from our governments, but we must expect much from ourselves. And there is no time to lose. Because there is no way an informed and therefore empowered people can lose. Because first, we must get together personally and electronically in an imagining of where we want to go. And it's our choice, not the President's, not the controllers, not the politicians, and not the media's choice . . . but ours. So let's make tools like Facebook work for us . . .

210. We are the most conditioned, programmed, beings the world has ever known. Not only are our thoughts and attitudes continually being shaped and molded, our very awareness of the whole design seems like it is being subtly and inexorably erased. Most issues of conventional wisdom are scientifically implanted in the public consciousness by a thousand media clips per day.

--Tim O'Shea

In his epical book: "The Doors of Perception" . . . On Why Americans will believe almost anything.

211. Whatever you do . . . stay away from corporate news. It's highly toxic, dangerously addictive propaganda is intended to disempower listeners and viewers with a depressing litany of unending disasters about which they can do absolutely nothing, except go to the mall or go buy a burger.

Michael L. Urias

"All Fall Down, The Politics of Terror and Mass Persuasion,"

By: William Thomas

212. Now this thought that you are about to read you may not think is important. But this thought contains some of the most pivotal information in this book concerning the development of one's self. Now what I'm going to speak on is the extreme prevalent reluctance of the masses of people to be creative. Because if you only knew right now in the world today there is an inordinate massive shortage of creativity so there is a lot of room, and a dire need for people to be creative in the world today. But because of fear and a lack of confidence people are not creative. And the fear that people feel is that they think that if they're creative and therefore start to create what has not yet been created, that they might fail or not succeed. And then add to that their own lack of confidence of what they think people might say or think about them being creative. In other words those breaking free from the status-quo and not being like the rest. So for mostly them 2 reasons fear and a lack of confidence the world is now suffering from an extreme lack and shortage of creativity. And remember that creativity means to create or form a new. And the world can never, and I say again, never get or have enough of that. And don't just read this thought . . . . One time read this thought 2, 3, or maybe even 4 times and ponder on it deeply. Then and only then will you get the reality of what I'm saying here.

213. Always remember that one of humanities greatest innate attributes is creativity, especially when cultivated, and developed, and not hindered by "I can'ts", "that won't work," "that's not possible," and all of the like that has been indoctrinated, and programmed in us from birth by our parents, our teachers, and especially the main stream. Because I want you to know and understand that creativity is really and actually one of our most puissant attributes. Why? Because creativity has no limit, it's infinite. And how much you exert or possess only depends on how much you've cultivated and developed it. And that's without the after mentioned impediments the "I can'ts," "that won't work," and 'that's not possibles" that have been indoctrinated in most of us over here in the western world.

But it's never too late. So now that you know start deprogramming yourself from that bullshit today. Because let me tell you something . . . one of the coldest and most severe regrets in old age and even when you pass over is knowing that you didn't even try. Because even if you fail at something, at least, you know that you tried God damn it. And that right there is very comforting. But if you don't even try, then just keeping it all the way real with you, then you are a failure . . . and a real loser. And you know that I don't even advocate regrets, but this is just the truth. Because remember you never know what will work until you try.

214. Always remember that even extremely smart people and geniuses don't know it all and can make mistakes. How, you might ask? Well here is how. A smart person or genius may think by plain reason or logic that something goes or may go this way or that way. But in all actuality be straight wrong. Because all things no matter what they are have their own individual way of working or going and if you're not familiar with that then nine times out of ten you're liable to make a mistake. And the same thing goes for understanding, because people don't understand that there is a hierarchy of understanding. Because before you can understand higher concepts or foreign concepts or concepts in which you have no experience in you must understand lower concepts and/or concepts that you have experience in. Then you can work your way up to higher concepts or foreign concepts. But you must go through the hierarchy of understanding. But all too often people try to go form a concept that they understand and know to one that is foreign or of a higher order and they think that they can comprehend or understand it but they really don't. But you can't tell them that, because they'll swear that they understand and/or comprehend. But like I said they really don't. So when in dialogues or discourses with people or when you're trying to explain something to somebody, remember, the hierarchy of understanding.

215. Alright, I've postulated that the basic building blocks of all the material physical world was thought. Well, I just thought that it would be nice for me to substantiate what I said based on

modern quantum physics. Okay. It goes like this as you break matter all the way down to its essentials you get atoms. Now follow me here . . . and atoms the basic building blocks of matter are not solid entities as you might of thought, but are a hierarchy of states of information and energy in a huge void. And atoms are made up of subatomic particles that are moving at lighting speeds around huge empty spaces. And these subatomic particles are not material things. They are fluctuations of energy (string theory) and information in a huge void. And I'm just going to say this, what is thought if not vibrating fluctuating energy and information. And all this I'm saying here comes straight from modern quantum physics. And when you look at matter through the eyes of quantum physics matter is proportionately as void as intergalactic space. Now that's deep, but very much true . . . and not just that, but did you know that in quantum physics it's now a known and accepted fact that 99.999% of matter is empty space. And the 0.001% that appears to be material is also empty space. It just gives the appearance of solidity. So in other words according to quantum physics matter is really made out of nothing. And we know better than that, because we know that matter is made out of thought. But as they say modern quantum physics, which is the most advanced physics of today is slowly catching up with ancient esoteric wisdom and knowledge that nothing is what quantum physics says that matter is made up of is really thought. But like they say themselves in quantum physics, the universe is made up of vibrating and fluctuating energy and information, which is nothing but thought. But those in the physics world just don't got the guts to say that yet. And lest we forget what is the main activity of the universe if not vibrant or vibrating and fluctuation of energy and information and at a quantum level a particle changes once you look at it. So what does that tell you, that once you focus your intent on something at the quantum level it starts to change? So therefore, in all actuality at the quantum level you are creating second by second, as you think. Meaning that you are creating via thought virtually all the time, incessantly. If you're thinking whether you know it or not you're creating. And I'm just going to say this and bring this thought to a close even if the whole of the physical universe were to be abolished or destroyed, it energy which is synonymous with thought would still go on existing and would be capable of creating a whole new universe.

216. John D. Rockefeller Sr. once said in 1899 when his holdings were estimate to be worth some 100 million that he was 60 years old, but in mistakes made he was at least 200 years old. And so my point is that mistakes are nothing but a natural part of life . . . they're inevitable and you're going to make them. So the thing is to make them, be resilient, learn from them, and keep moving. But never, absolutely never let mistakes keep you down or hold you back. And if anything just think of John D. Rockefeller Sr. one of the richest men to ever walk the face of the earth.

217. Always remember to build your life one line at a time, like you're writing a book until you get to where you want to go and or be.

218. Humanity is consumed and overwhelmed by fear and it's multifaceted expressions. And whenever anyone is in fear they will give their power away to anyone they believe will protect them.

--International Author and

Researcher, David Icke

219. So the plain lesson to be drawn from all this is that man must in the first place make the effort to have only good and pure thoughts and desires from his inner self. And next he must avoid those objects and associations that tend to cause to arise in him evil thoughts. And thirdly he must learn the truth that when he has these evil thoughts he attracts to himself spirits of evil who by their influence can do and do intensify these evil thoughts and desires. And they should learn this other fact that when their thoughts are pure and free from defilement and negativity they have surrounding them the influence of good spirits who work to increase and make permanent their good thoughts. And as these good thoughts continue, the natural love in man develops towards its pristine condition of purity and man comes nearer to his designed condition of existence.

--Lawyer and Renown Medium,

James E. Padgett, 1852 to 1923

220. Always remember that it's better to have a mind opened by wonder then one closed and locked by belief.

221. If you have a goal and you are 100 percent convinced about that goal, you will reach it.

--The Late Millionaire Aviator,

Steve Fossett

222. Always remember that whatever life is for you or whatever life turns out to be for you in the future, it is more times than not nothing but your own concoction via your thoughts. So you can't and please don't blame nobody for your life, because it's usually only your concoction.

223. Always remember that if you want to get your life together, you must start with your thoughts.

224. Always remember that the stone cold realities of life fuck people up, and people are incredulous to them, because people in the depths of their heart and soul don't want them to be so they wish most of the time them realities whatever they may be were not true. But yet, and so, realities will always be just that . . . . realities. And all I can say to that is that people need to wake up and face the music in their life, as well as, in the world.

225. Always remember that if you want to be the best at something, then you must learn from the best.

226. Always remember that the more corrupt a government becomes the more laws it will enact. And I'm going to tell you this and you can check it out if you like . . . legislators and governmental agencies have passed more laws, rules, and regulations in the last 10 years than has been passed in the last 200 years. And I just wonder what that makes you think!!!

227. The truth is usually the opposite of most of what you've heard or been taught all your life.

228. Always remember that people sneak, cheat, and manipulate more than you could ever imagine or believe.

229. Always remember to always absolutely believe in yourself and that sometimes you're going to have to fight verbally, physically, or otherwise, but you're going to have to fight sometimes. It's an inevitable part of life, and you must be ready and willing to rise to the occasion.

230. God's purpose for each of us was to go out into the world and do great things.

The Late Great Editor of Forbes,

Jim Michaels

231. Always remember that if you're afraid to take risks or afraid of failure then whether you know it or not you have a propensity to not go too far in life.

232. We are what we believe ourselves to be and the illuminati's most important goal is to tell us what to believe ourselves to be.

--David Icke

233. Always remember that every time we think and feel, no matter what our state of being may be. We are sending out broadcast waves that vibrate to the frequency of the particular thought or emotion. And we feel these frequencies coming from other people in what we call vibes.

234. Always remember that you can either live life or let life live you. And only you can make the choice. And sad to say most people either knowingly or unknowingly let life live them. And that's sad, very sad, because it doesn't have to be that way.

235. Now I just want to say something in regard to the power of thought and that's that the controllers of this world, which are

those that clandestinely control the U.S. government are themselves completely and totally infused with the power of thought to a degree that's just ineffable. And that's how they do what they do. They are masters and are completely proficient at using thought to create what they want . . . and that's how they do what they do. And I can't make it any simpler than that. And that power, the power of thought, which they the controllers have been using for eons to control the world in a negative way . . . I'm trying to give and convey it to you, for you to use in a positive way. Because you best believe me it's there for the taking. It's just they the controllers don't want you to know that.

236. Alright in this thought here I want to speak on something that is pretty important to most people, and that is the issues of baggage. Because a lot of people . . . some knowingly and some unknowingly carry baggage and that's not good. Because baggage hinders, impedes, and is nothing but negativity. And baggage can be the sole reason that keeps one from reaching his or her real and true potential. And to kill all ambiguity the baggage that I'm speaking on is the baggage that people carry from failure, past hurts, let downs, bad relationships, trauma, dysfunctional upbringings, or family relations, past abuse, emotional scars, fears, superstitions, irrational thoughts or beliefs, conflicts, misjudgments, past mistakes or losses, or any adverse or negative past experience. That is the baggage that I'm speaking on. And like I said baggage is nothing but negativity and can and will hinder a person from achieving his or her real and true potential. So therefore it is imperative that if one is carrying around baggage that one recognize it and know it. And then take effective steps, and measures to eradicate and neutralize all and any such baggage. And for those who have no idea of how to eradicate or neutralize such baggage . . . let me give you a great exercise that if done with diligence will have a great eradicating and neutralizing effect on all and any such baggage. And the exercise is this, and that's to at least 3 times a week go into a meditative state with a strong and positive frame of mind very important and while in this state empower yourself with nothing but empowering thoughts such as you're great, you're a winner, you can most definitely do or accomplish whatever you're trying to do or accomplish,

Thoughts on Life And the Absolute Power of Thought

you will absolutely succeed no matter how long it takes you . . . whatever happen in the past you will only learn from. You have no doubt whatsoever that god is on your side no matter what you have did or are doing, because God's love is beyond unconditional and we can never fully understand it. And that you know in the depths of your heart and soul without any doubt whatsoever that if you put out enough thought energy and exercise your will you can accomplish and or do anything that you wish. Now these thoughts are just an outline and you do not have to follow them to the letter they are just an example of the kind of thoughts you should be entertaining while you're in the first half of your meditative state of which should last at least 30 minutes. Now at the conclusion of the first half of your meditative state you should feel sufficiently positive, good, and empowered. But in this second half you're going to see and clearly visualize yourself carrying suitcases to a pier and in the suitcases is all your mental and emotional baggage, whatever it may be and you are just going to throw the suitcases over the pier and into the water. And you are going to know for a fact that whatever's hurting you or happen in your past or whatever the baggage may be it is in them suitcases that you're throwing over the pier and once you throw them suitcases over the pier you are going to know and feel that whatever that baggage was it is now completely and totally gone, lost forever in the ocean. And you are free of it. Now you must perform this exercise until you know for a fact that you are totally and completely free of all your baggage.

237. Always remember that positiveness is power. And real rock solid belief is power. And to constantly and incessantly project and put out those thoughts is implementation of that power. Now I'm going to give you a very real, and powerful state of mind when dealing with and eradiating problems and believe me it gives me great joy to do so. Because I know beyond the shadow of any doubt that innumerable people have various and all kinds of problems in a vast assortment of different capacities. And the state of mind is: I don't have no problems, believe that none, and the problems that I do have will most definitely take care of themselves. And it's not complex but just that simple. And I like it and love it that way.

Now that state of mind in the forgoing when really believed in the depths of one's soul and constantly and incessantly projected and put out in thought is very real and powerful. And believe it or not eventually becomes one's reality.

238. A genuine leader is not a searcher for consensus but a molder of consensus . . .

--Martin Luther King Jr.

1929-1968

239. There is a wheel on which the affairs of man revolve, and its mechanism is such that it prevents any man from being always fortunate. . .

--Croesus

560-545 B.C.

240. Always remember that you must fill your thoughts with emotional desire for them to be potent.

241. Let me say this because this is so real and will without a doubt become more and more noticeable as times goes on. And that's that synchronicity is most definitely on the rise now, and time, and things are moving faster and faster and will continue to do so until it seems that time and things are moving so fast that it will actually be scary. But this is nothing it's all part of a natural cycle that occurs on earth once every 26,000 years. And we are at the end of one of those cycles now . . . and the cycles changes in 2012 if you didn't know. But what I'm saying is that as time and things began to move faster and faster, people who are oblivious to this and don't know what's going on will feel as if they have to move faster and faster to keep up with what is going on, which is a straight lie. And will therefore wear themselves out and drive themselves crazy. But the thing to do is to slow down . . . think, get in tune with yourself, and know that synchronicity is on the rise and will continue to be. And the important and good thing is that thoughts once put out and projected will began to materialize faster and faster. So for those who know this. This is a very beautiful thing, because

they will be able to fix, create, or correct for themselves and their life whatever they want in a very short span of time and as time and things move faster and faster the time span for thoughts to materialize will get shorter and shorter. And for those of you reading this the truthfulness of what I'm saying here is self evident for those of you that are alert and conscious as to what has been happening and taking place in your life recently.

242. Always remember that all people have become what they are because of their dominating thoughts and desires.

243. It has been said that over 90% of the world's peoples sit back and wait on their leaders or rulers to tell them what to do because they lack the knowledge, education, courage, know-how, willingness, impetus, etc., etc., to get up and do their own thing and/or create their own reality. But this is just the way that they the controllers want it.

244. Always remember that no association or experience is really by chance, but is the outgrowth of the 2nd law of the universe known as the law of attraction. Each individual constantly meets him/herself in situations, people, and experiences that reflect their current and dominate thoughts and/or beliefs – whatever they may be.

245. Always remember to never, absolutely never take nothing for granted, because hear me, and hear me well, you never know what you got until it's gone.

246. Know that man, as has been expressed, was given dominion over all. And in the understanding of the same may use all the laws pertaining to the same for his benefit.

--Edgar Cayce

Clairvoyant and Mystic

1877-1945

247. Always remember that one can always sit back and think of innumerable reasons why one can hate, dislike, and basically think bad of, and not like the world. But at the exact same time one can also sit back and think of just as many reasons why one can be positive, love, and think good of the world. It's nothing but a choice, that's it and that's all. It's how you choose you can either be positive, or negative, optimistic or pessimistic. It's your choice and that's with everything in life.

248. I have and this is from experience created the impossible by simply using the power of thought . . . and that's real talk.

--The Author

249. Always remember that adversity can and more times than not does build strength and the saying that something can make you or break you is very true.

250. Always remember that thoughts are synonymous with energy and they are not only some of the most powerful things in the world, but in the universe. You are and/or will become whatever you believe. And you have all the power you could ever want, believe that! Thoughts are energy and energy is power. And you can harness any and whatever power you need via and through your thoughts. Meditate and learn how to do that and you will most definitely become powerful and in more ways than one.

251. Now this book if you didn't already know will provide you with the keys to the joy of living and the abundant life. This book will show people how to change their entire life, the course of history or the world if they want. And people need not great money, power, status, or even armies. All they need is a sincere passion, and belief in the power of thought meaning that they know how to project thought to create their own reality, they know how to project and hold a frame of mind, or put better, a frame of thought, because thoughts create our realities. And if you can project and hold a frame of thought or thoughts better known as thought frequency then you will be able to create damn near anything without exception that you want. Now, when you project this thought frequency whatever

you're trying to do or create you want to project it as fully done or created just the way you want or want it to be. And not just that, but you want to feel, and I mean actually feel the feeling of how you would feel, to actually accomplish or acquire, whatever you're trying to do. And another pivotal point is when you project your thought frequency you don't want to just project it or put it out for a day, a week, a month, or even a year, you want to fall into the state of mind of ceaselessly and perpetually projecting your thought frequency until it comes into manifestation without any regard to time. Basically it becomes a way of life until it comes about. And believe it or not what I just said in the forgoing works like magic all you go to do is project in thought whatever you're trying to do or create in completeness, keep the thought frequency constant and continuous and last but not least keep the thought frequency infused with desire and if you want it to be expedited into manifestation then keep it infused with hot emotional you can feel desire. Remember I was telling you about feeling? Now before I bring this to an end there's a flip side to projecting thoughts, frames of thoughts, AKA thought frequency's, because some people and this is truly inadvertently or without them knowing or being aware of it, get locked into states of mind where they are projecting and this is incessantly, and perpetually, negative or adverse thoughts, frames of thoughts, AKA thought frequency's and therefore these negative and adverse thoughts become reality and manifest in these people's lives as things and situations. And these people in turn have no idea where these bad, negative, adverse, and not good things and situations in their life came from . . . huh! They're creating them themselves, but such is the power of thought it can work for you or against you. And on a last note you want to stay away from anything that hinders, impedes or distracts you from projecting your desired thought frequency, i.e. Things you see, hear or come in contact with. And on the other hand you want to be around things that help, support, or facilitate your thought frequency that you're projecting. Like for example, if you want to be a billionaire then you want to eat, sleep, and read nothing but about billionaires . . . period. And the same holds true for anything else that you're endeavoring to create via projecting thought frequencies.

252. If man will only think, and in thinking understand that all sin and error and the resulting unhappiness and sorrow in the world are children of their own creating and not the children of God. And that in the economy of God's great universe he leaves the control and management and even the existence of these children to the will of their parents (mortals) and they will understand why evil exists, why wars and hatred and misery continue on earth. The universe and inhabitants thereof and the greatest production of his power man were all created by god, but sin and error and their awful following are the creatures and creations of man. The laws of God's universe all work in harmony and all is good. And even the apparent in harmony which man has created does not affect the great harmony, but is confined in its workings to man himself. Only man is apparently out of harmony in the universe and that is caused by man himself. And love is the great principle that enters into all knowledge of things spiritual. And without love it is utterly impossible for man to rightfully conceive the truths of God and possess them.

--Lawyer and Renown Medium,

James E. Padgett

1852 – 1923

253. Always remember that life was never meant to be or is it a vacation or a walk in the park. Life always was and is a labor of hard work, learning, and experience.

254. Always remember that you only have a problem if you first agree, and accede, that you have a problem . . . other than that you have no problems . . . you might have puzzles, or challenges, or opportunities in disguise, or whatever but you have no problems until you personally accept, and agree to that connotation . . . then and only then do you have a problem or problems.

255. Energy is always moving in us, through us, and out of us. That's why the vibes have to right before you can read someone

without static. Because every emotion is a different energy vibration.

256. The illuminati have no shape or form and they work through all people and all things – so therefore anybody who tries to describe their operations sounds like a paranoid.

257. The underground seas . . . are real they have just never been talked about or exposed . . .

258. The illuminati control all sorts of organizations and national governments without any of them being aware that the others are also controlled. Each group thinks it is competing with others while actually each is playing its due part in the illuminati's plan.

259. The FBI, the CIA, and all other agencies spy on each other endlessly.

260. The 1927 narcotics act made over a 100,000 harmless junkies straight criminals overnight. Then 10 years later in 1937, because giant corporations like DuPont who wanted to kill off the hemp industry for their own ends, all the harmless pot-heads in the country became straight criminals as pot was outlawed by an act of congress. And if you don't believe me you need to check it out for yourself.

261. Corporations and companies are infiltrated all the time so their products and services can and are compromised. More times than people know or think . . .

262. Advertisements placed in newspapers and in T.V. and other media are a lot of the time codes from certain people to other people. Like for example the thanking Jude for favors granted.

263. We don't have telepathy because we lack a hormone that causes it.

264. Mass human sacrifice can and is masked as other things, such as war, famine, and plagues.

265. The dishonest book of lies . . . The honest book of truth . . .

266. Always remember there's always an exoteric version and a real inside story to everything.

267. The pentagon might house an evil spirit, because a pentagon is the inside of a pentagram.

268. Always remember the truth does not change its identity in the process of being understood. Meaning that truth does and will not change. You either understand it or you don't, but nonetheless truth will still be truth.

269. It's been said that every man should have a plot of earth separate from all worldly concerns where he might go to ponder the realities of life.

270. The initiate learned why the great truths of life cannot be imparted by words alone.

--Lectures on Ancient Philosophy

By Manly P. Hall

271. Always remember that this book may seem profound at first to you, but that's because you're still a neophyte, but once you read, learn to learn and your understanding starts to open up you'll see and understand that the principals in this book are really rudimentary. And what I just said is very true, because once you see that knowledge is really and absolutely infinite, and truth is immutable. And there are some truths so abstruse, and so recondite, that they cannot in no kind of way even be articulated or described in human words or diction, and you may not be able to see or understand that right now, but like I just said once you start to learn, regenerate, and develop your mind you'll start to see and understand what I'm talking about. And that's that this book is really simple and rudimentary when compared to the great truths of the universe. This book is not even on the scale it's nothing and that's an understatement.

272. Proclus (410 to 485 AD) declared that the philosophy of Plato was given to men for the benefit of their terrestrial selves i.e.

That universal law might be authority instead of statutes, rationality instead of churches and/or temples, understanding instead of institutions, truth instead of mortal leaders, and that man who are now, as well as those who shall exist hereafter might now wander about the earth lost, deceived, and in ignorance.

273. It was said by the ancient Greek philosopher Pythagoras: that every substance, object, element, and agent in the universe is capable of instructing man in those phases of its order which are involved in its own constitution. In other words everything can teach us of itself, which is very true.

274. Always remember that the true source of man's education is not to be found in books, but lies in his observation of natural phenomena, and in his accumulation and understanding of his practical experiences.

275. Always remember that as we look about we see a universe which, whether we know it or not, is simply our inner convictions reflected back to us. Because life is for each of us nothing but a solitary cell whose walls are mirrors. And we terrify ourselves by the faces we make so I tell you to laugh in the mirror, and start seeing your life happy, good, and productive, and just the way that you want it. And then you will start to live as a guest, instead of a condemned prisoner in your life.

276. Know that man, as has been expressed, was given dominion over all. And in the understanding of the same may use all the laws pertaining to the same for his benefit.

277. Now what I'm about to say a lot of people need to really consider, because once again it's very real and very true. And that's that if you want something you have to be willing to pay the price for it and there's no and if's or but's about it. And I'm not necessarily talking about things that can be bought with money even though they fit into this too. But I'm not necessarily talking about them. What I'm talking about is say for instance someone is 100, 200, or 300 pounds overweight and they want to lose weight and be slim and trim. Now the

thing is they want to lost weight and be slim and trim . . . right? But and that's the key word here, but are they willing and actually ready to pay the price to lose that weight??? And the price to lose that actual weight is not really monetary but consist of getting up every day and indulging in strenuous physical exercise for at least, and that is at the minimum two hours every day for at least 6 months to a year and not only that but drastically decreasing their calorie intake and only eating certain things at certain times. Now that's the price that one would have to pay to really and actually lose weight. But again are they really and actually ready to pay that price to lose weight? And that question can only be answered and answered truthfully by the individual who wants to lose weight. Are they really ready to pay the price? And this applies to everything in life without exception that you want, are you really ready and willing to pay the price for it? And if you're not then please don't lie to yourself because trying to minimize, taking short cuts, and cut corners that's out you're only lying to yourself. And that's something you never want to do. And if you are doing it then I'm here to tell you straight up that you are in a state of straight denial and you need to wake up out of your delusion, because in life there's no free lunch only hard work baby.

278. Always remember that one of the first things of becoming enlightened is learning to doubt everything. And did you know it's been said that nothing is true until irrefutably and absolutely proven? And one of the oldest terrors or horrors when first becoming enlightened is the realization that you can't believe anything that you've ever been told. And just think about it you're only a baby, and I don't care if you're 20, 30, 50, 60, or 100 years old you're still only a baby in a world that's 4 billion years old and in a universe that's even much older than that. So what do you really know about what really goes on in the world, and has went on in the world aside from what the controllers have told you via religion, the media, so called formal education, and all the other facets of the mainstream? And for those of you out there who think you know something and call yourselves experts or whatever in whatever is your particular endeavor let me just tell you this in order for you to honestly and truthfully call yourself an expert in whatever your endeavor

is you must first from start to finish and as a whole possess more knows then I don't knows about your endeavor. And I'll tell you this I've met many people who called themselves experts in my life and everyone without exception possessed more I don't knows and questions than knows about their particular endeavor, but hey that might of just been my experience.

279. We are what we believe ourselves to be and the controllers most important goal is to tell us what to believe ourselves to be.

280. Is Bush's war on terror a fraud? You bet, says lawyer Michael Wildes. While representing a Saudi Diplomat who defected to the USA with 14,000 documents implicating Saudi citizens in financing terrorism, Wildes went to see FBI agents who told him they were not permitted to read any of his evidence.

--All Fall Down, the Politics of Terror and Mass Persuasion

By: William Thomas

Pg. 55

281. Always remember to listen to other people and to each other's stories. If you believe them to be truthful. Why? Because there is more wisdom in personal experience than damn near in anything else.

282. Always remember that you cannot and will not understand a person's actions unless you understand their beliefs.

283. Always remember that you can live life or let life live you. It's your choice.

284. The illuminati have used two apparent "opposites" to control the reality of people: official science and the greatest form of mind control ever invented . . . religion. These are seen as opposites, as polarities. But they are oppo-sames. They are the same outcome by a different route. Science has basically told us that the world that we see is all that exists and that what happens to us in our few years of consciousness is as random as

life itself. Religion tells us that if we do as it says we will go to paradise as a chosen one. If we do not do as it says we will spend our eternity in the fires of hell. Both opposites have a common theme. You are not in control of your life – you are either a random accident or the pawn in the game of some dictator God who is so loving He will condemn you to an eternity of suffering for having the nerve not to do what the men in the flocks tell you. The common theme is that you are ordinary and powerless. And you must look outside of yourself to others to tell you what you should think, do, and say.

--David Icke

In His Highly Acclaimed Book:

Alice in Wonderland and the World Trade Center Disaster

285. Ye have locked yourselves up in cages of fear, and behold now ye complain that ye lack freedom.

--The Honest Book of Truth

286. The Disciple asked the master where he might find the secret of life. And the master responded to the young neophyte and said you already have it my son. And the young neophyte responded and said no master I've searched the highest mountains, and the deepest oceans, and plowed the farthest plains of the earth . . . all to no avail. And the master responded and said no my young son you have it all wrong, the secret to life is within you.

287. Let me tell you something that came on ABC news about 25 years ago that I believe that can be adaptively applied to this book: If humanity decides to get behind a single message, the possibility to communicate that message is limitless.

ABC New Special

On Live Aid

July 13, 1985

288. All the breaks you need in life wait within your imagination. Imagination is the workshop of your mind, capable of turning mind energy into accomplishment and wealth.

289. Always remember that thoughts are real and actual things.

290. Thought are things, powerful things when they are mixed with definiteness of purpose, persistence, and a burning desire for their transmutation into the material physical realms. When projecting and putting out thought to do or create whatever you're trying to create. Remember emotional desire is the fuel for your thoughts. And you must focus your thoughts like a laser on whatever you're trying to create. For whatever time it may take to create whatever you're trying to create. And time or the length there of should not even matter. Because projecting thought to create your own reality is not something one does for a week, a month, or a year, it's a way of life. It's how one lives his or her life. And remember when projecting and focusing your thoughts to create your reality emotional desire is the only fuel. There is no other fuel for thoughts and to bring them into manifestation emotional desire is the one and only fuel. So the more emotional desire you pump into your thoughts the quicker they will manifest. And on a last note and this is very pivotal all objects, situations, or hindrances that are contrary to what you are endeavoring to create know that they're there. But after that please completely forget about them and do not so much as give them a scintilla of thought or thought energy because you will only be empowering them and you do not want to do that. So therefore you must not focus or think about the hindrances that you must surmount at all. You must think about and focus only on what you want to create and nothing else and I don't give a damn what it is outside of this it don't matter. You must live and actually act like you have already created or attained whatever you're trying to create or attain . . . period.

291. Always remember and this is absolute truth, that one of the most powerful things in the world, and known to man is a frame of mind that says I will not be stopped, I will succeed I don't give a damn how many difficulties, failures, or trials, I may

have to go through or surmount. I will succeed. Now that frame of mind when said with real conviction and sincerely adhered to is one of the most powerful things known to man. It's called absolute and immutable determination.

292. Thomas Edison dreamed of a lamp that could be operated by electricity and began were he stood to put his dream into actions, and despite more than 10,000 documented failures, he stood by that dream until he made it a physical reality.

293. Always remember that every adversity carries with it the seeds of a greater benefit.

294. It is said that man can create anything that he imagines.

295. Always remember that no one is ever defeated until defeat has been accepted as a reality.

296. Always remember that if one is really to be great and actually succeed in life one must be ready, and able to surmount staggering obstacles whenever the need presents itself.

297. This book that you are now reading is so, so powerful that I just want to beat and bank on this table that I'm writing on, and just holler and holler and holler, because the power in this book is just ineffable and please believe me people that's no lie. And when you get done reading this book you'll know what I'm talking about. Because you're now holding in your hands a master key to acquiring, attaining, or gaining absolutely anything that you so do wish in life if, and that if, is a big work, if you apply and put into actual action the principles mentioned in this book.

298. Always remember that you need only a few things to become wealthy. And one of those things is desire.

299. Always remember that no successful or great person has attained or acquired success or greatness without first encountering much failures and or defeat. And if you don't believe me just ask any great or successful person as to the truthfulness of this statement. And if you don't know nobody who has attainted or acquired a good deal of success or

greatness in their life, then I suggest you read some autobiography's of great and or successful people.

300. How to create one's own reality through and via one's own thoughts is the key to life. And that key right there has been and still is right now being systematically suppressed by those who clandestinely control the U.S. government via, and through their complete, total, and unequivocal control of all the tentacles of the mainstream. That's why you were never taught in school or on T.V., the news, or in church, or through any religion, or any other tentacle of mainstream society that you are the master of your own destiny, and are able to completely control, and create your own reality via, and through your thoughts and that everything starts within you. And this is why those who clandestinely control the U.S. government have given you the masses of people mainstream science, and organized religion and copious other pseudo beliefs, ideologies, and doctrines to feed upon. While all the time keeping the real and true arcane knowledge of life, nature, and the universe suppressed and to themselves.

301. Always remember that everybody isn't determined, and everybody isn't driven, and everybody does not have desire, and persistence, but everybody can it's simply a choice . . . your choice.

302. Remember what the great end we all aim at is: is it not to be happy here and in the hereafter?

--Taken From the Preface

To Long-livers Published

In 1772 By, Eugenius

Philalethes

303. Always remember that life is permeated with sin so therefore all kinds of bad and evil things are going to happen, and do happen every day, things like people getting killed, maimed, and myriad other unspeakable and unutterable evil, bad, and

negative things happen all day everyday in this world. But what I'm here to tell you is that we create our reality via our thoughts. So we are no more than what we think. So when we see or hear about these evil, bad, or negative things happening, because it's inevitable these things are going to happen as long as the world is permeated with sin, and if we are influenced by them and therefore start to ponder or think about them either consciously or subconsciously then we are actually aiding, supporting, and strengthening the evil, bad, and negativity by giving it thought energy. So what I'm telling you is when you see or hear about these adverse things happening or taking place do not and I say again do not ponder, or dwell, or think about them for any amount of time. Because that will only be feeding them and giving them power to manifest in your life. Because we are not more than our thoughts, and our thoughts create our realities and our worlds. So when you see or hear about these evil, bad, and negative things happening pay them no mind and do not let them distract you or throw you off from what you're trying to do or create in your life for yourself. Meaning keep your thoughts positive, and on what you're trying to create. And not on the evil, bad, and negativity, that's happening or taking place in the world.

304. Always remember that you don't know it all, and you going to make mistakes, and fuck ups. But the thing is to take these things in a learning process and not get stuck. That's the thing, and anything else is out. Meaning all the way dead.

305. Always remember that life if full of double standards and if you think not then you're crazy. And I'm not in the no kind of way saying that's right but that's just the way it is.

306. Now if this book can become a national movement which I really believe it can and will via word of mouth, blogs, the internet, text messaging, you tube, and even Facebook. Then this book will do good for America, and the world.

307. Now one of the most beautiful things in God's universe is that damn near all things are possible and if you don't believe anything else I say please believe this and that's that the universe as it was ordained and created by God was made to

specialize in creating the impossible and unique. I mean just look at all the countless stories of people saying, I never thought in my wildest dreams I'm make it this far, or I came from completely nothing to something. And people think stories like that are strange, or should not happen, or in their words impossible. But no, no, if they only knew how the universe really works, and was set up to work, they would know that the universe was made to specialize in creating what people not knowingly call the impossible or the unique. And once again if you don't believe me, just ask Oprah Winfrey to tell you her story.

308. Always remember that life is real, and no one ever said that it was going to be easy . . . life is hard. And emotions are real, and can do more times than not run deep. And whatever you do you don't want a sad and boring life. Because you live once and you only got so much time down here and after that you're gone out of here. So please believe me while you're here and while you still can you want to live your life to the fullest. You want to be vibrant, and exciting, and you want to take risks, and chances, like I said while you still can because believe me a day is coming (when you're old) and when whether you want to or not you will not be able to take risks, and chances. So live, and live to the fullest and stop making the mistake that so many make, and that's taking their lives for granted. Because you best believe me just ask somebody who has had a near death experience you could be here today alive and fully well and gone dead tomorrow . . . just that quick. So please take heed to these words.

309. Always remember that life is always going to have ups and downs, good times and bad times it's absolutely inevitable and this applies to everyone without exception and the only thing that differentiates us when the bad times come is how we think and how we choose to act and re-act either positive or negative when bad or adverse times hit us. And it was once said that when things are up and life is good you better enjoy yourself and take advantage because you never know what tomorrow may bring.

310. Always remember that you must always strive to be, and or, become more than the propensities that heredity and environment had planned for you.

311. The exterior physical universe this is where our attention is usually focused. It is entirely constructed by our senses and our projected thoughts as modern physics and ancient mystics both testify – but it is what most people call reality. They are conditioned to accept it, and not to inquire further, because only in this dream-walking state can they be governed by those who wish to govern.

312. Always remember the state is based on threat, if the people are not afraid of something, they'll realize they don't need big government.

313. Check this out . . . supposed our society crippled every infant's legs systematically. Instead of our minds? And the ones who tried to get up and walk would be called crazy, and neurotics, right? And the awkwardness of their first efforts would be published in all psychiatric journals as proof of the regressive and schizzy nature of their unsocial and unnatural impulse toward walking, right? And only those who knew the secret would be superior. Right? Well that is exactly what is going on concerning our minds true abilities and potentials, i.e. psychic abilities, and our innate potential to create our own reality via our thought projections.

314. Always remember that people exist on a spectrum from the most adamant to the most flexible. The latter, unless they are thoroughly trained in psychodynamics, are always at a disadvantage to the former in social interactions the adamant do not change their script, the flexible continually keep changing theirs trying to find a way or relating constructively. Eventually, the flexible ones find the proper gambit, and communication, of sort, is possible. They are on the set created by the adamant person, and they act out his or her script. The steady exponential growth of bureaucracy is not due to Parkingson's law alone. The state, by making itself every more adamant, incorporates more and more people into its set and

forces them to follow its script. Pay attention people to what you just read – and think about it.

315. For not all true things are to be said to all men.

> --Bishop clement of Alexandria,
>
> Egypt – Who was An Early
>
> Christian Father

316. Now what you just read in the previous thought I want you to know, and understand that it virtually applies to all groups, associations, organizations, institutions, etc, etc, and it makes no difference how lofty or prestigious they may be. They go by Bishop Clements tenet . . .

317. Always remember that most people have dreams in their youth that get shattered or worn down with age. They find themselves disappointed by people, events, and just plain reality itself. But I'm here to tell you with all the emphasis that I can muster to not let that happen to you. And this book will show you how to not let it happen to you. Please believe that.

318. The unlearned and the ignorant scoff and doubt the existence of evil cliques of men bent on global dominations.

> --Texe Marrs

319. There are two views of history: (1) History happens by accident or (2) It is planned. The general public is taught that history happens by accident. However, the upper echelons . . . know that history is planned.

--R.E. McMasters, Jr. In His Excellently Researched Book: The Power of Total Perspective

320. Since I entered politics, I have chiefly had men's views confided to me privately. Some of the biggest men in the United States, in the field of commerce and manufacture, are afraid of somebody, are afraid of something. They know that

there is power somewhere so organized, so subtle, so watchful, so interlocked, so complete, so pervasive, that they had better not speak above their breath when they speak in condemnation of it.

--Former President Woodrow Wilson,

In His Book: The New Freedom

321. Those who manipulate the unseen mechanism of society constitute an invisible government which is the true ruling power of our country. Our minds are molded . . . . largely by men we have never heard of.

--Edward Bernays,

In His 1928 Book:

Propaganda

322. Now in this thought here I'm going to tell you a story, and this story has been told many times prior to this. This is a story about the absolute power of determination, belief, and desire. And the story goes as follows: the morning after the great Chicago fire, a group of merchants stood on State Street looking at the smoking remains of what had been their stores. They went into a conference to decide if they would try to rebuild or leave Chicago and start over in a more promising or better place. They reached a decision – all except one to leave Chicago. The merchant who decided to stay and rebuild pointed a finger at the remains of his store and said, gentlemen on that spot I will build the world's greatest store, no matter how many times it may burn down. That was almost a century and a half ago. The store was built. It stands there today a towering monument to the power of determination, belief, and desire. Now the easy thing for Marshal Field to have done would have been exactly what his fellow merchants did. When the going got rough and all looked bad they succumbed and packed up and went elsewhere, where the going seemed easier and better. But mark well the difference between Marshal Field and the other merchants because it is the same difference which distinguishes practically all who succeed from those who fail.

And that difference is that Marshall Field possessed and absolute determination, belief, and desire, about what he was doing and/or wanted to do.

323. The key to happiness is to discover it in every moment, not to wait for it to arrive with the achievement of some future goal.

> --The Passion Test
>
> By Janet Bray Attwood
>
> & Chris Attwood

324. We've come to realize that anything is possible. You just have to be clear on what you want to show up in your life.

> --Nicole Wild, Executive
>
> Director of the Women's
>
> Alliance

325. You have no limitations until you set them.

> --Tibetan Mystic

326. Always remember that there is no death only the end of an experience and eternity is incomprehensible.

327. Meditation is a special place that is different than sleep and different from just thinking it is unique unto itself.

> --Edgar Cayce, Clairvoyant
>
> & Mystic, 1877 – 1945

328. It is either understood or misunderstood, that within the planetary awareness, the minds of humanity in combination are the conscious awareness of the planet itself.

> --The Handbook for the New

329. Timothy Leary said it: People have to go out of their minds before they can come to their senses. Because what the world calls sanity has led us to the present planetary crisis. And people have to break up and/or dismantle the conditioning, programming, and brainwashing that the controllers via society have laid on us all. Antonin Artaud and Andre Breton put it in a nutshell in the first surrealist manifesto: total transformation of mind and all that resembles it.

330. Always remember that the first man to think a new thought advances it very tentatively. New ideas have to be around a while before anyone will promote them hard. In their first form, they are like tiny imperceptible mutations that may eventually lead to new species.

331. The idea is to find out if a person will listen, really listen, or just shut their minds at the first really shocking idea.

--Howard Hughes,

1905 to 1976

332. If I learned one thing in the last few years, it's that the crazier an idea is the more likely it is to be true.

--Howard Hughes,

1905 to 1976

333. For those who can see it and for those who can catch it this book contains tons of knowledge.

334. Artists also arrive at truth through their imaginations, if they let themselves wander freely. They're more likely to arrive at the truth then more scientific minded people.

---Paul Klee

1879 to 1940

335. Always remember there is always an exoteric version and a real inside story to everything.

336. It was once said that people living in the modern western world know the price of everything and the value of nothing.

337. Why not secretly install fear in the people, to create turmoil? Why not set up and control your own opposition? In this way, changes favorable to them, the rulers, the illuminati, could be engineered and caused.

--Texe Marrs

The Circle of Intrigue

338. The media and the education establishment provide not a clue to the actual operation of society and the real history of the world.

--Texe Marrs

The Circle of Intrigue

339. To be effective we must direct our attacks on the real criminals, the super wealthy, and the powerful and secret elite of the entire world – the conspirators laboring day and night to enslave us.

--The Late Novelist

Taylor Caldwell, 1974

340. See you got to understand that there are many ups and downs in life and that any and all things that you can possibly conceive do come to pass good and bad. And that can be a good thing or a bad thing but it's for a certainty a real thing. And that just means that the unlikely, and impossible, do come to pass, and can come to pass in your favor if you believe that and stringently and honestly focus on that. Now did you understand what you just read? If not you need to re-read it.

341. Always remember that those who clandestinely control the U.S. government A.K.A. the illuminati have no shape or no

form they are the epitome of amorphous only with definite organization. And they work through any and all people and any and all things without any shame whatsoever. So therefore anybody who tries to describe their operations sounds like a paranoid. Like for example in World War II they worked through Hitler and at the same time were working through allies who eventually took Hitler down. Pretty ingenious, huh?!

342. Always remember that mistakes, and slip ups, in your life can hurt, and can cost. Think about that cause; it's very real. But most people tend to over look it.

343. I believe that this is one of the most profound and powerful, books written for the exoteric populace in the last 200 years.

--The Author

344. Human beings tend to live to far within self-imposed limits.

--William James

345. If one approaches the self believing that it is power and might, that one becomes might and power.

--Isreal Regardie,

The Tree of Life,

A Study in Magic

346. All the world is a stage.

--Shakespeare

347. Always remember that one of the best things of being successful is that it makes you forget all your failures.

348. It has been said that when we're born we are innocent and pure. But what we become when the world is through messing us over is something else. And it's either going to be positive or negative but whatever it is, it's going to be completely up to you.

349. Always remember that your future is nothing but your reincarnated thoughts of today. And I don't give a damn what your situation, or circumstances are you could be living in one of the poorest countries in the world, such as Haiti's Cite-Soleil where people literally eat cookies made from dirt for dinner. If you project and focus your thoughts, and thought energy, for enough length of time and absolutely let nothing distract you, you most definitely can bring about to manifestation whatever situation, and/or circumstances you want in life.

350. Always remember that you're not always all the time going to lose at everything, just like by the same token you're not always all the time going to win at everything . . . believe that!

351. Always remember never depend on somebody else's power, strength, or faith, never. Why? Because they will more times than not let you down . . . believe me.

352. Always remember that what you think about, where your thoughts go. Meaning where your energy goes will determine where you go in life.

353. Now in this thought here I just want to say like I been telling you all along it's about believing, faith, and projecting thought energy to create what you want, your own reality. But what I want to convey to you is that when you're projecting through energy to create whatever your endeavoring to create that the how part, how something going to happen or manifest should not at all concern you and if you do focus on the how part it can actually be deleterious to you . . . and deleterious is the key word here. And the reason I say that you should not concern yourself with how something is going to come to pass, or manifest, is because that is not your business or your concern that's the universe's business and concern and it's very pivotal that you know that. Because your only business and concern is to believe in the depths of your soul, to have absolute faith and to incessantly project the thought energy of whatever your trying to create. And let me tell you something else the universe sometimes brings things to pass and to manifestation, through the back door meaning that just because something

looks bad, negative, or adverse. It just may really look that way on the surface. But the truth might just be the universe bringing something to pass or manifestation through the back door. And this is why I say that no matter what stay believing in the depths of your soul, keep your absolute faith and stay incessantly projecting that thought energy of whatever your endeavoring to create or do. And you best believe me and I speak from vast experience everything will work out.

354. Always remember this and never forget it and that's that fear is failure. If you fear, or are afraid, you have already lost. Now it doesn't have to be that way because you can actually stop fearing or being afraid. Anytime you choose and take your power back and start winning.

355. Alright now what I'm about to convey in this thought is very important to those who are endeavoring to consciously create their own reality's via their thoughts and that's that did you know that it's a psychological fact and like I always say you can check this out for yourself that over 75% of people's daily thoughts are straight negative, indirectly negative, guilt-ridden, fear based, or adverse to them in some way, form, or fashion. Now that's not good, and that's the American Psychological Association's own statistics for the thoughts that the average person daily entertains. Now if you're endeavoring to consciously create your own reality via your thoughts that must change if you're trying to create good and beneficial things in your life. You must actively and consciously censor your thoughts and endeavor to think and project only those thoughts that are conducive to what you are trying to do or create in your life. And not only that but you want to fuel, and give those thoughts power, by infusing them with hot you can feel emotional desire. Remember thoughts are energy and that same energy is the bases of all manifested creation in this world the 3rd dimension.

356. The presidents and prime ministers are the ones who make the underground deals and speak the true underground idiom. The corporations, the military, the banks, this is the underground network. This is where it happens. Power flows under the surface, far beneath the level you and I live on. This is where

the laws are broken way down under far beneath the speed freaks and cutters of smack.

--Don Delillo

Great Jones Street

357. I personally am convinced that the justice department is against the best interest of the United States in terms of stopping drugs. What has the DEA agent who puts his life on the line got to look forward to? The United States government is not going to back him up. I find that intolerable.

--Representative Larry Smith,

Chairman of The House Task

Force On International

Narcotics Control

358. Always remember that the average person lives his or her whole life powerless because there moving so fast and virtually never take the time to slow down, focus, concentrate and meditate, and get into themselves, and put out thought energy in a coherent way with profound desire of what their trying to do and/or create in their life.

359. Now in this thought here I'm going to briefly speak on logic and illogic and how these two basic concepts are understood, applied, and used. Alright logic is derived from one's accumulated experience, and one's accumulated knowledge. Because you can only reason and rationalize things from what you have experienced or from what you have learned or have been taught, meaning what you know. So therefore if something is outside of your realms of experience and/or knowledge it is more times than not going to be illogical to you. Just like for example if you were living in the year 1850 and I told you about broadcasting T.V. live around the world via satellite you wouldn't begin to know or understand what I was talking about. It would be completely and totally illogical to

you. Why? Because it would be completely and totally outside of your base of accumulated experience and knowledge. Just like certain concepts in this book are going to be outside of a lot of people's accumulated experience and/or knowledge. And I just wrote this brief thought on logic and illogic so that when you see, hear, or read something and not just in this book but anywhere for that matter and it's something that you have never heard of, been told about, or seen. Meaning it's outside of your accumulated experience and/or knowledge you will not just dismiss it as impossible, not true, or illogical.

360. Happiness it was once asked, where is it, and how can one attain it. And the answer came back that real and true happiness is within oneself and starts with one's thoughts. Because how you think really determines how you feel. Like let me give you an example you could be a billionaire and straight miserable because of the thoughts you entertain, or you could be poor, broke, and penniless and in state of quintessential contentedness. Because of the thoughts you entertain. So once again only you can decide, and only you can make the choice, will I be happy or will I be miserable? And as I bring this thought to an end let me just say this in everyday practical life things, and situations, are going to inevitably occur that piss us off, make us mad, or bring us down. Now the thing is and this is one of the beauties in life that you are the sold arbitrator of how long you are going to stay in that state . . . smile.

361. Always remember that you are your thoughts and whatever you're thinking at a particular moment is what you're resonating with, emitting from yourself in the form of energy, which energy is real, and most definitely can be felt. And not just that but I'm going to tell you a little known secret every thought, ever thought, by any human at any time is indelibly taken note of and recorded by the universe. So that's why I say that it's just so good to just sit back and think positive and good thoughts. So therefore you're projecting, resonating, and emitting, nothing but positive energy from yourself. And this is why I say that one should just and this is for protracted amounts of time project thought. And therefore be resonating, and emitting that thought energy of what one wants to create in his or her life. Thought is your form of communication with the

universe and the universe does hear you. And not only that but that's the way it was set up and ordained by God. You got to do for yourself. Just like if you want God to feed you He will provide the means but you and only you have to perform the physical act of eating or you'll surely starve. And it's the same thing with the universe, God has already provided everything that you could ever want or conceive of in the universe. It's all there waiting for the taking. You just got to know how to go about getting it and to actually go get it . . . and if not you just won't have nothing it's that simple. It's once again just like the food God provided all the means the agriculture, the plants, the soil, the seeds, the sun, the animals. But man has to one knon how to go about getting meaning cultivating his food. And two, man has to go and actually do it. And it's the same with everything else in the universe you have to one know how to go about it, and two, actually go about it. And how you go about bringing what you want in your life is by incessantly projecting, resonating with, and putting out the thought energy of what you want or are trying to create. You just don't sit back and say I'm waiting for God to do for me, and do nothing for yourself . . . you will surely die.

362. This book will teach you the principles that form the foundation for directing the flow of thought into the coagulated energy that creates what is known as manifested reality. And not just that but it will teach you how to empower yourself simply by changing your attitude from that of victim meaning why me, why me, to that of winner. And remember that in life there's always going to be winners and losers and everything else in between and if you want to be a winner you must absolutely program and condition yourself to win at any and all costs, period. Remember it's not how many times you get knocked down but how many times you get back up. And remember in this book I'm simplifying some highly recondite, Arcanum, and abstruse principles concerning how creation flows into manifestation via thought – remember that!

363. Always remember that it's all freewill choice you can either choose via your thoughts to be powerful, rich, and strong or you

can choose to be and/or to stay broke, weak, and in negativity. Please understand people it's all "free will" . . .

364. The victim attitude is deeply ingrained within humanity as a whole.

--The Handbook for the New Paradigm

365. Always remember that politicians are not chosen for virtue, but for their skill at playing roles.

366. It was once said that if voting really could change the system it would have been outlawed a long time ago . . .

367. Always remember that you can never achieve anything big by thinking small.

368. Always remember that everything is in a state of movement, and perpetual change and it's totally, and entirely, up to you whether things change for the good or the worst for you.

369. Always remember that you are where ever you are in life because you chose to be there either consciously or subconsciously via your thoughts. But nonetheless you chose it.

370. Always remember that time as we now know it is and this is whether we know and accept it or not starting to move faster, and faster, and faster. So therefore we as people must absolutely slow down or actually not just risk being all disoriented, and out of whack, but actually risk-going literally straight crazy it's that serious folks. Time is actually and really moving that fast and is picking up momentum every day and the reason for that is a phenomenon that culminates in 2012 but that's a whole different issue the point here is that time is moving faster, and faster, and will continue to pick up pace until 2012. So therefore I'm here to tell you that it is beyond pivotal and that people need to slow down and take time out for themselves quiet time. Time in total solitude, time to think and gather one's thoughts, time to create and project those thoughts

which you are trying to bring into manifestation, time to get in tune with yourselves and just resonate with and put out that positive energy for yourself and for the world where it's also so desperately needed. Basically people need to take time out to create to sit back and project the thoughts that they want to manifest in their life a constant and structured program of daydreaming if you like. And your daydreaming if you want to call it that should be infused with feeling and real and active desire and last but not least you must be constant with the time spent there , I'll just say this the more protracted all the better. These are very crucial days that we're now in and time is moving at an exponential rate so if you don't want to lose your mind or go crazy I strongly suggest that you slow down and take some real time out for yourself.

371. Now let me tell you why people get frustrated and overwhelmed when dealing with problems and the reasons is that if they can't fix the problem or problems immediately. Right now. They get frustrated and overwhelmed and deem the problem or problems unfixable which is wrong, and just shows there impatience and that there moving too fast, because any and all problems are rectifiable and fixable if you focus on them long enough it may take a day, a month, a year, or years depending on the problem but the point is that all problems are rectifiable and fixable, if you slow down, focus, and have patience. Now the beautiful thing is that while you're focusing, and concentrating, and projecting thought energy to rectify the problem no matter what turn for the worst the problem may take as long as you keep believing, focusing, and projecting thought energy to rectify the problem believe me in the end the problem will rectify and or work to your advantage because everything is nothing but energy manifesting and you can have a direct hand in manifesting energy via your thoughts. I'll tell you right now I had a crux once that took me 3 years to rectify and another that took me 10 years to fix but in the end it all worked out.

372. Always remember that man potential wise, and otherwise, is a giant that has been tricked, manipulated, and conditioned, to live in a pygmy's hut. Now if you understand the meaning of that, that's deep. Think about the reality of that because it's so

very true. Man, potential wise, is an ultimate giant that has been forced to live all his days in a pygmy's hut; which is nothing but in the words of the controllers the self imposed limitation system that is inculcated and programmed into the people via the mainstream and other overt and covert tentacles that are under the control of the controllers. And if man meaning the people ever wake up to their real and true potential then and only then will the controllers have a real and formidable problem on their hands. Because right now and this is real and uncut talk the controllers through their vast phalanx of tricks, deceptions, and manipulations have the people and this is potential wise confined and living in straight pygmy's huts. And the people have absolutely no idea that they are ultimate giants that are being forced via trickery and deception to live in pygmy's huts. And that's the sad but absolute truth concerning human potential in the last 100 or so years on this planet. Now I'm just going to say this that if people would only wake up from all the false inculcating, programming, and conditioning, and think. And in the thinking assert their God given heritage and realize contrary to all the bullshit that's put out, and this includes all the religious bullshit out there that they are dear children of the most high God, and His highest creation, and that He prizes them above all His creatures and wants them to know that they are beings of such limitless, and wonderful qualities, and possibilities that it would then come to them an overpowering and conviction sense of what they really are and how necessary it is for them to assert their unalienable rights as such exalted creatures of the living most high god. And they would then realize that they are the absolute masters of their lives, and of their realities. For they have always been controllers of the same. And now as I bring this thought to an end I wrote the foregoing to let people know and understand that God only wants the best of the best for His highest creation "you" if and only if you will assert your will and claim what's always been yours – meaning your potential is limitless and the only one who can put a limit on it is you and that's via your thoughts and actions . . . going back to what the controllers call the self imposed limitation system. Now on a absolute last note for all those who have been conditioned and programmed to believe that God wants them broke, or that god wants them to take a vow of poverty, or that god is somehow against them being prosperous materially or otherwise. All I can say to them is that they are crazy and that all such beliefs, and thinking is negative and I cannot say this more forcefully contrary to God's will. Because God created man perfect and man through the rightful exercise of his will in a good and positive way can therefore regenerate himself and regain his former state of perfection. Meaning everything depends on your beliefs, the thoughts you project and what you will into action for yourself because you're potential and your power really is limitless.

373. Now in this thought here I want to speak on something, and that something if not properly recognized can be very pernicious to one's over all thought process. And that something is influence and that influence I'm talking about is not so much the direct influence that one can get from people. But the influence that one gets, and picks up from the basic mundane activities of everyday life such as the influences that one gets, and picks up from reading books, magazines, newspapers, billboards, articles, etc., or watching the T.V. or listening to the radio. Now the human brain works in such a way that when it takes in information via visual, audio, or whatever that information can and most times does influence the brain in a number of ways and in one of the main ways that the information influences the brain is that the brain starts to ponder, and form opinions about the information and therefore generates thoughts about it so if the information is frivolous, negative, or of no real importance now your thinking about it, and are therefore projecting thought about it, which is not good. Because now instead of projecting thought on what you want to do and create in your life, your thinking and projecting thought on whatever was the information that you picked up on and the information might be good or bad. I don't know. But I'll tell you this there is copious amounts of information out there and that might be an understatement, coming from a plethora of polygenetic sources that are doing nothing but promulgating, and imparting, frivolousness, negativity, and straight useless bullshit but the information is covered by a guise of plausibility. So what I'm saying here is that you don't want to be influenced at every turn because that's basically what it is, by the flood of information out there. And that's why I said that solitude, and

seclusion, for protracted amounts of time is beyond pivotal so that one can gather his or her self, think, free from all distractions, and can create meaning project those thoughts one is trying to being into manifestation into his or her life. This is very pivotal shit people so let's wake up and get smart. And on a last note that's the same thing advertisers do flood you with information get you to thinking about something next thing you know you're buying it.

374. It's been said that in the beginning we are all basically good and pure, but what we become when the world is through messing us over is something else.

375. Now in this thought here I'm going to briefly speak on reality, and it's been said that in our grand universe there's an infinite number of small multiuniverses all existing simultaneous in our one grand universe. Now that's true to the extent that each person walks through life encircled in their own world or universe created for them by their thoughts and is therefore in their own universe within the one grand universe. So if there are 7 billion people on the planet then it's fair to say that there are 7 billion smaller multi universes all simultaneously co-existing on the planet. Now reality, the reality that most people hold is something that has been basically programmed in to the masses of people by the controllers via the media and all the other multitudinous tentacles of mainstream society. And people just accept it and don't think for themselves, and the cold thing is that people have been programmed so good and for long that they don't even know that there not thinking for themselves. They sit around and wait to be told what to do, how to think, and how to act meaning they believe whatever the media, society, or the government tells them. Like for example when the news comes on and the newscaster says well official sources said that, or the government said this, people just believe it and say well that's what they said or are saying. It must be true. How crazy or stupid can you be. Just because they said it don't mean that it's true. Wake up people and start thinking for yourself and stop being yes men and programmed robots. And when it's said that 99% of the world's people sit back and wait for their leaders to tell them what to do. It's true . . . you God damn right it's true. For example let me tell you

one of the biggest lies ever perpetrated on the American people and that's democracy which means rule by the majority and that's whether something is wrong or right, so long as the majority wants it. And you must remember and think for yourself that just because the majority is in favor of something doesn't mean it's right. But people don't see that because they don't think for themselves. And another grand lie and scam that's perpetrated on the people is that of the legislature when they pass and make laws, people never stop to think are these laws just and right and in accord with God's universal laws but they don't think about that they just blindly follow and accept them not knowing that the legislature and specifically the American legislatures (and that's plural). Are some of the most corrupt in the world. And now you may call me cynical but the truth is that when most lawmakers make and pass laws they have some kind of hidden or ulterior motive meaning there under some type of venal influence. And people better wake up and understand and know that. And most important of all start thinking for themselves. And before I bring this thought to an end let me just say this to all those people blindly following and accepting laws without thinking for themselves. And that's if a law Is not right and just and in accord with God's universal laws and you accept and follow it then you're wrong, and guilty, and you will be held accordingly . . . believe that. And that goes for any law whether the law was enacted or passed under venal influence or not meaning that just because man with good intentions and no venal influence, and no hidden or ulterior motives makes a law and passes it does not mean the law is right, and just, and in accord with God's universal laws. And I say that to say that people need to deprogram themselves and start thinking for themselves.

376. Always remember that there are 3 things that are absolutely and 100% inevitable in this earth life and that's, one death, two aging, and three the craftiness, deception, and perennial manipulation now so prevalent in the world.

377. Always remember that the thoughts in this book are deep, and one of the keys to understanding them is meditation.

378. Now in this thought here I'm going to speak on human potential once again which the real and truth of I can honestly say is not known to the masses of people, but I can tell you with absolute certainty that the real and truth of human potential is known and has been known for a long time to the upper echelons of those who clandestinely control the U.S. government and that's why they have been and are keeping that truth suppressed via the T.V. reality shows, propaganda, public schooling, and myriad other mainstream tentacles designed to program, condition, and basically keep people stupid and away from the truth. Now human potential, meaning the potential of humans to do, and to create for themselves when fully known, and realized is and please believe me nothing short of astonishing and that might be an understatement. Because listen to me humans – people have no idea. And I say again, have no idea how much potential innate and otherwise they have at their disposal. If people would just stop, and I know that the exigencies of life are demanding but take time out, slow down, and start thinking, and I mean really slow down and think, really focus. And get in tune with their selves they would start to see so many opportunities that they would not even believe it. And the other thing is the virtually unlimited potential you have to create with via thought of which a great deal of this book is about. But the foundation to all of this knowing that you can, meaning believing, putting out that thought energy incessantly of doing, or creating, whatever your trying to do or create, and infusing that thought energy with emotional desire and not only that but to be able to possess the virtue of patience making putting out that thought energy a way of life no matter how long it takes until whatever you're trying to do comes to pass. And now I'm going to tell you the absolute key to all of this and that's faith meaning that while you're putting out thought energy to do, or create whatever your endeavoring to do the how part should not at all concern you for example if you're trying to become a billionaire the how part, how are you going to become a billionaire should not at all concern you. You should just know with all your mind, heart, and soul that you will become a billionaire period and incessantly put that thought energy out and not only that but put the thought energy out of how it would feel and feel is the key word, of how it would feel to be a billionaire and marinate in

that energy. And last but not least you must get rid of all of the I can't the what will they think or say about me, blocks, barriers, and other limitations inculcated in you all your life via the mainstream and other sources. And know that if you believe and put out the thought energy for enough time anything is possible. And know that if it looks like there's no way or opportunity at all, if you believe, think, and be persistent enough ways, and opportunities will most definitely show themselves. So all I can say in closing this thought is that you're a being of unlimited power and potential you just got to know it, and believe it to be so . . . you might want to re-read this thought.

379. Always remember that everything that exists is energy. Everything is a unique vibrational pattern of energy created by thought and emotion. All that exists is energy. But these infinite patterns of energy create infinite forms, just as water can manifest as liquid, clouds, steam, and ice. They look and feel very different, but they are all still water in different forms. And the same is true with energy it manifests in infinite forms, such the human body, it's organs, the birds, trees, insects, water, the sky, the air, and ad-infinitum. But yet in still at the bases of all physical matter is nothing but pure energy and at the bases of that energy is nothing but thought. In a nutshell all is thought. So now do you understand how powerful thought really is, thought is the bases of all there is in the material physical world. And did you know that certain mystics, and shamans, can actually see the thoughts as thought forms hovering over the heads of people as they think and project their thoughts. And according to the mystics, and shamans, since all the bases of the material physical world is thought, all thoughts, that are thought and projected by people can and do affect not just the people who project them by coming back to manifest in their lives. But all thoughts that are thought and projected by people affect the plants, the grass, the animals, everything because all is thought at it bases and/or core. And not just that but there is something known as the mass-consciousness where all human thoughts exist in a live state and if people or humanity I should say get to thinking to many or a preponderance of negative thoughts then the mass-consciousness will hit a critical mass or

a majority of negative thought and if and when that happens we're doomed because then negativity will reign supreme on this planet and it will then be excruciatingly hard for people to even think a good or positive thought. And that is just what those who clandestinely control the U.S. government want and are relentlessly working towards and that's a total and complete negative planet. So I sincerely and strongly hope that you don't help or assist them by thinking bad and/or negative thoughts in any kind of way. And this is why I say that it's so very important and pivotal that one only think and project positive and good thoughts not only for his own benefit, and well-being, but for the benefit and well-being of all humanity and the planet. Because just like those who clandestinely control the U.S. government and those that control them which are the negative forces of the universe are now working over-time from a myriad of polygenetic avenues, ways, and means to get people to think and project nothing but negative thoughts in any and all capacities so that they can get the mass-consciousness to a critical mass of negative thought. And thereby create a total and complete negative planet. So our only hope or the only hope for humanity on this planet is to think and project only good and positive thoughts and therefore get the critical mass of the mass-consciousness to a majority of positive thought then positiveness will reign supreme on this planet then those of negative intent will unequivocally lose because then it will be excruciatingly hard for them to think or project negative thoughts and right now the fight between those of negative intent and those of positive intent is head to head and only you the people can make the difference via your thoughts and that's for positive, the good, or for the negative, the bad. It's your choice.

380. Now in this thought here I'm going to explain to you why it's so extremely inordinately bad for you to think bad or negative thoughts which are nothing but negative energy. Because the negative thoughts which are nothing but negative energy like I said will not only adversely affect you. But will adversely affect everyone living on the planet at the time. And this is simply because of the way that the universe is set up and I'll try to briefly explain it to you but it works like this. Within the cycles of energy that maintain manifested creation in the

various dimensions there are critical points which allow for changing the vibratory parameters of these dimensions. And there is within this opportunity ways that the negative forces and there hierarchy have worked out to create a downward spiral into negative energy rather than the upward spiral of lifting in energy vibration as was intended. Now this can only happen when the mass consciousness of the people (majority of people) at the vibratory level of planetary existence have their focus on negative energy and or experiences which are at the lowest level of that dimension. Now do you understand what I just said what I just said is that when you think or entertain negative thoughts which are negative energy they the negative thoughts not only come back to you and manifest negativity in your life. But the negative energy that you put out along with every other human beings negative energy that's being put out at that time in your dimension/planet is helping the negative forces and there hierarchy attract more problems, hurt, pain, distress, unbalance, agony, evil, and adversity for every single human being and even the animals that are living in that dimension/planet at that time. So when you think or entertain negative thoughts in any kind of way you're not just hurting and affecting yourself in an adverse way but you're hurting and affecting every single human being and even the animals in an adverse way that are living in your dimension/planet at the time. And I'll just say this that it is extremely sad that real truth and the laws of the universe have been with held and suppressed away from you the masses and you are left to discover them by trial and error. So all I can say is please don't allow yourself to think, dwell, or entertain negativity in any kind of way because your not just hurting yourself but you're hurting every other living thing on the planet. So when negative thoughts come your way turn them negative thoughts around to the positive into what you would rather experience or have. Now I'm just going to say this all the wars, conflicts, calamities, upheavals, unrests, terrorist attacks, and so called natural disasters caused by those who clandestinely control the U.S. government are caused in part to keep the masses of people thinking and putting out negative thoughts, and energy, i.e. being fearful, worried, scarred, and just thinking pessimistic, bad, and negative thoughts which in turn when done by the mass majority of people in a dimension/planet will have the effect of bringing that dimension/planet vibratory rate down into the negative, Then the inhabitants of that dimension/planet will not be able even if they want to. To think positive thoughts and that's just what those who clandestinely control the U.S. government are attempting to do, to planet earth. That's why I've belabored you throughout this book why it's so very pivotal that you, we, think positive, and stay thinking positive, no matter what. Now there is a way that we can reverse what's being done to us, and that's for us as a collective to think positive, and just to be honest, and truthful with you there's no other way . . . that's the only way.

381. People here in America and the world as a whole are feeling more and more frustrated, and tired, now days and that's for various reasons. But as you read this book and like I've belabored you before if you take heed to the principals it imparts you will without question grant yourself some relief. And not only that but this book will show and teach you how to take charge and control of your life. But and this is the pivotal thing only you, and you alone can determine if you will come anew in your life or stay the same.

382. Our job, Huxley wrote before death . . . is waking up. Now what did Huxley mean by that? He simply meant that we must wake up from the spell that has been cast on us by those who clandestinely control the U.S. government via all their conditioning, programming, and brainwashing apparatus's such as the media, public schooling, and all there other sources of public information. Now a lot of people think that they're smart enough to know that the aftermentioned sources of information do not put out all the truth and that much of it is deception and misleading. But and this is pivotal here most people falsely think that there able of editing the deception, disinformation, and beguile propaganda out of what's true, and what's real, and I'm here to tell you that that's just not so. Because no matter how you edit the information that comes out of the aftermentioned sources you are still not going to get the truth concerning the big picture you might get insignificant and miniscule truths such as who robbed a bank or something like that. But you will never get like I said real truths or the big

picture. Like for example the presidential election going on now in 2008 between Obama and John McCain now with all the perennial coverage that the media is giving to the election and to Obama and to John McCain you will never get the real truth or the big picture concerning Obama and McCain and the real truth and the big picture concerning Obama and McCain is that they are both completely and totally controlled by the same people which are those that clandestinely control the U.S. government so it really and honestly does not matter who gets elected because either way you're going to get the same thing. Now that's what I mean by you never getting the real truth or the big picture out of or from the aftermentioned sources of information no matter how much editing you do unless you just go ahead and edit it all out but most people are not going to do that. Now that is what Huxley meant that you must wake up from the reality that has been fed to you all your life because you best believe me that it has been grossly manipulated and distorted. Now it's a known fact that people construct there reality, beliefs, etc. from what they have seen, heard, and been taught and if what you have seen, heard, and been taught is not true or right but has been distorted and manipulated then your view of reality, what you believe is possible, your beliefs, and everything else that has to do with reality especially with how reality comes into manifestation for you is going to be for lack of a better term distorted and fucked up. Like Huxley said you must wake up. Because the truth about reality is not known or is it taught to the exoteric. And that is just the way that those who clandestinely control the U.S. government want it. And one of their main plays is making people think or believe that reality is a linear affair when in reality, reality is a multileveled affair. But people think because that's how they have been taught all there life that if they can't perceive something with their five physical senses then it isn't real or doesn't exist but nothing could be further from the truth. Reality is most definitely not linear or just what you can see with your eyes but multileveled. And extends infinitely past what you can physically see. And it is sincerely hoped that when you get done reading this book that you will know and thoroughly understand that you have total and complete control over creating your own reality it may take a little time to change over from the reality that has been fed to you all your life but once you change over and get it started and you find yourself living the reality that you know, that you yourself have created for yourself then that's what I call the closest thing that you can get to nirvana here in the physical. And for those of you that are new to these topics, notions, and precepts, it is strongly recommended that you read this book at least 4 or 5 times so that you will get the subtleties and all the nuances of this material. And for the one who takes real heed to the advice that I just gave he or she will most definitely be a most happy person. And will be thinking that God has most definitely bless them which may or may not be the case but what definitely is the case is that they have learned how to put there God given innate power to work for them. And it's in all of us we all have the ability and/or power of creating our own reality and if you just think about it. It only makes sense because what you think that God would create us without an avenue for us to be able to get or attain everything or anything that we could ever want or need. Come on now, if you say that, or think that, you're saying that God is not omniscient and omnificent. I rest my case.

383. Now in this thought here I just want to speak on the absoluteness of belief, and that one has to thoroughly, and fully in the depths of one's heart and soul, believe before something can be brought about and before the projection of thought energy can really and actually be efficacious. Like for example people inadvertently or consciously all the time absolutely and thoroughly in the depths of their heart and soul believe things like if someone has a lucky shirt, thing, or object. They really in the depths of their heart and soul believe that thing or object is good luck for them and because they absolutely, and thoroughly, without the slightest doubt believe that then therefore that thing or object is good luck for them. Now you must understand because this is my point here the thing or object is good luck for them not because of any inherent power in the thing or object but because as they say in magic the thing or object has been charged with one of the most absolute powers in the universe the power of thought via absolute belief. And mine you this can work both ways if you believe that something is bad or bad luck to you or for you then it is. And

just in case if you didn't know this is the same principal used in magic when magicians charge (infused with power) there symbols, pentacles, and seals. To do and mean what they want, they do it via absolute belief and this is both in white and black magic. But any practicing magician worth his weight is pretty proficient at directing his thoughts (thought energy) or consciousness absolutely at any given objective or thing. And before I go on I just want to let you know that this absolute belief is the same thing or principal that makes placebos work and possible. And a placebo as we all know is nothing but a water pill and placebos please believe me do work it's just that the medical community likes to keep that type of stuff suppressed. But like I've said before this book was written for the sole purpose of informing and enlightening the people. So for those of you who may have physical or health ailments and are looking to heal yourself via thought then I strongly suggest that you check out the work and the books of Dr. Deepak Chopra who has written 23 bestselling books on the power of thought, consciousness, and on the power of placebos to heal the body profound shit believe me. Now moving onward cause we're flowing here see talking about the power of thought excites me cause once you understand the principals of this most exact science please believe me there is absolutely nothing you cannot do or accomplish and like I've said before this science of the power of thought has been used for eons by mystics, shamans, magicians, and many others who practice and indulge in the esoteric. But now this profoundly august arcane science is being divulged to the exoteric. See you got to understand that thoughts are real things and exist in their own realm or dimension in a live state and this realm or dimension where all thoughts exist has been called by many different names such as: the mass consciousness, the astral plane, the divine matrix, the morphic field, the universal collective mind, the 5th force, and the akashic records, now you may call it what you want, but just understand that thoughts once you think them or project them are living their own very real, and dynamic realities, in this thought world. Like for example like I just got done telling you if you absolutely without any doubt what so ever believe that a certain object or thing is good luck to you then it most definitely is because you have charged that object or thing with the power of thought via your absolute belief to be good luck to you or for you. And therefore in the thought world and for this work will just call it the akashic records that thought of this object or thing being good luck to you is alive and living its own reality. And those who have the ability to astral project can actually in there astral body go to the akashic records and view the thoughts in live 3-D form. And if you would like to learn all about astral projecting what it is and how you can acquire the ability I suggest that you check out the work of Robert Monroe or get the book: Astral Travel for Beginners, by Richard Webster. And when thoughts are projected or thought in this physical world especially highly charged emotional thoughts they can be seen by certain mystics and others who have that ability and the residue of these thoughts, and thought forms, can be seen hanging around for long, long periods of time in the place where these thoughts were projected and or thought. Now the Akashi records is where creation for this world starts because before anything and this is without exception can be manifest here in this world it was thought first meaning that it was first manifested in the Akashi records then and only then can it manifest here in the physical world. Even things that apparently no one projected or thought like a glass of water falling off a table first had its reality in the Akashi records and I know you are going to ask how so, since nobody directly projected or thought that thought of the glass of water falling off the table, yes, but the glass falling off the table was the unseen ramifications of other thoughts that were directly thought by somebody. And each thought with all of it's possible consequences, and ramifications, in their totality are known how by color and other energies around the thoughts that denote in the Akashi records which consequences, and ramifications, are more likely or less likely to happen or manifest. Now you're probably going to ask about things that are known as acts of God such as earthquakes, and hurricanes, which you would say nobody could have projected or thought into existence you would be completely surprised. But anyway when they do happen naturally they still had their origin first in the Akashi records and how you might ask will now you're getting into what the basic building blocks of all the material physical world are and that's thought. Thought is the basic building block of the entire material physical world. And this is a very, very, simplistic explanation of an extremely labyrinth process. But it's going to have to do for now. Because my intent is not to break down the intricacies of how creation flows into manifestation here that's for another time. But just remember that thought is the bases of the entire physical material world. And something else that you must understand and know and that's how God set the universe up to run and operate and I don't mean all the arcane and abstruse intricacies of the operations of the universe shit we couldn't understand them with our mind in this 3rd dimension even if we wanted to or if we lived for eons down here that's just not happening. That's not what I'm talking about. I'm talking about the basic most rudimentary function of how God set the universe up to run and operate concerning us human beings of how absolute and supreme our free will is and you can take this how you want to but it's straight, and uncut, truth and that's that even God's divine angels who are doing nothing but the will of God cannot infringe upon our free wills to carry out god's will and that's deep but it's very much true. But people don't know that. God's divine angels have to wait for opportunity to carry out their work and the will of god. Just like thoughts when you project them have to wait for an opportunity to manifest themselves unless your indulging in black magic or some other negative practice then of course you don't give a damn about somebody else's free will your free to do that, and nobody is going to stop you, not God, not his angels, not nobody. Have you ever heard of psychic wars? Well they're very real and that's where people send malevolent energy to harm one another, people die and get killed in psychic wars all the time. Most definitely very real and dangerous stuff. But I just said all that to say that our free will reigns supreme . . . physically or psychically, you can do whatever the hell you want. Now like you know that there are consequences behind actions if you break laws in the physical world you'll go to jail. And psychically and in the metaphysical sphere if you do bad or wrong things well God or anybody else doesn't have to do anything to you because just like in the physical too this is where the great and immutable law of compensation you would call it karma comes into play which will most definitely exact payment for any and all transgressions committed in God's universe. God does not sit back and arbitrarily run and control the universe like some people think. No He has laws that He put in place to do all that. And these laws are absolute and immutable and one of those laws is the law that says that our freewill is absolute and shall not be infringed upon by nothing or nobody. Now anybody can infringe on anybody else's freewill but when they do it they are violating one of God's laws and will therefore have to suffer the consequences. And people need to stop saying things like god made this happen to me, or God allowed this to happen to me, or God is mad at me because I didn't do this, or because I did that. Hear me and hear me well all such talk is nonsense and does not contain the least bit of truth. You could kill a million people in the worst way and God would still only love you and send you nothing but love because He's not capable of anything else. Now what His universal law of compensation does to you is something completely different because that's what it's there for to exact payment for all transgressions committed. So basically you're free to do as you will and nothing or nobody's controlling you or making things happen to you but you. One has to be absolute and positive about where, and what, one wants to do in life. Then one has to focus all of his or her thoughts and thought energy on those objectives and one must be 150% real about this. And if you're half hearted, or hesitant, or wavering, about this in anyway then you need to forget it and go sit down somewhere and get the hell out of the way until you're ready to be absolutely real about this commitment. Because in life you make your own lot, please believe that. There is extreme darkness, and hate, and negativity, in this world just like there is extreme light, love, and positivity in this world. So it's all on where you choose and want to be. And that's just raw and uncut and real talk my friend. But I also very much understand that everybody isn't ready for raw, and uncut, talk or truth. And I can't make it any simpler than that the bottom line is your in complete control, and are the ultimate decision maker of you, and are you ready, and willing, to pay the cost for what you want in life. And maybe you need to think or go back a few thoughts and re-read the whole thought I wrote on being ready and willing to pay the cost for what you want. Because this is real life here people and this is how it works in the real world. And you got to understand also that everybody experiencing and going through life is going to go through and experience extreme pain, hurt, dejection, distress, dissatisfaction, anger, unpleasure, sorrow, and trouble in many different ways, fashions, and assortments, and for different degree's and lengths of time and that's just the way that it is. Just like I told you in the preface to this book I'm going to give it to you raw and uncut. Let me see if I could use the expression of a roller coaster as an allegory to symbolize life because life is like a roller coaster ride it's fast and you going to have ups and downs and we all most of the time like the ups, it's the downs that we don't like. And sometimes when you're going through the downs you got to go through all kinds of shit, unforeseen twists, and turns, that we most definitely don't like and not just that but sometimes on the ups we go through the same shit. But the thing is on this roller coaster ride of life is to hold on stay believing and thinking positive, and to know that there are an infinite number of tracts or ride configurations and to a good degree you can choose via your beliefs and thought projections what kind of ride you wish to take on this roller coaster ride of life. And I said that you can choose to a good degree what kind of ride you wish to take because even when you project your thoughts and create your own reality you are still going to have problems, and unforeseen twists and turns. And for me or anybody else to say otherwise they would be a goddamn lie. But at least by you creating your own reality via your beliefs, and focused, and concentrated thought projections, you'll be on the roller coaster ride that you for the most part created. Meaning that you're on your ride whatever that may be. Not just riding blindly . . . big difference.

384. U.S. Senator Henry Bellmon in 1969 said: in a recent conversation with an official of the I.R.S. I was amazed when he told me, if the taxpayers of this country ever discover that the I.R.S. operates on 90% bluff, the entire system will collapse.

385. Now for a word on the federal income tax that was passed into law in 1913 now I'm going to ask you a question do you know the history on the federal income tax law, and how it was brought to be? Well nine times out of 10 you don't because if you did, I don't believe you would be giving your hard earned

money to the federal government. And one more thing before I start my discourse and that's what I'm about to say in this thought just like anything I've said in any other thought, if you don't believe it, or doubt it, in any kind of way please feel more than free to investigate, and check it out for yourself. But anyway back to the federal income tax and how it became law. But yeah it was required that at least 36 states agreed on it, the federal income tax because there had to be an amendment to the United States Constitution the 16th. Now here comes the shocker did you know that only 2 states agreed, so they were then, and still are right now 34 states short of making the 16 amendment which is the federal income tax a legal amendment and law. Now you're probably going to ask how did they do this, or how did this come about well I'll tell you. It was done through and by the then Secretary of State, Philander Knox who was associated and affiliated, with those who clandestinely controlled the U.S. government and when Congress asked him did the necessary number of states agree on the 16th amendment he simply said yes and Congress took him at his word. And the 16th amendment which is the federal income tax became an amendment and law. Now mind you there are people who know this and know that the 16th amendment is not actually law and many of them have took the IRS to court on that bases and won or I should say the IRS settled out of court with them, and with the out of court settlement the IRS made them sign what's known as a nondisclosure agreement meaning in a nut shell that they couldn't alert the public to the 16th amendment not being an actual law. But never the less this knowledge has leaked out. And to substantiate what I'm saying here I've procured a copy or should I say a replica of an internal revenue service internal memo that was from the IRS commissioner Roscoe L. Edger Jr. to all district directors and this memo was sent out back in 1985. (Please see next page) And if you want to learn more about the great income tax fraud, and how the IRS is actually operating illegally then you must get the following books: The Great Income Tax Hoax, by Irwin Schiff; Become a Nontaxpayer and Save, by Floyd Wright; The Law that Never Was Vol. #1, by Bill Benson & M.J. Red Beckman; How to Save 100% on Your Income Tax, by Len Martin; IRS Humbug and IRS Weapons of Enslavement, by Frank Kowalik; and How Anyone Can Stop Paying Income Tax's, by Irwin Schiff, and this book was a New York Time's best seller. And there are many, many more books on this subject which the mainstream media tries to keep suppressed but these right here are just a few, or you can go to your computer at www.LiveFreeNow. org to learn more about this subject.

Department of the Treasure

Internal Revenue Service

To: ALL DISTRICT DIRECTORS

April 4, 1985

On March 5, 1985, a change of tax evasion was filed in U.S. District Court in Indianapolis, Indiana, By U.S. Attorney George Duncan. The charges were dismissed: The Defense Attorney Lowell Becraft of Huntsville, Alabama presented irrefutable evidence that the 16th amendment to the U.S. Constitution was never properly ratified. This amendment which established the income tax was signed into law despite serious defects. In reality only 2 states ratified the amendment and ratification requires 36 states to be valid. The effect of this is such that every tax paid into the Treasury since 1913 is due and refundable to every citizen and business.

The official position of the Service is, as it has always been, to aid and assist the citizens of the United States. We will not publish or advertise this finding as a total immediate refund would cause a serious drain on the resources of the Treasury. For those citizens who become aware of this finding and apply for a total refund expedite their refund documents quickly and as quietly as possible.

Advise each of your managers that they are not to discuss this situation with anyone. There will be no written communications and you are to destroy this memorandum.

The Secretary of the Treasury assures me that there will be no reduction in the workforce as this refunding activity will take a minimum of 5 years to complete. Further directions will be forwarded as the need arises.

Signed: _____
Roscoe L. Egger, Jr.
Commissioner of Internal
Revenue Service.

386. Now in this thought here I'm going to speak on gun laws, gun control, and so called gun reform laws, and I'm going to tell you why it's all a sham put out there by those who clandestinely control the U.S. government to disarm law abiding taxpaying citizens. Alright, the heinous crimes committed with guns are committed by people for whatever reason or reasons chose to do those things. Now anybody can wake up tomorrow and say I'm going to get a gun, and go to work and shoot all my co-workers, and believe me no amount of gun laws, gun control, gun reform, or even a total gun band would be able to stop that individual from doing that. Why? Because once somebody chooses to be a criminal or disregard the law, then all laws in their totality become negated, and null, for that person. So what I'm saying here is gun laws no matter how harsh they are or any law for that matter can only stop crime if people abide by them. Criminals and lawbreakers, if you didn't know, do not abide by them. They could care less about a law, its penalties, or consequences. That's why there criminals, so now that you understand that criminals and those that commit crime which are lawbreakers could care less about any law, and are going to do, what they are going to do regardless of any law. Now that you understand that, I hope that you understand that laws, and in particular what we're talking about here are gun laws, and gun control, is only going to affect those that abide by laws, which are who the law abiding, taxpaying citizens which are

going to have their 2nd amendment all but eroded by all these gun laws, gun reforms, and gun controls. But that is the plan of those that clandestinely control the U.S. government, and that's to disarm the law abiding citizens of America and have the citizens do it themselves by having them vote all them gun laws, gun reforms, and controls into law. But it's all a sham like I said . . . why? Because like always the real truth has been kept from you. But I'm about to disclose that truth to you by one of the most commonly asked questions by law abiding Americans, and that's won't more gun laws, gun reform, and gun controls make it harder for criminals to get and obtain guns. And the real answer to that is no. But the media and the rest of mainstream society unequivocally controlled by those who clandestinely control the U.S. government will tell you yes. But like so much else it is a straight lie. And like I've said one of the reasons I wrote this book was to make known and impart suppressed knowledge, and suppressed truths. And this is damn sure one of them. Now why more gun laws, gun reforms, and gun controls, won't, and I say again will not make it harder for criminals and for those who wish to break the law to get guns is because the CIA just like it has been running drugs into this country for decades, and in a vast variety, and assortments it has been running guns. And these guns are channeled, and distributed, in the black market, and underground economy through the mafia, drug cartels, and other criminal elements, and please believe me there is no shortage of guns, or weapons in the black market of America. It's like this the CIA has made buying guns on the black market as easy as they made buying drugs in America on the black market. Now that's pretty fucking simple. And if you don't believe me well the proof is in the pudding. Have you ever heard of CoBray makers of the Mack-10, and Mack-11, machine gun well that was and is CIA created, owned, and operated, and have you ever heard of Samuel Cummings one of the biggest gun dealers in the world. Well he was a CIA operative, meaning his armory was CIA controlled, and operated, and these are just a few, because the CIA didn't just start running guns into America, as some people would like to believe. They been doing it for decades since at least the 1950s, and there networks are long established, and highly proficient. And the CIA is the arm, and tool, of those who clandestinely control the U.S. government. And that's why I say it's a sham for law abiding taxpaying citizens to vote in all the gun laws, gun reforms, and gun controls. Because there doing nothing but eroding their own 2nd amendment which is their right to bear arms, while those who wish to commit heinous crimes with guns, the criminals, the lawbreakers, and the rest of the opposition has literally an unlimited supply of them. Wake up people. And I'm going to say this if you don't think what I said in this thought is true. Well that is because you have only been getting your information and knowledge from the media, and mainstream society, which is like I've previously told you unequivocally owned, and controlled by those who clandestinely control the U.S. government. And if you would like to learn more about America's black market, the CIA and there gun running, and drug running, and the CIA's vast criminal enterprises then you must get the highly acclaimed book: Defrauding America, by Rodney Stitch there is even a website at www.DefraudingAmerica.com.

387. Did you know that those who clandestinely control the U.S. government are surreptitious programming your kids and teaching them how to think and what to believe? And did you know how there doing it well there doing it though public education, government schooling, the public school system. And those that clandestinely control the U.S. government have been for many, many years now and are right now still using the public school system as nothing but a tool, and a tool, for programming children in a way that those who clandestinely control the U.S. government want. And the masses of people who 8 out of every 10 themselves were programmed by the public school system don't know this, or even have the slightest idea of this, and still right now today don't know the real agenda of public schools who are funded, controlled, and operated though the government by those who clandestinely control the U.S. government, and I haven't even begun to talk about the drugs like Ritalin better known by doctors, and psychiatrists, by its pharmaceutical and pharmacodynamics name methylphenidate and other psychotropic drugs that the public schools are now giving to children for the slightest behavior infractions and these drugs people just don't know have myriad detrimental and irreversible side effects on

children's ability to think, there behavior, and personalities. And then there's the performance and the efficaciousness of the public schools in teaching the children the basic skills such as reading, writing, mathematics, and basic thinking skills such as logic and reason that is so low that it's a shame it should be criminal. Well let me tell you the public schools are doing such an extremely bad and poor job of teaching children the basic aftermentioned skills that nearly half of all graduates from public high schools are illiterate meaning that they are lacking the basic skills of reading, writing, mathematics, and basic thinking. And that's not even to mention creative thinking. And the children may have a diploma but that doesn't certify that they know anything it just certifies that they have graduated and that's it and that's all. And further more the government has completely took God and prayer out of the public schools and replaced it with the teaching of secular humanism and for God fearing and loving people that right there is nothing but a straight debacle. And then there's the school shootings there's been so many school shootings in the last few years, Santana, Granite hills, and Columbine to name a few and the Santana, and Granite Hills, shootings were just 17 days apart of one another. And it's only going to get worse for public schools just look at the Anchorage, Alaska, elementary school slashings of 4 helpless young children on May 7, 2001, just a couple of months after the Santana and Granite Hills School shootings. Now in this extremely malevolent and malignant act of a man by the name of Jason Prichard walked into Mountain View elementary school with a knife and slashed the throats of 4 completely innocent and helpless young children while they waited in line for their breakfast. And as for the school shootings don't think that any amount of gun laws, of gun reforms, or laws period, is going to stop these sort of things from happening. Because just think about it for a second people have been owning firearms, guns, knives, and all kinds of different weapons in this country since it's inception in 1776 and these sorts of things school shootings, school slashings, and kids killing kids did not start to happen until recently. But anyway remember that the public schools which is government schooling has been and is nothing but a tool, and a tool that's being used by those that clandestinely control the U.S.

government to program your children in a way that those who clandestinely control the U.S. government want. So that once they program the child from K-12th grade with is 13 straight years the child nine times out of ten will stay programmed that way for life and that means stuck on stupid, not knowing what's really going on in the world, or what the U.S. government is really about or doing and most definitely not knowing or if even told about those who clandestinely control the U.S. government he or she would not believe it simply because of the way he or she was taught and programmed that such things as a certain group, oligarchy, plutocracy, aristocracy, having de-facto control of the U.S. government and actually the whole world just doesn't exist, and it sounds and is totally surreal to them because they have never heard of or been taught anything like that before in their entire life. So therefore there mind is going to naturally reject it. Like for instance the conspiratorial view of history which talks about those who clandestinely control the U.S. government and speaks on a lot of the things that there aristocracy was responsible for in history is not taught in any public school and do you know why? Because those who clandestinely control the U.S. government do not want you, or anybody else for that matter to know or even hear about them, or their actions. So therefore in the public schools they teach the exact opposite to the conspiratorial view of history which is the accidental view of history that says that historical events just occur by accident for no apparent reason and rulers are powerless to intervene. And that right there the accidental view of history could not be further from the truth, it is nothing but a straight lie, and that's what's taught, has been taught, and always will be taught in public schools. And that is just to keep the people stupid and away from the truth as much as possible. So if you do not want your kids to be programmed by those who clandestinely control the U.S. government or killed in some senseless school shooting then take them out of public schooling and put them in a God loving private school. And if you would like to read more about how those clandestinely control the U.S. government control education here in America, then you must get the following books by: Anthony Sutton – America's Secret Establishment, and introduction to the order, and how the order controls education. And Dumbing Us Down, the Hidden Curriculum of Compulsory Schooling, by:

Thoughts on Life And the Absolute Power of Thought

John Taylor Gatto . . . and if you're interested on how and why our kids are being drugged unjustifiably then you must get Toxic Psychiatry, by: Peter Breggin.

388. Now did you know that navigating systems in automobiles were purposed by the U.S. government to all automakers foreign and domestic? And this is simply because those who clandestinely control the U.S. government want navigating systems in all cars and trucks. Now the natural question is why? Well let me tell you, so they can listen to you in your car, know exactly where you're at, at all times when you driving. And most important of all so they can virtually control you're automobile if they so do wish. Now this is all nothing but part of their plan for their new world order. And if you have never heard of, or don't know what the new world order is please read thought #616. And these navigating systems in automobiles are compatible with, and communicate with the satellites in space that are hooked up to the super computers in the underground cities and if you have never heard of the underground cities please read thought #412. And the U.S. government had and probably still has a covert off the books deal with all automakers again foreign, and domestic, to get these navigation systems implemented in all automobiles. Now use your common sense here and just think about that for a minute. Why would the government care so much about getting navigating systems implemented in automobiles? If they didn't have a hidden agenda!!! I mean the government doesn't even care that much about the poor, the homeless, and the hungry. And the automakers and car dealers push these navigating systems to unknowing, and unsuspecting consumers by telling them the customers all the good, and beneficial things a navigating system in the automobile can and does offer, which is pretty much true because a navigating system in the car can do a whole lot of novel, helpful, and good things. But there's 2 sides to every nickel, and they the car dealers don't disclose the other side of the nickel and tell you the consumer what else the navigating system can do and be used for, like by the navigating system being hooked up directly the cars central computer, the navigating system can virtually control your car. For example if you got a general motor's made car and therefore have the on-

star navigating system, if you lock your keys in the car you can call the people at on-star and they will via satellite pop your doors for you. Now just think for a minute if they can pop your doors via satellite what else can they do or control on your car via satellite???? And who else besides the people at on-star might have access, and or the ability of controlling the navigating system in your automobile which essentially controls your vehicle. Now before I end this thought let me tell you something else and what I'm about to say is already the law in Britain as of now 2005. And what I'm about to impart to you is that all 2005 automobiles made or sold in the United States will come with black boxes, with transponder chips in them. And these black boxes will virtually record in real time every time you ever use your car, and everywhere your car ever went. And not only that but these black boxes have a vast assortment of functions and capabilities one such function which is not yet fully operational because of the law enforcement agencies that are going to be the receivers of this particular function have not yet as of now 2005 fully upgraded to accommodate it. But by 2007 they should be fully upgraded to accommodate this particular function. And the function that I speak of is that whenever you speed the black box will send a signal to law enforcement (the police) letting them know how fast you were going, where you were at, what time and date you did it, and how long you did it for. And they in turn law enforcement will send you a ticket. And this is just one of the many functions these black boxes are capable of. Now I'm not saying that this function will be activated in 2007, 2008, 2010, or 2020 just know these black boxes are capable of this. And now I'm going to drop the bomb on you and that's if you disable or remove the black box, now mine you this is on your car that's your own personal property, it's a felony and you can and will be prosecuted and sent to prison. Now this is serious and grave stuff folks and I strongly recommend that you investigate. And I'm going to tell you now car dealerships are instructed and encouraged to engage in duplicity when you inquire about the true nature of these black boxes. And just in case if you didn't know they got a national toll system in the making where all roads in the United States will be toll roads by 2020. And the way they plan on selling this to you is by telling you that there is no money for roads and they need money to maintain and fix the roads, which is a straight lie . . . people don't buy it. They get billions from their tax on gasoline. And get this, and this is a real and actual story the pentagon lost track of, or can't account for 5-trillion-dollars. And yes . . . I said 5-trillion-dollars you get the details to this story on the Alex Jones web site at www.infowars.com so they the government can totally and completely miss me with that shit that they don't have any money . . . please.

389. In this thought here you are going to learn the real and true history of aids. Now do you know where aids really came from and who or what put the horrible plague of aids out there on humanity? Nine times out of ten you don't, because if you been listening to the media, T.V, or the newspapers which are all directly or indirectly controlled by those who clandestinely control the U.S. government then you do not know the truth of where aids came from. Well the truth of where aids came from is that it was developed and put out by those who clandestinely control the U.S. government for the sole purpose of ridding humanity of its most undesirable elements or people which in their eyes are all minorities, Blacks, Hispanics, and homosexuals. Because it was decided by those who clandestinely control the U.S. government that since the masses of people must be reduced for control purposes it would be in the best interest of humanity to rid of it its most undesirable elements or people. So there for they ordered CIA Project MK-NAOMI (AIDS) into existence and you must know and remember that the CIA since its inception has been and is the black hand of those who clandestinely control the U.S. government. So aids and the cure which nobody but those who clandestinely control the U.S. government have were developed by a Dr. Aurelio Peccei in 1973 it took him 4 years because he started work on it, CIA Project (MK-NAOMI), in June of 1969 but see the thing about CIA Project (MK-NAOMI) was that it was not yet aids because the microbe that was to be developed was to be one that was almost impossible to cure. So therefore it was recommended by a group of scientists that a microbe be developed that would directly attack the human immune system so without esoteric arcane knowledge make the development of a cure or vaccine damn near impossible. Because remember

that without an immune system you would die of a common cold. So that is why Dr. Aurelio Peccei developed a synthetic microbe that would directly attack the human immune system (AIDS). And the first population to be infected with aids was the African continent and they did it via a small pox vaccine in 1978 that was administered by the World Health Organization and the next population to be infected with the deadly aids virus was you guessed it the U.S. population and they did it in 1979 and 1980 and 1981 with the hepatitis "B" vaccine that was administered in New York and San Francisco and a few other major metropolitan American cities by the Centers for Disease Control. And check this out the ads that they ran in those cities' newspapers were specifically asking for promiscuous homosexual males. And that is sad, I can't say it enough but it's true very much true. And those vaccines the hepatitis "B" and small-pox vaccines were manufactured and bottled in Phoenix, Arizona and whatever causes aids was in those vaccines. And if you can ever get a chance to check the record, CIA Project (MK-NAOMI), is still to this day and always will be probably classified information. Also you might want to check out house appropriation committee HB-15090, 1970, vol. VI, pg. 129 Ref. U.S. Senate Library.

390. Well do you know how contagious aids really is well like I said in the last thought if you been listening to the media, the TV., the news, of mainstream medical science, which are all directly or indirectly controlled by those who clandestinely control the U.S. government then you've been lied to about aids in it's totality. But don't feel bad because they even deceived honest reputable doctors though the centers For Disease Control, and the World Health Organization, (which those who clandestinely control the U.S. government also control), into believing that aids was not that contagious and that people could not catch aids from a sneeze, a cough, a kiss, a salad bar, a dirty eating, utensil, or even a mosquito. Because the truth about aids is that it is highly contagious and can be transmitted from person to person by all of the aftermentioned and especially by mosquitoes because remember that it's a well known medical fact that mosquitoes can carry all kinds of serious diseases because they bite and suck blood out of people and animals. So what would make you think that if a mosquito bit a person

infected with aids that the mosquito would not then be infected with aids and therefore give aids to the next person or animal that it bites. And it's true that mosquitoes die after they bite a human or animal. But that does not negate that the mosquito will not get a few more bites in on people or animals before it dies or that it couldn't carry the disease. And besides that there are 3,550 species of mosquitoes all with different capacities for carrying diseases. But like I said don't feel bad because those who clandestinely control the U.S. government did not only deceive you, but deceived medical doctors and professionals. But they were able to do it only because the disinformation was directly put out but the same entities that put aids out, or were used to put aids out. The disinformation was accepted by the medical community as valid and true and therefore pushed out to the masses of people. And for those of you who might be dealing with aids close to home and would like to read or learn more about the truth of aids there's a few good books on the truth of aids. (Aids, What The Government Isn't Telling You, by" Lorraine Day, MD.; The Aids Cover-up, by" Gene Antonio; and Aids Silent Killer, by Don Boys, PHD.)

391. Now in this thought here I'm going to speak on foundations, the so called benevolent and great tax exempt philanthropic foundations that everybody holds so dear. Now when you get through reading this thought I can bet you a 1000 to 1, that you will never look at the great philanthropic tax exempt foundations the same way again. Now the foundations that I'm about the speak on are foundations that for the most part have been around since the turn of the 20th century and all of them without exception, were started by, and/or have been infiltrated and are therefore controlled now by those who clandestinely control the U.S. government. Now the foundations that I'm talking about are the very prestigious and powerful Rockefeller Foundation, The Rubin Foundation, The Carnegie Foundation, The Russell Sage Foundation, The Ford Foundation, The Lily endowment Foundation, The Heritage Foundation, The W.K. Kellogg Foundation, The Kettering Foundation, and The Thyessen Foundation, and the most newly added one to the bunch which is the Bill and Melinda Gates Foundation, and by the way is overtly now the one with the deepest pockets. And

all of their allied organizations, and subsidiaries in there orbit and under their control. Now these foundations you might not know it, but these foundations are very pivotal tools of those who clandestinely control the U.S. government for population control, and mind programming, and indoctrination reasons. Now very few people know or understand how much actual influence and control these foundations wield over the National Education Association (NEA), which is America's public school system, and over all of America's institutions of higher learning. And not just that but also over the financing and writing of scholastic textbooks which are used virtually nationwide in higher learning, and in the public school sector. Now you must remember that whoever controls the education of a nation will inevitably control the nation, through indoctrination of ideas, thoughts, and beliefs. Now the way that these foundations do this is by way of grants, endowments, and funding like for example the Rockefeller, Carnegie, and Ford Foundations alone have in the last 20 years furnished 3 quarters of the total endowment funding of all institutions of higher learning in America. And the grant making power of these foundations is really just ineffable because there resources are virtually limitless. And if an educational institution does not want to go along with the foundations behests then it is denied grants, and endowments. And mind you these foundations act in concert so if one denies you they will all deny you. Now I'm going to give you a quote from William H. McIllhany's great book, Tax exempt Foundation's:

They came to the conclusion that for complete control they (those who clandestinely control the U.S. government) must control education. And then they approached the Rockefeller foundation and they said: "Will you take on the acquisition of control of education as it involves subjects that are domestic in their significance", and it was agreed. Then together they decided that the key to it was the teaching of American history and they must change that. So they then approached the most prominent of what we might call American historians at that time with the idea of getting them to alter the manner in which they presented the subject.

So remember that those who clandestinely control the U.S. government through their foundations control what history and how history is taught in America and this control of America's educational system did not just start. It has been going on for at least the last eight decades. Now I want you to understand and know that these foundations don't just control America's educational system, but also exert tremendous influence and control over America's scientific and medical community's by way of research funding, and myriad other grants and endowments. And just as absolute is there control over America's educational system is just as absolute is there control over America's scientific, and medical communities. Now congress has tried to investigate these foundations and their activities more than once the first of the congressional committees to attempt such an investigation was the Cox committee, created in 1952 under the leadership of Congressman Eugene E. Cox, a democrat from Georgia. And Warren Weaver notes in U.S. Philanthropic Foundations that the official purpose of this committee was to determine which foundations and organizations were using their resources for purposes for which they were established and especially to determine which such foundations and organizations were using their resources for un-American and subversive activities or for proposes not in the interest or tradition of the United States. Now those who clandestinely control the U.S. government did not like this in no kind of way. So first they had their elements in congress delay the appropriation of funds for the Cox Committee, and then the Cox Committee was only given 6 months to conclude an investigation that would have properly taken several years to conclude. Cox hoped to expose the foundations for what they really were and that's involved in fraud, racketeering, deceit, and a number of other un-American activities. But as Dwight MacDonald pointed out Cox's strategy misfired and an elaborate counter-intelligence program was launched by those who clandestinely control the U.S. government against an unsuspecting, and unknowing Cox. And he Congressman Cox fell gravely ill during the investigation and died. So now with the impeccably idealistic chairman out of the way those who clandestinely control the U.S. government were able to have their elements whitewash the whole investigation. But one member of the committee refused to go along and play a part in the whitewash cover-up. He was Congressman Carroll Reece of Tennessee, a former chairman of the republican national committee. And he promptly demanded a new investigation. Now those that clandestinely control the U.S government were frantic and had their media, newspapers, and virtually the entire establishment press ridicule, and scream, that the Reece probe was wholly unnecessary, and a stupid waste of public funds. But even as the media and the establishment press, unleashed an enormous barrage of vilification against the new probe the probe went on but as researcher Carroll Quigley noted in his book: Tragedy and Hope,

"It soon became clear that people of immense wealth would be unhappy if the investigation went too far and that the most respected newspapers in the country closely allied, and controlled, by these men of great wealth, would not get excited enough about any revelations to make the publicity worthwhile."

So what did the media, newspapers, and establishment press, didn't get excited about were the Reece Committee's official finding which were that" The rich and super rich banking families give money to the foundations without losing control of how it is spent. The major foundations are interconnected and work as one to a common policy. They took and have complete control over America's educational system. History books are being funded which keep the truth away from the people, they have the power through grants, and endowment funding to suppress those people of ideas whether they be great or small that disagree with their plans or agendas. And in the medical and scientific community's research sponsored by the foundations is slanted to conform to the conclusions the foundations funder's demand. And that the Ford family had long lost control of the Ford foundation, that it was only Ford in name but completely controlled by the Rockefellers. And these findings that I just mentioned and many more came from the 1953-54 Reece special house committee to investigate tax exempt foundations, which issued its report in 1954. And all of this almost became public in the mid 50's when the Reece committee issued its official report in 1954. But the tight control of the media, the newspapers, and the whole establishment press by those who clandestinely control the U.S. government suppressed it. But the 1954 Reece report on tax exempt foundations is still around today and can be looked up at the library of congress, via your internet. And not only that but many great books exposing the truth about these foundations have been written like: Tax Exempt Foundations, by William H. McIllhany, Foundations There Power, and Influence, by Rene Wormser, who was counsel for the Reece committee when it was investigating the tax exempt foundations. So now that you know the truth about the so called great philanthropic foundations you'll probably think twice before thinking that there nothing but benevolent.

392. Thus for my own part I have more than once been deceived by the person I love most and of whose love above everyone else's I have been most confident.

-Baldassare Castiglione

1478 - 1529

393. Everybody steals in commerce and industry, I've stolen a lot myself but I know how to steal.

-Thomas Edison

1847 – 1931

394. What more obvious prison can we live in then to see laws passed in which the people have had no say. And those same people to believe that even though the law is ludicrous or fascist, they must respect it.

--David Icke

395. The law is just a piece of paper that results from a group of mostly uninformed or corrupt politicians voting for whatever reason or reasons it's introduction.

Michael L. Urias
--Former U.S. Senator

396. Always remember that right now, as we speak we are living in what's known as fascism here in America, and the masses of American people don't even recognize it, or know it. And fascism as we all know is when you the people own property, such as businesses, houses, land, cars or vehicles, or whatever but the state and/or government controls it. Now let me give you a few examples of how fascism now exists here in America right now. All right, it's like this. If those who clandestinely control the U.S. government want you to do something with your property, or they want you not to do something with your property, all they do is just get a law, ordinance, or regulation, enacted as such. It's that simple. And nine times out of ten that law, ordinance, or regulation will be in the name of public safety, or environmental good, or both. Now I want you to just sit back and think for a minute of how many of these laws, ordinances, and regulations, do we have in America right now. There's myriad. And when I say your property I'm mainly speaking of your business, your house, your real property, your land, and your car or vehicle. Now just think about all these laws, ordinances, and regulations, here in America right now and how they interfere, and intervene, with the otherwise peaceful use of your business, real property, house, land, and car or vehicle. But don't think about the purpose or effect the government says these laws, ordinances, and regulations, are for or have which is plausible, and false, until you've thought about the real life effect all these so called public safety, environmental good, or whatever they want to call these draconian laws, ordinances, and regulations, have on you and your property. Well, the real effect is if you haven't got it yet is control, because those who clandestinely control the U.S. government are surreptitiously controlling your property through laws, ordinances, and regulations. And if you own your property, but they the state or government controls it then your living under what's known as fascism. And the masses of people have absolutely no idea how many more myriad laws, ordinances, and regulations are going to be enacted to restrict the use of private property in the next five to ten years by those who clandestinely control the U.S. government. So that they can have complete and total control over you and your property.

And check this out did you know that the 1990 federal register leister more than 63,000 new laws, ordinances, and regulations restricting the use of private property, and in 2003 the federal register lists more than 150,000 . . . yeah, you read right . . . more than 150,000 laws, ordinances, and regulations restricting the use of private property. And I'm going to tell you something right now one of the most horrific, liberty eroding, and tyrannous acts ever passed into law in the history of America was the Patriot Act. But the vast majority of American people don't know that, they have no idea what the Patriot Act really is all about. But I'm here to tell you that the Patriot Act is the most liberty eroding piece of legislation ever enacted into law in the history of America, with clauses that mandate such sentences as 25 years to life for peaceful demonstrators, meaning anyone demonstrating against war, or the government in anyway, form, or fashion, could be prosecuted under the Patriot Act and if convicted will receive a mandatory sentence of 25 years to life. And if you don't believe me then I strongly recommend that you type Patriot Act compliance into any search engine and you'll get about 100 hits or procure you a copy of the Patriot Act 1 and 2 from the federal register via your internet and read it for yourself. And if you cherish your liberty, privacy, and rights because obviously there's people out there who don't. Then I personally guarantee that you will be totally and completely aghast after reading it. And you know what the sad thing is? The sad thing is that our freedom, and liberty, here in America is so vastly disappearing through laws, ordinances, regulations, and other so called measures that it's really just a shame. But do you know what's even a worse shame, is that the American people don't even see it happening. Be on the lookout for laws telling you how much alcohol you can and can't buy. And laws telling you what you can and can't believe and/or like.

397. Always remember that there are certain kinds of people in the world that are not to be trusted in any kind of way, and that you must watch out for. The following three types or kinds of people are the main kinds and/or types that you must never trust under no circumstances and you must always watch out for.

a. The kind of person who only cares about material possessions, and themselves living in opulence, and luxury. But they try to keep every part of this hid.

b. The kind of person that is down to earth, cool, likeable, and even lovable. But has ulterior motives and hidden agendas.

c. The kind of people that are intelligent, maybe even educated. But are crafty, sneaky, and manipulative. But they try to keep the crafty, sneaky, and manipulation part of themselves hid.

Now whenever you come across one of these kinds or types of people that I just mentioned, you better not trust him or her in no kind of way. And you had better keep your eye on them. Because there full of nothing but deceit, selfishness, and hidden agendas. And you best believe me they mean you nothing good.

398. Always remember that in the game of life anything is possible. And the game is dirty.

399. Always remember that you cannot shelter forever your kids from the cruelness, hatred, lies, hurt, deception, pain, and evil now so prevalent in the world. You can only prepare them for it.

400. Always remember that in life the good moments are going to come and go, just like the bad moments are going to come and go. But this is because we live in a universe where good and evil co-exist simultaneously and together. And the good and evil are incessantly and constantly at odds with each other in the physical, as well as, in the spiritual realms so only a fool would believe that he or she is only going to have all good moments non-stop with no bad moments in this life.

401. Now in this thought here I'm going to name a phrase and I can bet you 10 to 1 that you will not know who said if first, and the phrase is very common and I know you you've heard it many time before and the phrase is:

Thoughts on Life And the Absolute Power of Thought

An evil exist that threatens every man, woman, and child of this great nation. We must take steps to ensure our domestic security and protect our homeland.

So who said the foregoing phrase first? Do you know? Stop reading right now and make your decision. What is Clinton? Bush? Cheney? Rumsfield? Powell? Tony Blair? Condolelezza Rice? Or other? Now all of the after mentioned have uttered the phrase and sentiments to that effect. But they were not the first to use it. The first to utter and use that phrase was Adolf Hitler when he was announcing the creation of the Gestapo in Nazi Germany. But wait a minute there are more parallels between what's going on now and what happened in Nazi Germany. Have you ever heard of the enforcement act? Probably not. Well the enforcement act was an act instituted by Hitler in Germany after his rise to power. And guess what our Patriot Act and I kid you not is almost a carbon copy of it. And if you don't believe me then I suggest you procure yourself a copy of our Patriot Act and a copy of Hitler's Enforcement Act and read them. People you need to wake up before its too late.

402. Now in this thought here I'm going to show you, and you are going to see the populace or groups of people in society as they really are. And this is the way that those who clandestinely control the U.S. government view society because to them there are only 4 major population groups in society. Read them and see which group you fit into, and you'll notice that group A is the largest group or segment of the population with 55% of the people and this group is the group that is mostly responsible for keeping the machine running and the machine is the economy because this group consists of the everyday working person, all the way on up to doctors, professors, and various other everyday working professionals, and executives in various fields. But by these people being everyday working people and therefore having so little time to actually think. And by them eight out of every ten of them being programmed and conditioned by public schooling which is the indoctrinating tool of those who clandestinely control the U.S. government. And by these people getting mostly if not all of their information from mainstream society, these people in group A are the least

informed of what's really going on. There the least informed to how society, the government, and the world really operate. And they are the ones that are going to be most shocked by the revelations in this book. But like I said group A is the group mostly responsible for keeping the machine going and if group A ever wakes up to what's really going on and learns the truth, and sees that they have been mislead, tricked, deceived, manipulated, and lied to all there life. Then those who clandestinely control the U.S. government are going to have a serious problem. And that's why I'm endeavoring to wake up group A with this book, because the other 3 groups to more or lesser degrees already know the business. And when you look at the diagram notice the configurations groups A and B are in there own spree. And groups C and D are in there own spree. I made it like that for a reason. Because people go from group B to group A all the time. And people go from group C to group D, and from group D back to group C all the time. But rarely do people cross over whole spree's. So go head and read the diagram, study it, and you'll see what I'm talking about.

GROUP A is the middle and average working class. The largest segment of the population, those who believe in patriotism, justice for all, what's good and right, and have been raised with morals and that is why this group is manipulated so easily by Group C and believes everything Group C tells it.

GROUP B is looked at by all of society as the undesirables. Group C incessantly tells Group A that Group B are the only criminals in society which is a lie and that the majority of society's problems are because of Group B. But, if Group A only knew that the biggest criminals in society and the cause of 90% of society problems and ills are Groups C and D. None the less, Group A always believes whatever Group C tells it.

GROUP C ceaselessly manipulates both Groups A and B, lies to them and deceives them in a myriad of ways. Groups A and B have been programmed all their lives to trust and believe Group C.

GROUP D is 15% of the people and this is where the real criminals and evil is at. This group controls Group C through money and power. This group is where the real wealth and power of the world lies. If you would like to learn about the underground world economy and how it actually functions and operates and how the legal, and overt, economy is subject to it and depends on it, then you must get Jeffrey Robinson's book: The Laundrymen, or more recently The Infiltrator by Robert Mazur…or go to www.the-infiltrator.com.

403. First he said that the cure for cancer has been known for decades but they would not release this to the public because they did not want people to survive and were making far more money drugging the dying and treating the symptoms then they ever would curing the disease.

--Unknown CIA, Secret Agent

GROUP A 55% of the people
The highly educated, the educated and the average, middle-class or every day working person

GROUP C 15% of the people
Crafty politicians, crafty businessmen, corrupt government employees and officials and anybody else in the know about or associated with those who clandestinely control the US Government and anybody in the know about or part of the underground world economy.

GROUP B 15% of the people
The average thug, gang-banger, radical, small-time drug dealer, small time criminal, drug addict or non-the-less average uneducated or poorly educated person or minority and the ghetto population.

GROUP D 15% of the people
Those who clandestinely control the US Government. Those who make up the underground world economy, i.e. drug lords, Dons, members and associates of worldwide criminal syndicates, etc. which is where all the real wealth and money is. Second only to those who clandestinely control the US Government.

404. Now in this thought here I just want you to know that those who clandestinely control the U.S. government have been spreading cancer throughout our nation for the last 50 or so years. Let me explain . . . back around 1955 those who clandestinely control the U.S. government were informed by there so called advisers that people were beginning to outlive their usefulness because of technology and the advancement in medical science available to the common person. So therefore people would start to live to 80, 90, or even 100 years old unless something was done. So those who clandestinely control the U.S. government ordered there advisers to run think tanks to come up with a sound answer to this on coming population problem by the way this is also one of the reasons they those who clandestinely control the U.S. government created and put out aids, but I already told you about aids in a previous thought. But none the less this was one of the reasons for it also. But anyway the think tanks were conducted and they came to their conclusion about the oncoming population problem and their conclusion simply was that people must not be allowed to live to 80, 90, or 100 years of age. Because as the think tanks advised that people after the age of 60 and definitely at 80, or 90, and most definitely 100 years old are pretty much useless because there completely unproductive, and all there doing is taking up and using space, food, money, healthcare, and even air and all of societies other natural resources that sustain life. And all these resources that the unproductive and useless segments of the population over 60 years of age are using up could be better allocated to the younger more productive segments of the population. So therefore something had to be developed to get rid of and neutralize people right when they become useless and unproductive, right around age 55 to 70. So it was determined that they would give people cancer in installment plans meaning they would infect people throughout their lives in such microscopic and specifically designed time released amounts of carcinogenetic substances that it would take anywhere from 20 to 40 years for actual cancer to appear. So that by the time a person reaches 70 years of age they would nine times out of ten done at least one of 3 things. 1) battled cancer and survived; 2) currently battling cancer, or; 3) have

already died from cancer. So therefore neutralizing people right at or around the time they become unproductive or useless. And like the think tanks also advised that peoples should start to get ready to exit or in other words die in their late 40's to early 50's so by the time they get in there mid 60's to early, early 70's they will be fully ready to make the transition to the other side, meaning die. But the think tanks also found that mostly nobody wants to die at 65 or 70 so therefore they have to be neutralized or in other words killed without their knowledge and that's where the cancer in installment plans came in to play. And when they said that people should start to get ready to exit or die in their late 40's to early 50's they mean just that just look around you and that's about the time people have their first bout with cancer and if they survive there lucky. But in their mind believe me there stating to psychologically get ready to pass on because they know that they don't have too much longer left. So as always those who clandestinely control the U.S. government have met their goal and have successfully implemented a measure to get people ready or at least to start thinking about passing on in their late 40's to early 50's and actually having them pass on right around age 70 if not before. And mine you, that those who clandestinely control the U.S. government have got a cure for cancer they been had a cure for cancer that's old news. But I'll tell you one thing regular people will never get it. But anyway and now how they actually infected and are infecting the masses of people with cancer in installments well like I told you it's given to the people in microscopically specially designed time released installments so that it virtually can't be detected. But it's probably and this is not known for sure in something universally used that everybody without a doubt uses like sugar. But I'll tell you this and this is pretty much known for sure the microscopic time released carcinogens are in the hormones given to our livestock and in the pesticides sprayed on farm crops and its conjecture if there in the soda, coffee, cigarettes and alcoholic substances. And I already know that the average person is going to argue that if you smoke, and drink coffee and alcohol you're more than likely to get cancer. But no you have got to understand that these things have been deliberately spiked with special carcinogenic substances so that if you do any of them for any length of time you will without any doubt get cancer somewhere in your body. And we already know that cigarettes are carcinogenic, but that's not what I'm talking about . . . . they have been deliberately tampered with. And you got to remember virtually everybody loves soda and do you want to know why? Because there are special additives in the soda, the coffee, and the cigarettes, and in all alcoholic substances to get you hooked . . . believe that, it's a known fact. And now you don't have to wonder no more why eight or nine out of every ten people by the age of 70 has had cancer, is currently dealing with cancer, or has already died from cancer. And that right there is not natural as the media, the press, and the medical community makes it out to be. Because check this out there was a landmark study on the causes of cancer by Sir Richard Doll and Richard Pete that set on to determine the causes of cancer in the United States and according to Doll and Peto environmental pollution only accounts for 2% of all cancer cases in the United States. And that right there is contrary to the myths put out there by the media, the Environmental Protection Agency (EPA) and everybody else who wants to blame the environment and pollution for increasing cancer rates in America. And Richard Doll and Richard Peto are not alone in their conclusion that environmental pollution only account for something like 2% of all cancer cases in America. Renowned scientist Michael Gough affirmed the same thing. Gough analyzed the findings of the Doll and Peto study along with estimates of cancer causes in the EPA's report (unfinished business) and he came to conclusions extremely similar to that of Doll and Peto. Gough noted that only 2 to 3% of all cancers could be associated with environmental pollution. So now do you understand that it's not the environment or pollution causing cancer in America as they those who clandestinely control the U.S. government would want you to believe but rather it is them causing cancer in America. And last but not least check this out, did you know that those who clandestinely control the U.S. government have been and still do block and do not let in to the United States effective cancer curing drugs. Drugs that have been known to have the power to eradicate and neutralize cancer in it's tracts are not allowed in the United States. And those who clandestinely control the U.S. government do this through the (FDA) The Food and Drug

Administration which they surreptitiously control just like they do every other government agency. And for more on this topic on how and why those who clandestinely control the U.S. government block and do not allow effective cancer curing drugs in the United States you must read the following books on this unbelievable but true and very intriguing topic, books such as: Cure For All Cancers, by Hulda Clark PH.D; Murder By Injection, by Eustace Mullins; Racketeering in Medicine The Suppression of Alternatives, by James P. Carder, M.D.; and The Medical Mafia, by Guylaine Lanctot: and if you want to read and learn about why those who clandestinely control the U.S. government want to and are neutralizing the population then you must get the following books: The Population Bomb, by Dr. Paul Ehrlich; and The War Against Population, by Jacqeline Kasun. And just so you know cell phones are a major and leading cause of cancer, but that is being suppressed here in the United States and if you don't believe me then please go to www.willthomasonline.net and impartially peruse his information.

405. Now in this thought that you are about to read you are going to learn 2 things. First how those who clandestinely control the U.S. government use national crisis and wars to their own advantage. And two how a very prominent newspaper (The Wall Street Journal) deceives the people and prints plausible misleading information. Alright, and please read carefully . . . the following is a small excerpt from a October 23, 2001 Wall Street Journal article by a Jay Winik who started the following:

> 1. That in previous national emergencies U.S. Presidents took strong repressive measures against the American people and other U.S. residents of the country.
>
> 2. That the repressive measures implemented so far by the Bush administration are comparatively mild and,
>
> 3. That notwithstanding the Draconian measures taken during previous crisis normalcy returned and so did civil liberties invariably stronger than before. And the

Wall Street Journal concluded . . . "even if the Bush administration deems it necessary to enact more restrictive steps we need not fear."

Now that whole little excerpt that you just read is a straight lie and misleading, put out by the Wall Street Journal. Because as a matter of fact if you know your history you would know that each episode of a national emergency or war left the liberties of the American people not stronger then before but severely maimed and weakened. And if you don't think so, well we are going to take a little trip through history and take a look at the facts of how those who clandestinely control the U.S. government use wars and national crisis to their own ends, okay. Now during World War I the Wilson administration that was clandestinely controlled by those who had de-facto control of the government at the time took sweeping actions to suppress not only individual's freedom of action but even there freedom of expression. The 1918 sedition act must be read to be believed. Under it one might be as some 2,000 persons were prosecuted for daring to utter, print, write, or publish any disloyal, propane, scurrilous, or abusive language about the form of government of the united States or the constitution of the United States, or military, or naval forces of the United States, or flag of the United States, or the uniform of the Army or Navy of the United States, or any language intended to bring the form of government of the United States, or the constitution of the United States or the flag of the United States, or the uniform of the Army or Navy of the United States into contempt, scorn, contumely, or disrepute, not either was this all the statue forbad. And then when convictions under the sedition act were challenged in the courts the U.S. Supreme Court upheld the statue. And to his eternal shame Justice Oliver Wendell Holmes Jr. wrote:

"When a nation is at war many things that might be said in a time of peace are such a hindrance to it's effort that there utterance will not be endured so long as men fight and no court could regard them as protected by any constitutional right."

This decision and others upholding unconstitutional measures undertook by the Wilson administration might strike the ordinary person of today as odd because the constitution itself makes no provision for it's own evisceration during wartime or any other crisis that might befall the nation. Yet time and time again during national emergencies, crisis, and wars the courts have allowed the legislative branch, and especially the executive branch of government to transcend there constitutionally enumerated powers and to nullify individual rights proclaimed and protected by the constitution. And the Wilson administration conscripted some 2.8 million men 70 percent of those who served in the army. And the Supreme Court could find no constitutional infirmity in that involuntary servitude and it's ruling has been a decisive precedent for judges ever since. The government also intervened massively in economic affairs, setting prices, allocating raw materials, and even going so far as to nationalize the interstate railroad, ocean shipping, and telecommunications industries. Those measures established precedents that would return to haunt subsequent generations and undercut their liberties in later crisis, economic depressions, wars or whatever. And each time cutting more deeply into the fiber of American life. And with extremely malign effects on America's liberty. Now I'm going to speak on World War II for a second. World War II became the occasion for those who clandestinely control the U.S. government to have the U.S. government set unprecedented repressive actions against the American people. Starting with drafting more than 10 million young men against their will into the war to fight. That's about 63% of all those who severed in the armed forces in the war. And hundreds of thousands of them died or suffered serious injuries. Then the government imprisoned nearly 6,000 conscientious objectors and most of them were religious people who refused to obey the conscription law because of religious reasons. And then totally without due process of law the government confined some 112,000 persons of Japanese ancestry and most of them U.S. citizens at that, in concentration camps. Because they were perceived to be enemies of FDR's administration. Then the government built and implemented a massive apparatus of economic controls and other controls such as New York City's never abandoned rent controls between 1941 and 1945 and displaced free markets for the duration of the war. Then men, women, and children, were sent to prison for violating the price controls. And people were displaced from their homes to make way for military construction projects. War time taxation itself was no trivial assault. Then to pay for the gargantuan munitions production during the war for the government imposed new taxes and raised the rates of existing taxes to unprecedented heights. And this was when the now infamous income tax was born, implemented and never abandoned or repealed. And the reason given to the American people for all the tax hikes. And especially the income tax was that the government was in an imperative need of money because of the war, which is true. But that is just what those who clandestinely controlled the U.S. government wanted. Why? Because the war, World War II, cost the U.S. government over 200 billion dollars. And where do you think the U.S. government got that 200 billion dollars from??? They borrowed it, and they borrowed it from those who clandestinely control the U.S. government . . . (The Federal Reserve). Therefore swelling the national debt into astronomical amounts. And for those of you who don't know, the national debt is now in the trillions of dollars and the national debt is not money owed by our government to other countries, it's money owed by our government directly to those who clandestinely control the U.S. government . . . owed to the Federal Reserve. And you know who created, owns, and controls, the Federal Reserve. (Please see thought #460)

So now do you understand why wars are so beneficial to those who clandestinely control the U.S. government? And that's not it as the great economist Calvin Hoover observed World War II conditioned people to accept a degree of government intervention and control in their lives after the war, which they would not have accepted prior to the war. So you see the benefits of wars are myriad for those who clandestinely control the U.S. government. And now in light of these and countless other facts don't you wonder how the Wall Street Journal was able to conclude that in times of war, national crisis or whatever may be the case. We, the American people should not worry about the repressive measures, controls, or any other liberty depriving actions that the government takes against us, the people. But like I always say the history and facts that you just read in this thought are not taught in public schools. They omit stuff like this . . . why??? Because it makes the government look bad. And those who clandestinely control the U.S. government don't like or want the government to look bad. And again . . . why??? Because the government is what those who clandestinely control the U.S. government use to deceive and manipulate the American people. And I must say me personally, I've always wondered why people are so reluctant to question the government or it's actions. Well I guess that this is in due part to the outstanding jobs the public schools do of programming people to not question authority. I mean the public schools do a far, far, superior job of teaching and programming kids not to question authority then they do of teaching the kids how to read, write, and spell. I mean this is all good to some degree because of course we don't want a nation of criminals. But this is not good to the absurd degree that the kids once they grow up will under almost no circumstance at all question authority. Come on folks, that's absurd!!! And who's the supreme authority of the land??? The government! I mean the way the public schools teach and program people not to question authority is nothing short of brainwashing them, so that the government can virtually do whatever they want, and the people will not question it. The people will just say well if the government is doing it then it must be right and it must be for the good. Come on people . . . WAKE UP!!! And no matter how many laws, ordinances, and regulations the government enacts to erode America's liberties and intervene in the peoples personal and private lives. T he people will just say, okay . . . it must be for the good if the government is doing it. This is one of the main reasons that I'm writing this book and filing it with rare facts that have been suppressed and hid from the average American person, is to wake the American people up. And it is beyond pivotal that the American people wake up to what those who clandestinely control the U.S. government are doing. And what they're doing is using one of the oldest tricks in the book against America and that trick is gradualism. Meaning anything that's gradually done is seldom if ever noticed. And those who clandestinely control the U.S. government 70 years ago gradually burdened down America with taxes. Because if you know anything about the history of tax law and taxes, then you will very much well know that in 1913 there were 11,000 words in the U.S. tax code. And now today we have over 7 million words in the U.S. tax code. And not only that but in 1913 the average American paid about 5% annually in taxes. Now the average American pays annually in taxes about 38.2%. How did that happen??? Gradually. And now that we are paying 38.2% annually in taxes it's too late to do or say anything about it. Just like when we wake up in a totalitarian socialistic state because of all these laws, ordinances, and regulations that are being passed then just like the taxes it will be too late to do or say anything about it. And now that you know how those who clandestinely control the U.S. government benefit from wars in every way. I want you the American people to stop being fools and know the truth about the September 11, 2001 terrorist attacks on the nation. Those who clandestinely control the U.S. government caused and made it possible for the September 11, 2001 terrorist attacks on our nation to happen. Why? Well, there are myriad reasons. Why? But I'll give you a few of the more pivotal ones, 1) To break down America's resolution and to put the masses of people in a state of terror, fear, uncertainty, and discord. And therefore make the people malleable, 2) So they could declare a war of some type and therefore put the nation further in debt, by America having to finance the war, with them . . . those who clandestinely control the U.S. government loaning the money to the government via and through there bank (The Federal Reserve), which makes this money out of thin air and then turns around and loans it to the government at something like 5 ½% interest, if not more. And this is all 100% legal . . . it's shocking, but it's very true and legal. 3) So the government under the control of those who clandestinely control it can have a reason to implement more repressive measures, and controls, economic and otherwise, and have a reason to implement more laws, ordinances, and regulations to inch there totalitarian socialistic state, all the more on the American people with the American people asleep, not knowing what' really going on and thinking everything is all good. And all I can say is I hope America wakes up before it's too late. And now I'm going to mention a few facts about the September 11, 2001 terrorist attack. First there is absolutely no way in hell, and believe me

I know, that a terrorist organization the size of Osama Bin Laden's could have escaped detection or have somehow been overlooked by all of America's security and intelligence agencies. First of all the average American person has no idea of the technology and sophistication of the CIA and the other intelligence and security agencies. And those who clandestinely control the U.S. government know this. But I'll say this there are those who do know of the advance technology and sophistication of the CIA and the other intelligence and security agencies . . . But them people are mostly all spooks who work directly or indirectly for the government. So therefore they are not talking, but they know that the notion of a terrorist network the size of Osama Bin Laden's being not detected or picked up on by the CIA and the rest of the intelligence and security agencies without some serious high up help is a straight joke they know its bullshit. But like I said they aren't talking. And for how the intelligence agencies work please read (Intelligence Agency Thought #420). But anyway did you know that every single phone call wireless or not, fax, page, and email since something like 1984 has been monitored by the government and you can't go talking about they can't do that because this surveillance here is protected by national security laws which supersede all other laws. And agencies that do this surveillance don't share their information or findings with no one not no local agency, not no state agency, not even federal agencies can get their hands on this stuff it is strictly and completely top secret. You would have to be endangering the national security like Osama Bin Laden and his terrorist organization was for you to get a visit from these people. And I'm going to tell you something else these people also monitor just so you know every single frequency and transmission of information whether it's wireless or not that goes through the air and this is without exception no matter what it is, all T.V., and music radio included. And you already pretty must know that all these agencies including these super secret agencies are controlled by those who clandestinely control the U.S. government and for how they control all these super secret agencies, and virtually all the intelligence agencies you must read again thought #420. But all I'm saying is that there is absolutely no way in hell that

Osama Bin Laden could have pulled off 9-11 if indeed and that's a big if, it was Osama Bin laden, because maybe and more times than not in my opinion and in the opinion of many other skilled and renowned researchers people who have devoted their life to studying these who clandestinely control the U.S. government Osama Bin Laden is just accepting responsibility because he was told or asked too. Because the bottom line is Osama Bin Laden could not have pulled off the September 11, 2001 terrorist attacks without the help of those who clandestinely control the U.S. government. It is absolutely impossible, point blank. But I'll tell you this the average American doesn't know that and that is again where those who clandestinely control the U.S. government win again at. And those who clandestinely control the U.S. government have got the masses of people in America stuck on straight stupid and completely brainwashed and do you know how those who clandestinely control the U.S. government have done this? Well they did it through the T.V., the newspapers, the media and all the other outlets of public information and do you know how those who clandestinely control the U.S. government have got and kept their surreptitious monopoly on the outlets and different entities of public information. Well they buy the parent companies of magazines, T.V. stations, newspapers, etc. Therefore the magazine, T.V. station, or newspaper still looks and appears to the public as an independent entity and all those who clandestinely control the U.S. government then do is fill the board with their directors, put in their CEO's and supply the head editor for each magazine, T.V. station, newspaper, etc., to control content for them so all the myriad T.V. stations, newspapers, magazines, and other outlets of public information that you the public thought were independent of each other and independent entities are really all and the same and owned and controlled by the same people. And just so you know in recent years those who clandestinely control the U.S. government have been consolidating there media interests, because right now as I'm writing this there are 5 major media conglomerates here in America that own over 90% of all the broadcast media here in America, which is, 1) Time Warner, which has gobbled up America On Line, MGM, TNT, CNN, and countless other media entities, 2) Viacom, which owns CBS, UPN, MTV, and 39-T.V. stations including outlets in 15 of the top 20-markets, and that's most definitely not all just like Time Warner, Viacom owns countless other media entities, 3) The Disney Empire which owns ABC, 4) NBC Universal, and 5) News Corporation (FOX) which is owned and controlled by Rupert Murdock, and News Corporation owns so many magazines, newspapers, and other broadcast and publishing media around the world that it is estimated that news corporation has a demographic of roughly half the world 3 billion people. And each one of these media conglomerates is owned and/or controlled either overtly or covertly by those who clandestinely control the U.S. government. Just look at Time Warner CEO Jeffrey Bewkes who has been a long time member of those who clandestinely control the U.S. government. And the same goes for Viacom CEO Sumner Redsone, FOX CEO Rupert Murdoch, Disney CEO Bob Iger, and NBC Universal CEO Steve Burke. So the line that there all saying, so it must be true meaning all the collective media pushing or saying the same thing. Is a lie, and 100% negated. Because what you don't' know and are definitely not told is that what you get from the collective media is nothing but the same line, opinion, and scrip from a myriad of polygenetic sources, and those who clandestinely control the U.S. government have been doing this since 1915 when their predecessors bought up all the newspapers in America. So all I can say is it's pivotal that people stop believing everything they see and hear on T.V., stop believing everything they read in the newspapers stop believing everything they read in magazines and in periodicals, and just stop being stuck in extorvetism. And if you really want to know what's going on with your life or what's really going on in the world all you got to do is get in tune with yourself and then and only then will the truth about whatever you seek be revealed and be made known to you. But I'm going to tell you one thing you'll never get the truth about nothing being stuck in extorvetism you'll always get if not a straight lie, a throw off, or some kind of miss lead. And an excellent book on how those who clandestinely control the U.S. government make and cause wars and have actually made and caused every single war in America's history even the 1789 French Revolution is: the truth shall set you free by David Icke. And if you want details this book is full, replete with meticulous details about those who clandestinely control the U.S. government, their predecessors, there tricks and get downs, and how there execrate organization came about. And if you're specifically interested in wars and how those who clandestinely control the U.S. government cause, make, control, and benefit from wars then you must get the excellent book called: The Report from Iron Mountain. And this book is available from global insights at www.nohoax.com or 1-800-729-4131. And just in case if you're specifically interested in how those who clandestinely control the U.S. government planned, financed, and caused 9-11 to happen then you must get the most profound and excellent book ever written about the truth of 9-11, called: Alice in Wonderland and The World Trade Center Disaster, by David Icke ISBN#O-9538810-2-4 who has spent well over a decade studying and researching those who clandestinely control the U.S. government. And all the books that I just named and many more are available from global insights at the web site and phone number that I just mentioned.

406. Now in this thought I'm going to explain to you what those who clandestinely control the U.S. government are and how their organization somewhat works now. You must understand that this is by no means the first book ever written about them there have been innumerable books written about them since the middle of the 19th century to the present, books such as: Conspirator's Hierarchy, The Story of The Committee of 300, by Dr. John Coleman; The New World Order, Our Secret Rulers, by Eustace Mullins; The Truth Shall Set You Free, by David Icke; The Immaculate Deception, the Bush Crime Family Exposed, by Ret. General Russell S. Bowen; Secrets Behind the Societies, by Jon Rappoport; The Biggest Secret, by David Icke; The Satori and the New Mandarins, by Andrian Krieg; The Unseen Hand, by R. Epperson; None Dare Call It A Conspiracy, by Gary Allen – and many, many more. And those who clandestinely control the U.S. government have been called by many different names throughout the years from an all powerful conspiracy to the international bankers. But I will say this, international bankers they may be but a conspiracy they are not. Because a conspiracy means that everybody involved knows what's going on and that is just not so with everybody

that is involved, associated, or part of those who clandestinely control the U.S. government. Because those who clandestinely control the U.S. government are so secretive even within their own groups, associations, and ranks that it's a shame. But given what they're doing I guess it's needed. See I don't want people to think that there is some kind of all powerful omnipresent conspiracy going on in the U.S. government and all the senators, legislators, and lawmakers without exception are acting together knowingly with sinister hidden agendas. No, it doesn't work like that. Because they, most of the senators, legislators, and lawmakers are being manipulated themselves by those who clandestinely control the U.S. government. It works like this . . . this is how those who clandestinely control the U.S. government control it they have usurped power in the U.S. government just like they have in every other government, industry and commercial enterprise in the world. Now you must remember that this did not just start or happen it was started by the predecessors of those who now clandestinely control the U.S. government over 130 years ago. But anyway this is how they clandestinely control the U.S. government. They most of the prominent members of the government such as the prominent and powerful senators, legislators, and lawmakers and is does not matter what party they are from. Mostly all are members of the trilateral commission or the council on foreign relations or whatever they want to call the group or club these days. Because it changes names quite frequently. But none the less it is a pretty secret group, club, or association of the most prominent and powerful senators, legislators, lawmakers, judges, lawyers, government agency heads, CEO's, and many other successful, prominent and powerful people. Now you must understand that most of these people got to where they are by being members in good standing of this association and/or by the direct help of those who clandestinely control the U.S. government. Same thing. So these people know that they are who they are and got to where they're at because of this association, which is lead, ran, and controlled by those who clandestinely control the U.S. government. Now this association has rules and guidelines just like any other. But most of these prominent and powerful senators, legislators, lawmakers, judges, lawyers, CEO's, government agency heads, and other successful prominent and powerful people are nothing but the lower ranking members of this association. Therefore they don't know what is really going on because they are not told all they know is that they are part of a pretty secret association that's into philanthropy and is concerned with the betterment, upliftment, and progress of the world. But these lower ranking members when they are called up on by the association to do something and most of the time it something legal and well within the sphere of the law such as get a certain bill passed or change a certain policy or rule they don't ask no questions as what the effect of the bill will have or what the effect of the policy or rule change will have on the people. They just do it with no questions asked. They do as they're told. Thinking that if the association wants it, it must be for the good. So therefore they the prominent and powerful senators, legislators, lawmakers, judges, CEO's, government agency heads, and all the other successful, prominent and powerful people that are part of this association are being manipulated to just like everybody else. So that's why I say it is not a conscious all out conspiracy. And I'll say this so that you can have a clear view of what's going on most of the sensitive jobs in the government if not all of them such as CIA Director, FBI Director, some sensitive spots in congress and in the house of representatives and the president and his immediate cabinet are only given to the more upper ranking members of the association without exception. Now the people in these jobs know there in the know to a good degree, and they know a whole lot more than the other members. These people in these highly sensitive jobs have inside knowledge on those who clandestinely control the U.S. government. Now these people are not always but are more times than not nothing less than sinister there are 30% to 50% in the know not 100% in the know but they know enough these are the ones that will lie, cheat, and do whatever it takes to hold it together for those who clandestinely control the U.S. government these people 30% to 50% maybe more in the know of what's really going on while the rest of the lower ranking members in the associations are from 0% to 15% in the know of what's really going on. Just like former President George Bush Jr. he is a very high ranking member of this organization his father was a member and his grandfather was a member also. And just like former President

Ronald Reagan was a high ranking member of this organization and this is going to shock most people but those who clandestinely control the U.S. government deemed him a risk he knew too much and they thought he might talk so they surreptitiously had him infected with the mind deteriorating disease Alzheimer's so as to make sure he would not talk. Well as it turned out he couldn't even remember who he was. And now you're probably thinking, thinking to yourself well how big is this club, group, or association headed by those who clandestinely control the U.S. government. Well I'll say this they have chapters in virtually every part of the world and they have chapters in every major city in America. The higher ranking members and those who clandestinely control the U.S. government themselves are masons. And anybody that's extremely prominent, powerful, and successful in America is probably more times than not a member of this group, club, or association. But you have got to understand too that the person 8 times out of 10 probably does not know what he or she really is a part of because like I told you the truth and what's really going on is kept away from the lower ranking members. All they know is there part of a very, very prominent and affluent organization that's deep into philanthropy and is concerned with the betterment, upliftment, and progress of the world. And those who clandestinely control the U.S. government don't just recruit out of Harvard and Yale anymore even though Harvard and Yale and a few other ivy leagues are still prime recruitment centers for those who clandestinely control the U.S. government. They now recruit on an ongoing basis. If they spot someone who is extremely successful and prominent in their chosen endeavor or field and they deem him worthy or needed in some capacity they will inconspicuously approach that person and tell him that they are a group, club, or association of extremely prominent, successful, influential and none the less wealthy and powerful people and that they would like his membership in there esteemed organization and then they will lay down the rules and guidelines of their association and explain to him in a affable and plausible way that once you're in your in for life there's no out but I don't about that rule it might have been changed recently. And now only applies to the higher ranking members. But none the less they then invite him to one of their dinners. And there at the dinner he see's and is introduced to all the other extremely prominent, successful, powerful, and wealthy people local and otherwise that are members and are at the dinner and he is told that the club, group, association or whatever their calling it because like I told you they use different names to keep everybody thrown off even their own members, the lower ranking members that is. But they are the vast majority. But anyway they tell him that the club, group, or association is deeply into philanthropy and the betterment, upliftment, and progress of society and the world. And the prospective member looks around and see's all the other extremely prominent and affluent members and is genuinely flattered and nine times out of ten he accepts membership. But he just doesn't know just like 85% of the members don't know that he has just became a member of one of the most sinister if not the most sinister organization the world has ever known, or will ever know. He has just not knowingly become a member and a part of the long, long reaching hand of those who clandestinely control the U.S. government and virtually the world.

407. Did you know that Cuba only exists because those who clandestinely control the U.S. government allow it to? And because Castro obeys and does as he is told. Because if Castro did not do exactly as he is told by those who clandestinely control the U.S. government they would have been a long time ago got rid of, and eradicated Cuba, and Castro. I mean just think about it for a minute use your common sense here do you not think that if the United States really wanted to liberate Cuba from Castro' totalitarian control it could not. Of course it could and with no problem. But that will never happen unless those who clandestinely control the U.S. government want it to happen. But that won't happen because Castro listens and obeys accordingly he isn't no fool. And Operation Bay of the Pigs was a straight joke and for those of you who do not know that was the United States so called attempt to liberate Cuba from Castro's totalitarian control. It was planned and carried out by the black hand of the CIA and it was ordered by those who clandestinely control the U.S. government that this operation must fail and that's just what it did, failed in every way. But it was just a throw off to the world and to other

countries to make the United States look like the good guy. To make the United States look like it had really and sincerely wanted to liberate Cuba from totalitarianism. But had honestly failed which is a straight lie because like I said operation Bay of the Pigs was meant to fail from jump street. But like I said Castro is no fool he knows he got it good and he's had it good as the sole dictator of Cuba for the last 45 some odd years. And you best believe me that Castro is going to keep obeying every order and command of those who clandestinely control the U.S. government until he dies or steps down. But also you best believe this to . . . he's going to have a nice legacy in the history books as the only dictator this side of the western hemisphere to be able to have kept a socialistic totalitarian state for 45 some straight years with the big bad United States not able to do nothing about it, and/or he was able to keep the United States at bay . . . point blank. But none the less that is what the history books years from now will reflect and what the public schools and universities will be teaching the kids, which is not the truth. But the kids won't know that. Just like right now a lot of people still don't know the truth. And that is because of the public schools, so called Ivy League universities, the T.V. the media, the newspapers, magazines, and all the other outlets of public information and entities that are covertly controlled by those who clandestinely control the U.S. government that deceive, mislead, or straight out lie to the public. And whether they do it knowingly or unknowingly is not the point. And there are a few good books that have been written about how the media, the T.V. and the newspapers distort the news and even put out straight lies, such as (Bias, by Bernard Goldberg) (Newspaper Control in America, Published by CPA Book Publisher) (Tragedy and Hope, by Carol Quigley) and The Truth Shall Set You Free, by David Icke).

408. In this thought here I'm going to explain to you or at least try to explain to you how those who clandestinely control the U.S. government also control other governments, nations, and virtually the world. Well one of their main ways of controlling other governments, and nations, is by supplying them with money (aid) and therefore they those who clandestinely control the U.S. government can infiltrate and not just exert influence

but control foreign nations and governments through this aid. And this practice has not just started it has been going on now for well over 100 years. Those who clandestinely control the U.S. government have been using the United States to make and break governments and nations since the end of the 19th century and the practice dates way further back than that. And it works like this if a nation or government chooses to act hostile or does not want to listen to what those who clandestinely control the U.S. government tell it to do then the first thing that happens to that nation or government is that it's money (aid) is threatened to be sanctioned or completely stopped and if that doesn't work which nine times out of ten it does then that defiant nation, or government will find itself an a war with no support from the United States government or it allies. And therefore will be subsequently eradicated by another U.S. supported nation or government. And believe me no nation or government wants to find itself in that position. So therefore nations and governments when they are told to do something by those who clandestinely control the U.S. government they more times than not do it no matter what it is. Whether its start a war with another nation, or government or kill off some of their own population and or people in what's called effective population control and management. They do it with no questions asked. So do not think for a second that those who clandestinely control the U.S. government could not stop wars and conflicts among nations and governments if they wanted to. Because you best believe me they could. But as you should already know they won't because that is not in their best interest. Keeping wars, conflicts, famines, diseases and extreme poverty among some nations and governments is. It's all part of what they call effective and efficient world population management and control and those that clandestinely control the U.S. government really feel that there doing the right thing. Because based on their experts, advisers, social engineers, new science scientists and think tanks, wars, famines, and diseases are imperative for effective and efficient population control. Just like the cancer in installments plan making sure that eight to nine out of every ten people exit or die when they are no more useful to society. And poverty the thought goes that there are just not enough natural resources in the world to make every nation self-sufficient. The reasoning is some nations got to have a little or nothing so that other nations can have a lot or too much, and just so you'll know those who clandestinely control the U.S. government feel that the average person is to stupid and does not have enough intelligence to conduct his or her own affairs and control his or her own life and therefore must be assisted. Because those who clandestinely control the U.S. government believe that the average person has no more intelligence than dumb animals (cats and dogs) and dumb animals virtually have no intelligence at all . . . they work off instinct. And I'm going to give you a few facts like I always do on wars, conflicts, sanctions, deaths, and genocide, imposed on nations and governments by those who clandestinely control the U.S. government though the United States and it goes as follows: for more than 10 years the United States supplied money and weapons to Indonesia's Suharto to carry on a war of genocide against the people of East Timor. And in the course of that support a third of the population was killed as many as 75,000. And in Nicaragua the United States sponsored contra war led to the deaths of 30,000 of it's citizens. The bombing of Iraq in 1991 left over 200,000 dead and the bombing continued for 10 years. And the United Nations estimates that over one million Iraqis died and that 5,000 more died each month as a result of indiscriminate sanctions enforced by the United States military. And the United States claimed that any weapons of mass destruction Iraq had Iraq should of destroyed. Yet the United States refused to end the sanctions which were a weapon of mass destruction themselves that had killed more than a million people and most of them children. And all of these deaths that I just mentioned in the foregoing when you take them collectively over 98% of them were nothing but poor people and children. And these facts that I just mentioned are but a few of the known facts and they are for the most part suppressed away from the average American person because there are myriad other facts that are not known and may never be known. But this book is full of rare facts and facts that even if not rare that are not taught or put out in schools, or the mainstream, or almost anywhere else for that matter because of the far, far reaching hands of those who clandestinely control the U.S. government. But all I can say to you is that you must stop believing everything that you hear, read, and see and stop being stuck in extorvertism and looking for the truth outside of yourself and start looking for the truth within yourself because that's where it is. Because as long as you look for the truth outside of yourself you are always nine times out of ten unless you have been trained otherwise, going to be lied to, mislead, and deceived in some kind of way. And for more on how those who clandestinely control the U.S. government use money, aid, and other intrigues to control governments, nations, and virtually the world then I strongly suggest that you get the books by John Perkins: The Secret History of the American Empire, and Confessions of An Economic Hit Man . . . or go to www.expansions.com.

409. Now this thought right here is to let you know how those who clandestinely control the U.S. government plan to use nuclear war and weapons domestically and abroad in the not too distant foreseeable future. And how those who clandestinely control the U.S. government plan to use nuclear weapons here on American soil. Now that is totally crazy but that's what they plan to do and they will do it. Remember they those who clandestinely control the U.S. government caused 9/11 to happen with no problem. And those who clandestinely control the U.S. government will do virtually anything to implement and reach their sinister agenda's. But any way President Bush is now working overtime to satisfy his bosses who are those who clandestinely control the U.S. government to implement their sinister agenda's. Now I recently reviewed President Bush's recently released nuclear posture review (NPE) and I'm here to tell you that the average person would be absolutely shocked if not completely horrified at what it asserts. And if you don't know what the (NPR) is it is nothing but President Bush's pronouncements and policies of his administration regarding nuclear weapons and their use. Now the (NPR) said it envisions and foresees the possible testing, production, and use of nuclear weapons in the foreseeable future and throughout the 21 century and just that right there is a proliferation of nuclear weapons and use, which is a direct violation of and is illegal under the nuclear non-proliferation treaty of 1968. But what does President Bush care about the United States being part of the nuclear non-proliferation treaty . . . nothing! But I'll tell you this we the American people do care. And that's not all President Bush's (NPR) continues and states sovereign nations

that include but are not limited to Iraq, Iran, North Korea, Libya, Syria, China, and Russia. And now those threats to use nuclear weapons against other nations are another direct violation of the nuclear non-proliferation treaty and not only that but according to the international court of Justice is morally illegal and legally impermissible. And last but not least what Bush's (NPR) states about domestic nuclear weapons use. The pentagon under the Bush administrations directives is going to develop and test a new class of more usable nuclear weapons for use if need be in domestic conflicts and against terrorist within our own borders and against enemy combatants and American seditioners better known as dissidents. Now that right there is absolutely crazy but true. Now you must remember that President Bush is just a pawn in the game. He is just doing what he is being told to do by those who clandestinely control the U.S. government. He is there agent. And what those who clandestinely control the U.S. government want is to bring nuclear war out of the theoretical realm and into reality. So all I can say is that the American people need to stop being nourished on nothing but sitcoms, talk shows, and reality T.V., and WAKE UP!!! And I am not even spoke on President Bush's decision to withdraw the United States from the 1972 anti-ballistic missile treaty, a move that was highly criticized by world leaders around the globe because the treaty was seen and regarded as a cornerstone of global efforts to prevent nuclear war.

410. Now this thought right here is just to let you know about a few of the main banks and financial institutions that are owned and controlled by those who clandestinely control the U.S. government. Now the banks and financial institutions that I'm about to name here are without any doubt the most big and powerful in American. Alright! When you hear people say well Wall Street thinks this or that, or Wall Street thinks this or that about that company or industry. They are speaking collectively about the investment branches of these banks and financial institutions that I'm about to name because they are in reality Wall Street . . . point blank. And when you hear the phrases international bankers, the money lenders, the money magicians, the money changers, the money power of the world,

they are speaking about these banks and financial institutions. And the one's that own and control them, which are those that clandestinely control the U.S. government. Now these banks and financial institutions that I'm about to name the American economy virtually belongs to them . . . it's there's. And the same people that own and control these banks and financial institutions own and control the Federal Reserve. And like I've told you previously this control and monopoly of America's economy and money supply didn't just start it's about 130 years in the making and there cornerstone and pinnacle came in 1913 when they got there Federal Reserve system enacted into law. Now the banks and financial institutions are as follows . . . J.P. Morgan Chase. And if you didn't know Chase was previously Chase Manhattan Bank owned and controlled by the Rockefellers and still is. It just merged with J.P. Morgan and Co. And now it's J.P Morgan Chase, Citigroup, Bank of America, Deutsche Bank, Credit Suisse First Boston, Canadian Imperial Bank of Commerce, Lehman Brothers, and Merrill Lynch and CO., and Merrill Lynch before it was took over by those who clandestinely control the U.S. government was originally Merrill, Lynch, Pierce, Fenner, and Smith. But anyway the banks I just named in the in foregoing are without a doubt the most powerful banks and financial institutions in America and whether you can understand it or not they are all owned and controlled by those that clandestinely control the U.S. government. And there financial dealings and activities are so extremely intricate that it is actually impossible to track, audit, or follow them in any kind of real way. And these banks and financial institutions that I just named control myriad other banks and financial institution – both ostensibly and covertly – not just in America but throughout the world. And check this out I was only able to find money lending figures for 5 of the banks and the figures are nothing short of astonishing and astronomical. And these figures that I'm about to give you are only for one year they are for how much money each bank or financial institution loaned out in 2001 and they go as follows: J.P Morgan Chase 127 billion dollars, Bank of America 113 billion dollars, Citigroup 102 billion dollars, Deutsche bank 40 billion dollars, and Credit Suisse First Boston 35 billion dollars - now collectively these five banks and financial institutions loaned out in just the year 2001 alone a total of over 418 billion dollars which is almost half a trillion dollars. And check this out there is not no 418 billion dollars in physical U.S. currency in circulation the actual amount of all the physical U.S. currency in circulation is supposed to be somewhere around 200 to 500 billion dollars, even though some say it's 500 to 700 billion. But being able to loan out billions of dollars without the money actually existing or physically being available is just one of the many tricks of those called the money magicians. Now most of us can't even understand, comprehend, or begin to imagine how much money that is but that's the kind of money that those that clandestinely control the U.S. government loan out and play with on a daily basis.

411. Now this thought here is just to let the average person, taxpayer know that he or she might think he or she knows about what their elected officials like the senate and congress do and what kind of laws they enact on a daily basis. Well I'll start like this remember that I told you in previous thoughts that those who clandestinely control the U.S. government control directly or indirectly virtually all of America's biggest corporations and companies, okay. Now look at what congress just did in 2002 congress voted to repeal the alternative minimum tax law of corporations and companies. This law requires or did require because it's gone now that hugely profitable corporations and companies pay at least some tax. It's repeal will allow many hugely profitable and powerful corporations and companies to pay zero U.S. income tax a loss of more than 12 billion in 2003 revenue alone. But wait a minute you haven't even heard the jaw dropper yet. The repeal is retro-active . . . yep, you read right. Retroactive. Corporations and companies will get rebates for the last 15 years meaning let me give you a small sampling of a few of the companies rebates. IBM will get 1.4 billion in rebates. General Motors will get 833 million in rebates. General Electric will get 671 million in rebates. Chevron Texaco will get 572 million in rebates. And the now defunct Enron Corp got 245 million in rebates. And these are just a few of the companies and corporations that stand to get rebates. And just so you'll know and please believe me congress, and the senate passes laws like this on a daily basis every day. But you the average person, taxpayer does not know this and

congress knows that. So therefore they do what they want. And of course all the laws that congress passes or enacts are part of the congressional record which is open to the public. But how many average everyday people are really going to go looking though the congressional record on a regular basis. They probably would be absolutely shocked at what they might find if they did. And frankly I could write volumes that would be guaranteed number 1 best sellers on just that subject alone. But I like almost everybody else has not time to be pouring through millions of pages of congressional records. But anyway so now you know so the next time you hear the President, a senator, or politician talking and crying about some budget deficit you'll know he's just talking to hear himself talk. And like I always tell you this is one of the main reasons I wrote this book. To let the average person know what's really going on in the world and especially what's going on and has been going on within the U.S. government. And congress repealing the alternative minimum tax on companies and corporations was none other than the work of those that clandestinely control the U.S. government and if you believe anything other than that then I got a bridge I want to sell you in San Francisco too.

412. Now this thought, this thought right here that you're about to read is probably the most, if not one of the most incredulous and profound thoughts in this book and I ask that you keep an open mind because what you're about to read in this thought 98% to 99% of Americans have no knowledge of. But nonetheless everything in this thought is real and without a doubt true. And I'm going to give it to you just like it is meaning unabridged. So like I said please keep an open mind. And remember just because you personally have no knowledge of something or have never heard of something does not mean it doesn't exist or doesn't take place or happen. And with the exception of the Federal Reserve thought and a few others. I don't give lengthy introductions to thoughts. But the profoundness of this particular thought compels me to do so. That's why I'm giving you this introduction. But anyway in this thought you will learn the truth about UFO's and aliens . . . how long aliens have been living among us here in America . . . where they are house at, and live . . . and the astonishing

technology those that clandestinely control the U.S. government has and how they have built over 100 underground cities since the 1950's and that some of those cities are as big as major metropolitan cities such as Los Angeles, and New York. And these underground cities are mostly in remote areas under deserts, mountains, and forests. And these underground cities have virtually every function of a regular city on land. . . I mean absolutely every function. These underground cities are a 100% self-sufficient. They have their own factories and industries; they grow, make, and produce their own food and your probably wondering how they grow food without the sun. Well the incandescent lights they have down there are so technologically advanced that they light the cities up down there just as bright as the noon day sun would light up Los Angeles on a day when the temperature is in the high 90's. But there lights are temperature controlled and can give off heat anywhere from 60 to 150 degrees but they usually keep the lights given off heat at about 80 degrees year round. And they have a night down there too because at or around 6:00 pm what they call the night lights come on. And water wise well as you know the purest and best water comes from deep underground springs and these cities are built anywhere from 40 to 80 miles underground so they basically have an unlimited supply of the best and purest water. And the knowledge that there geohydrologists have down there is so advanced it's not like anything we got or know of up here. And like I said these underground cities have every function and amenity a regular city up here on land has and more. They have streets, sidewalks, houses, apartments, buildings, and freeways, better known as mass-transit systems, and their own power plants. Now like I said these underground cities were built surreptitiously in the 1950's by those that clandestinely control the U.S. government to house the alien presence and exploit the aliens of their extremely advanced knowledge and technology which has been successfully accomplished in these underground cities. Now out of the 100 or so underground cities they have a capital and the capital underground city is said to be nick-named Mount weather now this is supposedly the biggest of the underground cities and it's nick-named Mount Weather because it's under a giant Mountain and this mountain is located in a little town called

Bluemont, Virginia about 46 miles west of Washington, D.C. in an area of wilderness covering what has been called the toughest granite rock in the eastern United States. And you'll know when you hit the area because it's surrounded by signs that say restricted area. This area has been declared a restricted area by the U.S. government and unauthorized persons entering this area will be arrested and prosecuted to the full extent of the law. And this is the only area that gives any indication to those in the know of course that there is an underground city in that area or under that area. But to everybody else it's just a government restricted area. And all of the underground cities are connected to one another by a mass underground transit system. And a lot of the underground cities are in Pennsylvania, Virginia, West Virginia, Maryland, and North Carolina. And do you want to know what congress thinks about Mount Weather and the rest of the underground cities. Well, I'll tell you this much, congress knows they exist and that they're there. But that's about all congress knows. Because it's like this officially and for the record the underground cities were built by the federal civil defense administration, which is now the federal preparedness agency and the official name of the project was "The Continuity of Government Program" which was supposed to be a program to house and protect the President and executive branch of the federal government in case of an invasion or nuclear war. And congress has repeatedly tried to discover the real purpose of Mount Weather and the other underground cities but so far has been unable to find out anything about the secret underground installations. And check this out retired air force General Leslie W. Bray Director of the Federal Preparedness Agency (which is the agency that's supposed to have authority and control over Mount Weather and the rest of the underground installations/cities) told the senate subcommittee on constitutional rights that was investigating Mount Weather and the other underground installations/cities in September 1975, he General Leslie W. Bray states: I am not at liberty to describe precisely what is the role and the mission and the capability that we have at Mount Weather or at any other underground installation. And at that the Chairman of the Committee, Senator John Tunney (D) California expressed concern and he said my question is this: is there anyone like yourself General

Bray that is in overall control of these underground installations. And your answer as I understood it is No. Senator Tunney continued: General Bray I must say that I still don't know who's in control of these underground installations. And you say that you don't have that knowledge and we still don't know from the 3 witnesses that we had here today. But anyway the committee concluded that these underground basis/installations operate with few if any safeguards or guidelines. Senator James Abourzek (D) South Dakota, a member of the subcommittee said, I feel the entire operation has eluded the supervision of either congress or the courts. And Chairman Tunney said Mount Weather and the rest of the underground installations are out of control. But nonetheless nothing was done by congress to rectify the situation and Mount Weather and the other underground installations as Chairman Tunney said remain out of control. So well now at least you know that congress has knowledge of these underground cities. But why congress isn't doing nothing about these underground cities well you already know why that's because of those that clandestinely control the U.S. government. But I haven't even got to the good part yet on what they do and have been doing in these underground cities, but as you read on you'll know the reason why Mount Weather and the other underground cities were built. But anyway now I'm going to give you a glimpse of what they do down there in them underground cities. Well it all started back on February 13, 1948 notwithstanding Roswell when an alien craft was found on a mass near Aztec, New Mexico it was the first UFO/Alien craft ever found and documented and certified by the U.S. government to be an extraterrestrial aircraft which was crash wrecked but no aliens were found dead or alive. And then on March 25, 1948 in White Sands proving ground another UFO/alien craft was found it was about 10 feet in diameter and this time 17 dead alien bodies were found aboard the crash wrecked craft. And check this out of even greater significance was the discovery of a large number of human body parts stored aboard the alien craft. And then the U.S. government being basically the only ones in the know about the 2 crashed wrecked UFO/alien crafts and the 17 dead alien beings immediately deemed the alien phenomenon top, top, secret and the secrecy imposed was even tighter then that upon the Manhattan Project. Then the government implemented a special group of America's top scientists under the name Project Sign in December 1948 to study the alien phenomenon. Then Project signed evolved into Project Grudge then Project Grudge evolved into Project Bluebook then Project Bluebook evolved into Project Pounce. And then Project Pounce evolved into something else and you see the reason those in charge of the alien phenomenon kept changing the name of the alien project was to keep everybody even their own people thrown off because like I told you the secrecy imposed on the alien phenomenon was even tighter than that on the Manhattan Project. Now during these early years the United States Air Force and the Central Intelligence Agency exercised complete control over the alien secret. In fact the CIA was formed by a presidential executive order first as the Central Intelligence Group for the explicit purpose of dealing with the alien presence. Then the National Security Council was established to oversee the intelligence community and especially the alien endeavor. Now President Harry Truman's secretary of defense James Forrestal strongly objected to the secrecy. He was a very idealistic and religious man. He deeply believed that the public should be told about the alien phenomenon. James Forrestal was also one of the first known abductees. And when he began to talk to leaders of congress about the alien problem and secret. He was asked to resign by President Truman. And James Forrestal expressed his fears to many people and rightfully he believed that he was being watched. Now this was interpreted by those who were ignorant of the facts as paranoia. Forrestal later was said to have suffered a mental breakdown. He was ordered to the mental ward of Bethesda Naval Hospital. In spite of the fact that the Truman administration had no authority to have him committed the order was carried out. In fact it was feared that Forrestal would begin to talk again. So he had to be isolated and discredited. And his family and friends were denied permission to visit him. Finally on May 21, 1949 Forrestal's bother made a fateful decision. He notified authorities that he intended to remove James from Bethesda on May 22, 1949, sometime in the early morning hours of May 22, 1948 agents of the CIA tied a sheet around James Forrestal's neck fastened the other end to a light fixture and then threw James Forrestal out the window the sheet tore and he plummeted to his death. And all this was because James Forrestal believed the public should be told the truth about the alien presence. Now in 1949 with the so-called Ebe alien crash everything changed that was when the government recovered the first ever live alien found wandering in the desert. And they named him Ebe which stands for extra-terrestrial biological entity and just so you know the movie E.T. was a thinly disguised story of Ebe. But anyway with the finding of the live alien (Ebe) that's what got those that clandestinely control the U.S. government interested and involved in the alien phenomenon. That was when President Truman called his good friend Nelson Rockefeller and told him about the live alien found and that's when Truman and those that clandestinely control the U.S. government began planning the super secret underground cites which would become reality in a few years. Then in 1953 a new president occupied the White House, he was a man as you probably already know put there by those that clandestinely control the U.S. government and his name was Dwight D. Eisenhower then during Eisenhower's first year in office in 1953 ten more crashed wrecked alien crafts were found and out of the 10 alien crafts a total of 26 dead and 4 live aliens were recovered. So now those that clandestinely control the U.S. government deemed it imperative that the underground cities/installations became a reality. Now those that clandestinely control the U.S. government had 2 primary priorities and that was 1. To get those underground installations/cities built. And 2. To exploit the aliens of their superior knowledge and technology. But anyway those that clandestinely control the U.S. government and there specially selected group of scientists were able to establish a positive dialogue with the aliens and were able to persuade the aliens to make contact with their point of origin and with that contact being established those that clandestinely control the U.S. government couldn't wait to exploit the aliens of their advanced knowledge and technology and therefore ordered the construction of the underground installations/cities to begin immediately. And a super top secret facility was quickly built at Groom Lake in Nevada to house the aliens until the underground installations/cities were built and completed. And it was code named Area-51 and Area-51 is still around to this day but aliens are not housed there anymore. And at the time back in the 1950's when actual aliens were housed at Area-51 all personnel required what was then known as a (Q) clearance as well as an executive presidential clearance called a majestic. But this was ironic because of the fact that the president of the United States himself did not have or could issue a majestic clearance. Therefore he himself could not visit the site, because a majestic clearance was a clearance given out directly by the executive governing body of those who clandestinely control the U.S. government. By and through their top secret group called majesty twelve (MJ-12) which consisted of Nelson Rockefeller as chairman, and then director of the CIA Allen Welsh Dulles, then secretary of the state John Foster Dulles, then secretary of defense Charles E. Wilson, then chairman of joint chiefs of staff admiral Arthur W. Radford, then director of the FBI J. Edgar Hoover and 6 unknown men from the Council on Foreign Relations known only as the wise men. And you see this group consisted only of members of those who clandestinely controlled the U.S. government. And this group was established by a presidential executive order or by secret executive order NSC-5510 and NSC stands for National Security Council. And MJ-12 was to oversee and conduct all covert activities concerned with the alien presence. But anyway before the underground cities were completed the 4 live aliens made contact with their point of origin and called to earth at least 600 more alien beings who were housed at Area-51 until the underground cities were completed. And just so you know a second project code-named SNOWBIRD was implemented and carried out by the CIA to explain away any and all sightings of the red-light crafts as being Air Force experiments. And I'll say this project SNOWBIRD was extremely successful. And reports of sightings and UFO's from the public in those years steadily declined. And the CIA to this day still runs an extremely elaborate UFO debunking program. And even has people employed full time whose only job is to write books, articles, and anything else they can to keep you and the rest of the masses of people confused and thrown off about the truth of the alien presence. And remember back in the late 80's the show called "UFO COVER UP LIVE." It was nothing but a CIA backed T.V. production. And I'm going to tell you something else all of the major UFO research organizations since the 1960's when they started popping up and as they pop up are targeted for infiltration and control by the CIA and these endeavors are always successful don't think there not. Mufon is a great example, because hundreds of Mufon members from all over the world conduct investigations, and send to Mufon Headquarters physical UFO evidence such as footage and pictures of UFO's. And that evidence quickly disappears. Like for example some samples were collected of a liquid that had dripped from a UFO onto a school yard in Gulf Breeze Florida. The samples were sent to Mufon Headquarters where they immediately vanished without a trace. And any Mufon member who tells it like it is, is immediately debunked and barred from UFO symposiums. And the members are told what to believe and what not to believe. The members do not seem to know that they are being controlled. The members of the Mufon Board of Directors and the members of the Advisory Board of Consultants are 90% supported by the CIA/Government in the form of salaries, grants, and retirement checks. Now who can believe that this does not constitute a conflict of interest? Who can impartially investigate the hand that feeds them? And always remember that money is the basic method of control for anything. But anyway the first underground city was completed sometime in 1958 or early 1959. And the 600 or so aliens and a specially selected group of scientists and personnel were moved in to the underground city to learn and basically exploit the aliens of their superior knowledge and technology. But the aliens were in total agreement with this and had agreed to share their advanced knowledge and technology with us. So for the first time in the history of the world as we know it, aliens, extraterrestrials, coexisted with human beings. And the aliens, and human scientists, and personnel resided full time at the underground city. Now the knowledge and the technology that the aliens imparted was and is beyond belief it was beyond belief then in the 1950's and 60's and is beyond belief now in the 21st century. I'm going to give you a glimpse of the kind of knowledge and technology that the aliens imparted in the early 1960's and that knowledge and technology is so astonishing and so extremely far advanced that us right now today in the 21st century up here in the regular world have still not even come close to attaining or possessing any such knowledge and technology. I'm going to start with the technology first and then I'm going to give you a glimpse of the knowledge of the sciences that the aliens imparted in the 1960's. Alright the technology that the aliens had perfected and imparted in the 1960's is so profound and myriad that the best I can do here is just to give you a glimpse. Because it would be impossible for me to try to name explain, and describe all the different kinds of technology that the aliens imparted, because the space is just not available here I could write volumes on just that one topic. But anyway the aliens imparted in the 1960's in the underground cities such technology as how to construct and make anti-gravity aircraft, aircraft that gravity has no effect on and therefore the aircraft is able to defy the laws of physics. And these anti-gravity aircrafts are capable of some astonishing things such as the ability to take off vertically and at such great speed that to the naked eye it looks as if they just disappeared into thin air. And these anti-gravity aircrafts are capable and able to make interplanetary journeys. And they move and operate silently, and they got from the aliens and have perfected since the 1960's nano-technology which is the making of microscopic devices and things such as cameras, and robots, that are so small that you cannot see them with the naked eye. And the computers that they got in these underground cities well I'll just say this they are not like anything you or I have ever heard of or seen up here in the regular world. I'm talking about supercomputers that are capable of performing and this is no exaggeration this comes from people who are in the know more than one sep-tillion (1,000,000,000,000,000,000,000,000) functions a second and don't even try to comprehend or understand that because you can't you will literally hurt yourself trying. I mean just think about it in two seconds, three seconds tops one of those computers can analyze everything ever done by everybody who has ever lived. Now that's deep . . . but anyway moving onward. Artificial intelligence is old news down there. They also have and use down there something called programmed response systems. And a programmed response system in short is just something that will make a person or alien it doesn't matter do anything or it can teach them virtually anything. And programmed response systems are administered by a strobe light carrying high frequency microwaves being made to play on a individuals optic nerve through his or her eyes and therefore able to entertain patterns or whatever is desired on to that persons brain waves and or subconscious. And by doing this a person or an alien can be taught virtually anything or made to do virtually anything. Like for example a person can be given a programmed response system to learn the whole collegiate unabridged dictionary and that person will know every single word in the whole collegiate dictionary in a matter of about 15-20 minutes which is how long it takes to give someone such a programmed response system or a person can be given a programmed response system to say to kill him or herself or someone else that can be triggered in to effect or into conscious awareness same thing at a later time by a certain sight, sound, noise, action, or thing. And I'm going to impart this to you the CIA has been surreptitiously administering program response systems to the population for sinister, and malevolent, reasons since the 1960's creating crazed killers, assassins, sociopaths, suicide bombers, and all other kinds of kamikazes, and a lot of these people are programmed to live in the community sometimes for years as regular everyday functioning people until the time comes for their program response system to be activated, and then everybody who knew them said oh my God, he or she was such a nice and quiet person, why did they take that gun and shoot all those people. Thing is it wasn't them . . . there program response system was activated. So therefore they were not in conscious control of what they were doing. And the CIA was administering these program response systems through there now infamous mind control program known as project MK-ULTA. And if you doubt it, well on August 3, 1977 the CIA at a senate hearing admitted publically that they had been giving millions, countless people program response systems. And therefore mind controlling them without their consent and or knowledge. And it's a known fact that the CIA's MK-ULTA had involved over 200 scientists, 80 US institutions among them pharmaceutical companies, hospitals, and 68 medical colleges, and universities. But anyway we don't want to lose point here we're talking about the underground cities not the CIA. So now I'm going to briefly speak on the capabilities of their weaponry that they got in these underground cities which is just as unbelievable and astonishing as everything that I just spoke on if not more. But anyway there weaponry capabilities are most definitely not limited to but consist of such phenomenal weapons as laser beams which are fired from satellites that orbit the earth of which more than 2500 are already in orbit right now as we speak and orbit the earth 24 hours a day, 7 days a week. And these satellites are completely controlled from these underground cities and are able to fire there laser beams virtually anywhere on earth with unbelievable precession from hitting a dime on the ground, to hitting a mountain or an entire continent. Now these laser beams are unbelievable as it may sound. But you have got to remember that this is extraterrestrial and not regular terrestrial technology and these laser beams are capable of totally disintegrating any type of solid matter into ashes or something less than that in a split second. And that is just one of myriad of weapons that they got in these underground cities. And they got sound frequency, biological, and chemical weapons one such biological weapon that I've been made aware of has the ability through the use of sound and microwaves to cause instant decaying in any human being or living organism. Meaning that if you're hit by it you will start to instantly decay from the inside out. And of the chemical weapons they have certain agents that are odorless, tasteless, and colorless. That can be released into the atmosphere of any region and once inhaled by the populace will cause instant paralysis and suffocation. And they have highly sophisticated computer controlled weapons. With abilities only real now up here in the regular world in science fiction. And they have a vast assortment of death ray throwers, ray canons, ray rifles, and ray guns with unbelievable striking power. And they have a host of electromagnetic weapons to complex and sophisticated for me to describe here. And the underground cities are where those who clandestinely control the U.S. government keep their vast depositories of dossiers on every man, woman, and child. And it doesn't even matter if the person is dead there file is kept for 20 to 30 years after they are deceased. And you would not believe the personal information that these files contain they contain your most personal and private thoughts, ideas, and beliefs. And do you know how they do this? Well those who clandestinely control the U.S. government have satellites that are capable of reading your mind and those satellites are real and the computers they are hooked up to are in these underground cities. And it works like this every single human being has an individual biological field frequency AKA bioelectric field frequency that emits from them while they are alive and no 2 individual biological field frequencies are alike they are just like finger prints and DNA everybody has their own. But anyway that's how these satellites that read your mind distinguish who's who they lock on to your individual bioelectric field frequency. And because thoughts are individual electrical brain waves, these satellites are capable and able of picking up your brain waves, which are your thoughts and then they send the brain waves back down to the supercomputers in these underground cities to be deciphered at which point whatever you were actually thinking is filed and put away under your name and number with the exact time, date, and location. And all thoughts are meticulously and systematically, classified. So they know what you were thinking say 5 years ago on a certain data and at a certain time better then you do. And these satellites have been up and running 24 hours a day, 7 days a week since the early, early 1970's or late 1960's. And just so you know the supercomputers that these satellites are hooked up to in these underground cities. These supercomputers constantly 24 hours a day, 7 days a week stealthy access all known computer networks in the world without exception I mean the Justice Department, FBI, CIA, all police departments without exception, all local, state, and federal agencies, the national security agency, and all other intelligence agencies computer and networks, the pentagon, and all military computer networks, classified or not, all hospital computer networks, the internet and all the millions of PC's and other computers hooked up to it, all department store computer networks, all direct mail house computer networks, all cable telecommunications and telephone computer networks, all supermarket laser scanner computer networks and those RAFL's and Vons club cards that give you a slight discount on your grocery purchases but you have to give your I.D. and social security number on the application to obtain them is nothing but a way of knowing exactly what you buy at the supermarket and it goes into much greater detail than this. But anyway these supercomputers are hooked up to and like I said stealthy access all known computer networks imaginable in the world. Therefore incessantly, and constantly, feeding information of every kind to the massive filtering systems that organize and meticulously, and systematically classifies all information under the correct name and number and/or category. Then all this extremely exorbitant amount of information in it's entirety is meticulously scrutinized and intensively studied by a vast assortment of extraterrestrial and human scientists who have been studying human beings for the last 50 or 60 some years. But only in the last 20 to 30 years have their studies become more and more personified or individualized and this is only because of the added personal and individual information coming in from hospitals, insurance companies, jobs, all government agencies, department stores, supermarket laser scanners, the internet, the information data brokers, and myriad other sources with new sources being added each and every single day. But you best believe they know you individually and otherwise they know what you like, what you don't like, and a whole lot of other things you could not imagine, or even believe . . . they know all about you. And they have you placed in a category and they have categories for absolutely everybody from the president of the United States to the homeless bum on the street corner. Now collectively again you best believe they know the people or I should say humanity to it's very core, all human attributes, qualities, weaknesses, and potential, under any and all circumstances imaginable is known. And you know what the cold thing is, is that human potential when not hindered by disinformation, fear, and worry. (Technical name of system of self imposed limitation) human potential is astonishing to say the least and is very much capable of being in the stratosphere in all instances and circumstances are also very much known. And all human susceptibilities and weaknesses are well known and used against you. Where do you think overdosing the people with non-stop soap operas, T.V., talk shows, and reality T.V. came from?! These things weren't any accident these things were intensively studied years ago then put out there at a specifically designated time. Just like what you will be watching on T.V. and hooked on five or ten years from now is being designed and studied right now. But anyway you have been studied in every way imaginable, and/or conceivable, by mind and computer model. And they have comprehensive and all inclusive active, real, and live, computer models of all cities, localities, states, and the world. And these computer models because of the such advanced nature of the artificial intelligence incorporated in them act just like if not better then the real thing acting on real time that can be rewound or fast-forwarded. But anyway this is how those who clandestinely control the U.S. government have made their vast depositories of dossiers on every man, woman, and child, without exception. And I like to call these supercomputers the beast because you better believe they know everything about you. And this is one of the key ways that the executive governing body of those who clandestinely control the U.S. government control the world by knowing everything about even the thoughts of certain world leaders and certain prominent people and other unknown individuals of certain prestige and influence, by using this massive universal surveillance and human intelligence gathering system A.K.A. the beast. And like I told you 98% to 99% of the people don't even know that these underground cities exist let alone know what goes on down there. And of those who clandestinely control the U.S. government the only ones that have actual knowledge of these underground cities and of what goes on down there and actually go down there are the ones that make up the executive governing body of those who clandestinely control the U.S. government and these are the men that actually run and control the world. They are the elite of the elite they are the supreme aristocracy in the world and consider themselves above all other human beings either living or dead. But anyway, now for the sciences, sciences that we up here in the regular world have barely begun to understand and are still serious areas of exploitation and mystery for us. They are so advanced in them that it might be an understatement to say that they have perfected them. Sciences such as biotechnology, genetic engineering which is nothing but genetic manipulation – Eugenics, biogenetics, biotelemetry, embryology, biochemistry, bacteriology, microbiology, and molecular biology, and by them having perfected these sciences and many others they are more than able to create the unbelievable such as perfect human beings and when I say perfect, I mean perfect without a single flaw. Human beings that are nothing less than astonishing phenomenons. Let me give you a quick and brief overview of how they do this. And what I mean by flawless human beings that are nothing short of astonishing phenomenons – alright, it works like this . . . let's say that one person is highly intelligent in a certain way say creatively they clone that gene that makes that person creative. And let's say another person is a mathematician they clone the gene in the person that makes him, or her, a mathematician. Let's say another person is a great painter, artist they clone that gene that makes that person a great artist and/or painter. Let's say another person has a fast metabolism and therefore is naturally slim they clone that gene in that person. Let's say another is tall they clone that gene in that person. Let's say another person is very, very strong naturally, they clone that gene in that person. Let's say another person has a perfect or damn near perfect facial structure and is very pretty or handsome they clone that gene or genes in that person. Say another person has an exceptional memory; they clone that gene in that person. Say another person has the longevity gene able to live easily to 80, 90, or 100 years of age they clone that gene. So do you follow me because everything from our intelligence in all areas to our physical body structures, eye color, hair color, eye sight, height, reflexes and motor skills, natural temperament, and anything else that makes us who we are is determined by our genes whether they be bad, alright, or good or exceptional. Now what these scientists do is they get the human embryo and they strip it of all it's natural genes whether the genes be bad, good, or alright, it doesn't even matter. Because the genes these scientists use can be no less then exceptional. Then they insert the human embryo completely with handpicked extremely exceptional genes so then when that human embryo morphs in to a baby and is born, it is naturally perfect in every way, shape, and form and of course it has to learn and be taught. But it is like I said naturally flawless, super intelligent in every way and 100% perfect. And these are the kinds of people that they have been making and raising and that they have populated these underground cities with for the last 50 to 60 years. And also by them being able to make human beings as they wish they have also made some completely without feelings and with an innate need to commit murder. But they give these programmed response systems to control them. But they are also the ones who make up the secret armies. And the secret armies are the ones that are going to be unleashed up here in the regular world when the time is right and/or it's time for them to usher in their new world order in on us. So now that you know the uncut truth about UFO's and aliens, where there housed at, and what basically goes on in these underground cities, don't let nobody or nothing else tell you anything different. And remember this thought is nothing but a concisement of what goes on in them underground cities because everything that goes on down there would not fit in ten volumes. Believe that! And all the human engineering, experimenting, manipulating, and mutating that goes on in them underground cities I haven't even spoke on. And I'm talking about some of the sickest and most grotesque genetic engineering, experimenting, that you can think of such as animal and human hybrids of every kind imaginable and other things and creations that are only real up here in the regular world in the most surreal science fiction are real and everyday reality down there in them underground cities. And if you like to read further on UFO's, aliens, and the underground cities then you must get the following books: Contact of the 5th Kind, by Philip Imbrogno and Marianne Horrigan; The Day After Roswel, by Col. Philip J. Corso; UFO FBI Connection, by Bruce Maccabee PH.D. And if you would like to read more about the program response systems and mind control and how the CIA has been and still is right now giving countless people program response systems and therefore mind controlling them. And this is entirely without their knowledge and making them into what the CIA calls mind controlled slaves then you must get the following books: The Illuminati Formula to Create an Undetectable Total Mind Controlled Slaves, by Fritz Springmeter and Cisco Wheeler. And if you would like to learn further about underground cities, installations, and bases, there's a great web-site that you must want to go to at: http://www.angelfire.com/UT/Branton or you can go to John Rhodes web-site at http://www.reptoids.com. And if you're interested in exotic technologies that have been systematically suppressed up here in the regular world, such as teleportation and time travel then you must go to the following web-sites www.starfire.com and www.projectpegasus.net.

413. Now for a quick word on NASA and there so called space programs which are so fake that's it's a damn shame because they are nothing but straight lies, misleads, and throws offs. They are for one purpose and one purpose only and that's to keep you the public thrown off. Because the truth is that those who clandestinely control the U.S. government and their secretly selected people have been going to outer space, other planets, and even the home planet of the aliens since the early 1960's in antigravity aircraft that is as you already know made with advanced alien technology. And you must remember that you have been lied to all your life by the schools, the media, the news outlets, the T.V., and damn near everything else, and check this out just think about this for a minute . . . why do you think that every single space shuttle take off for the last 45 years or so has been covered and broadcasted by all the major media, T.V., and news? Do you know why? Well that's because their supposed to keep the space shuttle and it's take off in your (the public's) face, to keep you thrown off, mislead, and deceived into thinking that the space shuttle is the most latest marvel in technology, which in reality is nothing but a straight lie . . . and to the ones in the know a straight joke. Because the space shuttle as it is, is obsolete. It's beyond obsolete but it has a purpose and a big purpose and that's to keep you (the public) thrown off and completely mislead. And the Russians I'm going to briefly speak on them for a minute because they are the ones that we are supposedly to be having this great space race with which is another straight lie. Because those who clandestinely controlled the U.S. government have been clandestinely controlling Russia since 1917 when the Russian revolution that they (those who clandestinely control the U.S. government) financed overthrew the Russian Czar Nicholas II from power and those who clandestinely control the U.S. government at that time which included but was not limited to John D. Rockefeller, Sr. and Jr., William B. Thompson, Jacob Schiff, Paul Warburg, Max Warburg, J.P. Morgan, Thomas Lamont, Colonel Edward Mandell House, A. Piatt Andrew, Nelson Aldrich, Frank Vanderlip, Edward Harriman, Henry P. Davidson, Herbert H. Lehman, Charles Norton, Bernard Baruch, Will H. Hays, Charles Evan Hughes, Charles Gates Dawes, J. Ogden Armour, James Stillman, George F. Baker, Benjamin Strong, Otto Khan, Sidney James Webb, Williard

Straight, Henry Morgenthau, Douglas Dillon, Andrew Mellow, and many others even though they're all dead now they are still directly responsible for all those tens of millions of deaths caused in Russia under the U.S.S.R. Totalitarian Socialistic Rule. And everything that happened in Russia was more like an experiment for those who clandestinely controlled the U.S. government at that time. And check this out, in the February 8, 1920 illustrated Sunday Herald of London sir Winston Churchill wrote: "From the days of the illuminati leader Weishaupt to those of Karl Marx, to those of Trotsky, Bela Kuhn Rosa Luxembourg, and Emma Goldman, this worldwide conspiracy has been steady growing. This conspiracy has played a definitely recognizable role in the tragedy of the French Revolution. It has been the mainspring of every subversive movement during the 19th century. And now at least this band of extraordinary personalities from the underworlds of the great cities of Europe and America have gripped the Russian people by the hair of their heads and have become practically the undisputed masters of that enormous empire. And for more on this you can get the following books: Wall Street and the Bolshevik Revolution, by Antony C. Sutton; The Secret Driving Force of Communism, by Maurice Pinay; Tragedy and Hope, by Carrol Quigley; The Truth Shall Set You Free, by David Icke; and Pawns in the Game, by Guy Carr. But anyway, another great lie that the masses of American people and the masses of Russian people had been deceived in to believing was that we were supposed to have been Russia's greatest enemy which was a straight lie. But it was put out there and always kept fresh in the minds of American and Russian people alike to keep us and them completely thrown off and on pins and needles. What do you think the Cold War was all about? And now they're doing the same thing with Islam and the Islamic Nations they're supposed to be our greatest enemies, because they're supposedly terrorists . . . what a joke. But anyway, the truth is that Russia just like every other country in the world, and this is without exception, is surreptitiously controlled by those who clandestinely control the U.S. government and don't think that those who clandestinely control the U.S. government can't destroy the world or a great part of it if they want. Because they most definitely can. And they are the ones who have been making wars and conflicts happed in the world for the last 200 years or so. They even made and destroyed Hitler and if you would like to read about that there' s a few books on just that subject like: Wall Street and The Rise of Hitler, by Anthony c. Sutton; Who Financed Hitler, by James and Suzanne Pool, The Truth Shall Set You Free, by David Icke, and Hitler's Secret Backers, by Sidney Warburg. But those who clandestinely control the U.S. government keep a number of wars and conflicts going on in the world for their own benefit and sinister agendas. The United Nations, The International Monetary Fund, and The Bank of International Settlements are there's and were their brain childs and creations. And if you look at the governments involved to neutralize these wars and conflicts it doesn't take a genius to see that the policies that these governments implement to neutralize these wars and conflicts are designed to have little if any effect or completely fail and that is not by accident but by design. People need to stop being so gullible and believing everything that governments, Senators, Legislators, Politicians, and those so called diplomats, tell them and start judging things by their actions and effects, and therefore, for what they really are.

414. Always remember that one of the main purposes of the T.V. The Media, Newspapers, The T.V. News, and especially the T.V. News are to keep people pacified. Because it is a well documented fact that people have an innate need to know meaning that people are innately curious, and inquisitive. So therefore, The T.V., The Media, Newspapers, and especially the T.V. News are there and used to satisfy that need. And those who clandestinely control the U.S. government most definitely know this and use it to their full advantage. So therefore it is imperative for them those who clandestinely control the U.S. government through there long, long reaching hands to keep The T.V., The Media, Newspapers, and like I said, especially The T.V. News, good, enjoyable, interesting, and extremely plausible or they risk people going elsewhere for their knowledge and there for people to start stumbling on to the truth such as the truths and knowledge in this book which those who clandestinely control the U.S. government do not. And I say again, do not want you the people to know or find out about. And I'll say this there are some people out there who are pretty

damn smart and intelligent. But they get 95% if not more of their knowledge and information from the T.V., The Media, Newspapers, and especially the T.V. news, and therefore they really think and believe that they're very well informed. But in reality they don't know anything of what's really and actually going on. They only know what those who clandestinely control the U.S. government want them to know and believe. And that's sad but oh so true.

415. Now in this thought here I'm going to tell you and expose some of the ways and means that those who clandestinely control the U.S. government use to control, mislead, throw-off, deceive, and brainwash the masses of unsuspecting people. First of all do you know why CBS, NBC, ABC, and myriad other T.V. stations, networks, and newspapers constantly take polls? Well that is because most of these polls are coordinated through and at the National Opinion Research Center, which is a think tank and behavioral science research institute where as much as it will amaze most people they keep and develop psychological profiles for every segment of the population. And this National Opinion Research Center is just one of the myriad institutes funded and surreptitiously controlled by those who clandestinely control the U.S. government. Because they have think tanks, institutes, and research centers that do research into every imaginable facet of human life. Like the Hudson Institute, The National Training Laboratories, The Institute For Social Research, The Institute for Policy Studies, The Stanford Research Institute, and the Rand Research and Development Corporation. But like I Said these are just a few of the myriad think tanks, institutes, and research centers funded and surreptitiously controlled by those who clandestinely control the U.S. government. But anyway, back to why T.V. stations, and networks, and newspapers constantly take polls. Well, it is to find out how responsive or nonresponsive the public is to the policies, directives, and certain other current events orchestrated or handed down by those who clandestinely control the U.S. government. Because the masses of people are divided up into targeted population groups that consist of ethnic and social economic status. And one of the main things measured by the pollsters is how much resistance, is generated

to what appears in the nightly news. And this is all part of the elaborate opinion making process created by the public opinion makers at various research institutes. So now you know the truth about polls and there are myriad people out there who really believe that they are very well informed. But what they do not realize is that the opinions they believe and hold are not their own, but were in fact created for them in some research institute. Because remember much of what we read, hear, and see on the T.V. news, and in the newspapers, as in subjects and topics, has first been cleared by the polling and research institutes. And check this out, why do you think that in 70 some years of reporting the news and other current events . . . Time, Life, Newsweek, U.S. News and World Report, Fortune 500, People, Omni, Forbes, National Enquirer, InStyle, McCall's Vogue, CBS, NBC, ABC FOX, CNN, and myriad other T.V. stations, Networks, Magazines, and Newspapers have not . . . not even one time to my knowledge ran a story, did an article or even mentioned those who clandestinely control the U.S. government, and there beyond sinister hierarchy and agendas. Well that is because those who clandestinely control the U.S. government have through there infinite organizations, companies, front companies, and other entities and tentacles completely usurped all the outlets of public information. And for more about the public opinion makers and how they bring about the public opinion that's desired you must read David Naisbett's book: Trend Report. And I'll say this; it's a very good book and goes into great detail about all the techniques used by the public opinion makers.

416. George Orwell in 1984, his classic novel of big brother and a coming totalitarian state observed that very few people are awake and alert to the machinations and manipulations of the controllers. Thus the people as a whole fall victim to a colossal conspiracy out of ignorance and because of apathy and denial of reality. And note: George Orwell's novel was first published in 1948.

417. Did you know that the abolition of privately owned firearms is already in force in three quarters of the world. And only in the United States can the populace still own guns and rifles. But that legal right is being eroded and chipped away at such an

alarming rate by federal, state, and local laws, which violate the constitutional right of all citizens to bear arms. Private gun ownership will probably more times than not have become a thing of the past in the United States by the year 2018. And this is all part of those who clandestinely control the U.S. government's plan to bring about their new world order as will be described in thought #615.

418. Now in this thought I'm going to inform you not that I haven't already informed you about the infinite resources of those who clandestinely control the U.S. government. But first of all you must know and understand that those who clandestinely control the U.S. government have the power and the means to tell the people of this country and virtually the world anything they want and it will be believed by the vast majority of the people. And that the T.V., the media, the newspapers, the magazines, and all the other outlets of public information are used as a weapon against, and to discredit and debunk anybody who even attempts to expose those who clandestinely control the U.S. government. But what I'm getting at is that when this book comes out it's going to be an instant best seller because of it's contents and the things that it discloses. And because of it's contents and the things that it discloses it's going to be the target of a covert and highly elaborate debunking, and discrediting, campaign carried out by the black hand (CIA) office of disinformation and this office is so surreptitious that it is never ever even mentioned by it's name it is simply referred to as the service and officially the service does not exist and there are no official records kept. And the service has at its disposal the infinite resources of the CIA and the service has myriad agents who are polymorphous, and can assume virtually any pseudonym, rank, or title, such as PH.D., Expert, Specialist, etc., in any field. And most firms that it deals with don't know the truth about the service or that it's CIA related. So don't be surprised when you see all kinds of PH.D's, Experts, and Specialists in various fields on T.V. talk shows, and all over the T.V., radios, newspapers, and magazines, discrediting and trying to debunk this book. So now that you have knowledge of this book when you hear or see somebody discrediting or trying to debunk this book you'll know that there knowingly or

unknowingly working for and/or doing the bidding of the service. And the services primary functions are 1) to discredit and debunk all legitimate UFO sightings, and 2) to discredit and debunk anybody or anything that attempts to expose those who clandestinely control the U.S. government. And other then that the service known only to a few as the office of disinformation does just that, it incessantly floods the country with disinformation and false propaganda that's in favor of those who clandestinely control the U.S. government. Just making sure people don't stumble on to the truth about those who clandestinely control the U.S. government or there hierarchy or what there doing. And the service deals with and interacts with intelligence agencys around the world including but not limited to Gestapo secret agencies. And the service gets unlimited free air time on T.V., and in the media to put out it's disinformation and misleading propaganda because most T.V. and media moguls like Rupert Murdock, CEO of FOX and News Corp., Sumner Redstone, CEO of VIACOM, Jeffrey Bewkes, CEO of AOL TIME WARNER, and John Malone, CEO of LIBERTY MEDIA, and others are associated with, if not direct members of those who clandestinely control the U.S. government. So now at least you have some kind of idea what kind of unrelenting powerful attack this book is going to be under once it comes out. But like I always say people will know the truth especially those people that are in tune with themselves will most definitely know the truth when they see it.

419. Now in this thought here I'm going to give you a little brief history on the first television networks so you can see and understand that the first television networks and subsequently all other television networks had their origin with those who clandestinely control the U.S. government. First those who clandestinely control the U.S. government formed the Radio Corporation of America (RCA) from 3 of their other companies, G.E., a J.P. Morgan owned and controlled company, Westinghouse, which J.P. Morgan and Co. bought from founder George Westinghouse. And J.P. Morgan's, Morgan Guarantee and Trust Bank, and RCA's First President was Owen Young, a J.P. Morgan right hand man. Now all the first 3 major television networks first came as subsidiaries then as spin-offs from RCA. First National Broadcasting Company (NBC)

closely followed by American Broadcasting Company (ABC) and then 3rd was the biggest one, Columbia Broadcasting System (CBS) which still is to this day just like (ABC) (NBC) and all the other myriad major T.V. and media companies surreptitiously owned and controlled by those who clandestinely control the U.S. government. And the T.V., media, and entertainment industry is just but one tiny tentacle of those who clandestinely control the U.S. government. And you must remember that those who clandestinely control the U.S. government are the only organized power hierarchy in the world transcending all laws, governments, entities, public or private, and individuals no matter who they are. Joseph Stalin, former dictator of the U.S.S.R. was one of their products. And he use to refer to them as the all powerful family. And President Eisenhower another one of their products use to describe them as the dark forces. And other heads of governments around the globe refer to this all powerful group as the magicians. And that's simply because those who clandestinely control the U.S. government can make anything and I say again anything, and this is damn near without exception happen that they want in this material physical world.

420. Now in this thought here I'm just going to ask you have you ever wondered why the T.V., the media, the newspapers, and the rest of the outlets of public information hardly ever if ever speak on the intelligence community with the exception of the F.B.I., the now defunct KGB, and the CIA . . . oh, and now after 9-11, Homeland Security. So why is it that the myriad intelligence agencies, private and Gestapo, domestic and foreign, hardly ever if ever get any exposure or air time on T.V. in the media or in the newspapers, and when most if not all of the activities that the vast majority of these intelligence agencies engage in are questionable. Why don't they get the same exposure that say local and state law enforcement gets? Why aren't the myriad intelligence agencies, domestic and foreign, kept in your (the public's) face, via the media, even after the 9-11 attacks the only intelligence agencies that got any real exposure were the FBI, and the CIA, when there are myriad more domestic intelligence agencies that dwarf the CIA and the FBI, in all capacities. But they didn't get any exposure from the

T.V., media, or the newspapers on 9-11 or afterwards . . . why is that? Well, I'm going to answer that for you and this might come as a shock to the average person but not to those in the know or in the higher ranks of the intelligence community. But damn near every intelligence agency, Gestapo, domestic, and foreign, has been usurped by those who clandestinely control the U.S. government. And the reason the T.V., the media, the newspapers, and all the other outlets of public information don't speak on, give air time to, or expose the vast network of intelligence agencies, domestic and foreign is because for 1) those that clandestinely control the U.S. government don't want the masses of people woke up to the intelligence agencies or to what they do. And for 2) intelligence agencies of all types play a pivotal role in controlling the people and dispensing disinformation that's in favor of those who clandestinely control the U.S. government. And for 3) Intelligence agencies play another pivotal role in counter-intelligence programs of all types against dissidents and anybody or anything else that tries or attempts to expose those that clandestinely control the U.S. government. And 4) those who clandestinely control the U.S. government want the masses of people to think that intelligence agencies don't exist and if they do their activities are outdated and very minimal when just the opposite of that is true. And it is through their control of the intelligence community that those who clandestinely control the U.S. government are able to maintain and exert their power and control over us (the masses of people). And did you know that those who clandestinely control the U.S. government have new intelligence agencies, domestic and foreign, pop up almost every day some surreptitious and some not and the ones that are surreptitious no one knows they exist let along what they engage in, or what their called. Take for instance the National Reconnaissance Office (NRO) it has been around surreptitiously since 1960 but was just recently declassified in 1994 so therefore the masses or nobody else knew about NRO for the first 34 years of it's existence. And then when it was declassified in 1994 people thought it was a brand new, just created agency. And therefore just created and established in 1994 when NRO had been around for 34 years. Just like the underground cities that you read about in thought 412 will one day too be public knowledge . . . I say sometime in the next 30 or so years. But that is not absolute it is just conjecture. But anyway like I said there are myriad intelligence agencies, private and Gestapo, domestic and foreign, with new ones popping up damn near everyday some surreptitious and some overt. But I'm going to give you a partial listing of some of the overt intelligence agencies here in America now. Now you might have not have ever heard of these agencies I'm about to name but you best believe that each one of these agencies is an intelligence gathering and operating agency and each one is controlled by and does the bidding of those who clandestinely control the U.S. government. So have you ever heard of such agencies as: Combined DNA System (CDIS); The Law Enforcement Satellite System (LESS); Defense Message Agency (DMA); The Office of Naval Intelligence (ONI); The National Security Agency (NSA); The National Identification Center (NIC); The National Endowment for Democracy (NED); The Office of U.S. Military Intelligence (OMI); U.S. State Department Office of Intelligence (SDOI); Interpol (INPO); Air Force System Command (AFSC); Information Infrastructure Task Force (IITF); Directorate for Science and Technology (DST); Defense Intelligence Agency (DIA); The Army G-2 Intelligence Office (AGIO); Defense Information Systems Agency (DISA); Nuclear Emergency Search Team (NEST); Counter Information Terrorist Center (CITC); Financial Crimes Enforcement Network (FINCEN); National Strategy Information Center (NSIC); Man and Biosphere Program (MAB); Triple-1 National Central Bureau (NCB); Office of Special Investigations (OSI); Interstate identification Index (III); Integrated Fingerprint ID System (IFIS); Multi Jurisdiction Task Force (MJTF); National Crime Information Center (NCIC); The National Reconnaissance Office (NRO); The Super Secret 40 Committee (40); and last but not least, the CIA's Super Secret Assassination Bureau. Now this is another one of those so secret so surreptitious bureaus that it is not known or ever mentioned by it's name it is just simply referred to as the guys and officially it doesn't exist and there are not official records kept. But I'll tell you one thing and you best believe me that the assassination bureau is real and very much does exist and has been around for over 60 years now and it is used to carry out assassinations worldwide when all other remedies have failed. And just so you know

President John F. Kennedy was one of it's victims. But that's a whole 'nother story. But anyway the intelligence agencies that I just named are only the overt ones with the exception of the 40 Committee and the Assassination Bureau. But there are many, many more surreptitious intelligence agencies right here in America that no one knows exist with the exception of those that work for them and they might not even know who they're really working for. Because as a rule of thumb all intelligence agencies incorporate an internal policy of compartmentalization. But like I told you before, intelligence agencies are very pivotal to those who clandestinely control the U.S. government. Because it's the intelligence agencies that do all the underhanded and dirty work for those that clandestinely control the U.S. government including but not limited to starting and causing all kinds of insurgencies here and abroad, keeping conflicts going where they need to be kept going, and doing myriad other things whether legal or illegal that are in the interest of those that clandestinely control the U.S. government. And there are two intelligence agencies of special interest; one is the behemoth National security Agency. Now this might shock the average person but did you know that the National Security Agency by Executive Order of the President is exempt from all laws, local, state, federal, judicial, legislative, or otherwise and this is all in the name of national security. Now what does that tell you??? It tells you that the National Security Agency can do whatever it damn well pleases without exception. Now I'm going to let you know that the NSA covertly spies and eavesdrops on everyone and everything in the United States without exception via it's massive electronic surveillance networks 2nd only to the surveillance networks of the underground cities. Now the NSA is the agency that spies, watches, and eavesdrops on all the other intelligence agencies, private and Gestapo, domestic and foreign. Including the black hand which is the big bad CIA because the NSA is the hog with the big nuts of the intelligence community. Because like I just told you it's massive electronic surveillance networks super computers, and technology is 2nd only to that of the underground cities and the NSA runs and controls myriad other intelligence agencies overt and surreptitious around the globe. And runs myriad cover businesses, front businesses and legitimate businesses for surveillance, information, and covert reasons. And just when you were thinking that the NSA might have missed something well you were wrong. Because the NSA keeps track of and monitors all PC's and other computers sold in the U.S. without exception. This is part of the NSA's domestic intelligence and surveillance program. And it works like this the NSA's electromagnetic frequency (EMF) equipment can tune RF emissions from computers circuit boards while filtering out emissions from monitors and power supplies. The RF emission from computer circuit boards contains the digital information in the computer; coded RF waves from the NSA's equipment can resonate computer circuits and therefore access the data in the computer. Meaning the NSA can gain wireless modem style entry into any computer in the country. Almost like and damn near like the super computers in the underground cities that wirelessly access all computers in the known world 24 hours a day, 7 days a week. But there's no intelligence agency in the world like it that's why the NSA is the hog with the big nuts of the intelligence community. And the NSA just like all the other myriad intelligence agencies is a tool of, and is controlled by those who clandestinely control the U.S. government. Now the other intelligence agency of special interest is the International Criminal Police Organization or Interpol. And this agency is only of special interest because it's the biggest privately owned intelligence agency in the world owned and controlled by a very powerful member of those who clandestinely control the U.S. government . . . David Rockefeller. And the intelligence community as a whole is how those who clandestinely control the U.S. government, control, coordinate, and run, the illicit drug trade of the world. Yes if you didn't know! Well now you know that those who clandestinely control the U.S. government run, and control the world's illegal drug trade from the very top and the intelligence community is their liaison to the drug world. And I could write books, not one but numerous books on how those who clandestinely control the U.S. government have been and do control, and run the worlds nefarious illegal drug trade from the very top through there liaison which is the intelligence community. And if you would like to read about this more and want a complete history of how those who clandestinely control the U.S. government have been running, and controlling the world's illegal nefarious drug trade for more than 200 years you must get Dr. John Coleman's book: The Conspirators Hierarchy. And there are many other good books on this subject such as: Drugging America, by Rodney Stich; Michael Levine and Lauri Kavanau Levine's – The Big White Lie, and Terry Reed and John Cummings – Compromise Clinton, Bush, and the CIA. And there's one book that dramatically exposes the U.S. government's role in drug running and it's called Barry and The Boys, The CIA, The Mob, and America's Secret History, by Daniel Hopsicker and on the front cover of this book there is an actual photograph of the super secret 40 committee that author Daniel Hopsicker says he procured from a retired military intelligence officer and on page 26 of that book he gives you the history of the picture . . . very interesting. And the book as a whole is a great expose of the U.S. government, the CIA, the FBI, and the DEA in drug running, gun running and copious other intrigues. And I haven't even mentioned to you the myriad publications, magazines, and periodicals that contain polygenetic disinformation, and plausible propaganda that are surreptitiously put out by the intelligence community mostly through front companies, businesses, and other entities controlled by intelligence agencies. And I'm going to tell you one of the intelligence community's best kept secrets and that is that one of the best places to put disinformation and plausible propaganda is in women's magazines, such as Vogue, McCall's, InStyle, etc. And that's because women are known to be much more easily deceived then men and therefore are more gullible, and susceptible to disinformation and plausible false propaganda. And with that the thought goes that women will take in the disinformation and propaganda and spread it to their husbands, boyfriends, sons, daughters, colleagues, and acquaintances, and so on and so forth. So therefore the average middle class woman is seen as and is of great interest to the intelligence community because she's seen as a pivotal tool for spreading disinformation and propaganda. And the amount of disinformation and propaganda that's put out nowadays, and not just what's aimed at the average middle class woman. But what's aimed virtually at everybody and anybody is staggering to say the least. And it's not just put out by the intelligence community alone it's put out by the T.V., the media, the newspapers, institutions, organizations and myriad other sources. And the thought behind that is to completely bombard the masses of people with not just disinformation and false propaganda but with virtually incessant, myriad, amounts of information and propaganda. So therefore the people will be overloaded with information and the psychological distress arising from the excess load of information will affect the decision making mechanism of the human mind. Because it's a known scientific fact that there are clearly marked limits to the amount of information that the human mind can take in so therefore the people are left confused to such a degree to where they just don't know. They are left in a state of not knowing what to believe and in that state they are no longer able to make informed, intelligent, and sound choices. And the choices they do make whatever they may be they will feel insecure and uncertain about. And this is just what those who clandestinely control the U.S. government want so that the masses of people will be stuck in a state of apathy and will not give a damn what's going on either way. But that's why I've told you previously in this book that it's extremely imperative for one to at the minimum at least once a day to go somewhere and shut everything down and to be in total solitude with his or her self. And that right there is to get in tune with one self so one can tap into that innate unlimited power supply in oneself. So that one will not be confused about nothing or stuck in extrovertism. So now I hope you understand why the T.V., the media, the newspapers, or any other of the myriad outlets of public information don't really speak on, expose, or give air time to in any real kind of way to the intelligence community. And for a complete inclusive study on how those who clandestinely control the U.S. government control, and use, intelligence agencies for their own benefit you must get Rodney Stich's 750 page book: Defrauding America.

421. It is sincerely hoped that the truth contained in this book will be like a sword that cuts through all the armor of deception, and lies, that are now so prevalent in the world today.

422. Well in this thought here I'm going to show and explain to you how watching T.V. is extremely detrimental to your physical

health in more ways than one. But first I must explain to you the different vibratory rates or frequencies that the human body operates at and just so you know this is all scientific fact. But a brake down of the vibratory rates or frequencies of the human body goes something like this. The human body itself has been determined to operate optimally between 62 and 68 MHZ . The human brain functions and operates optimally between 72 and 90 MHZ. And when the body's vibration lowers to 58 MHZ, it can catch a cold and at 57 MHZ. the flu. At 55 MHZ. candida at 52 MHZ. Enstein Barr. At 42 MHZ. cancer. And at 25 MHZ. death begins. So now that you got a brief understanding of the vibratory rates of the human body. Did you know that the radiation that you take in from watching T.V. lowers the MHZ. or vibratory rate of your body. And when your body's MHZ. lowers you feel tired, lazy, and you're most definitely more susceptible to get sick. And not only that but when your brains MHZ. lowers you think much slower, you forget more, and you're just plain dumber. And not only that but research is being done right now that is still somewhat inconclusive that links the cause of Alzheimer's to the radiation that people take in from watching T.V. over the years. And just so you know the new digital T.V. sets and this is not by accident but by design put out from 5 to 10 times the radiation of the old analog sets. And now you can better understand why by 2009 analog T.V. sets will be a thing of the past. And broadcasting in America will be in the digital format and this was mandated by congress in 1998. But I'm pretty sure that you already know whose real agenda this was . . .it was the agenda of those who clandestinely control the U.S. government. Because just think about it since when has congress given a rat ass whether people watched black and white or color T.V., or now in this instance analog or digital T.V.? Congress could care less because congress has too many other innumerable, myriad things to worry about. Then what kind of radios the people are buying or what kind of T.V.'s there watching. But like I told you in thought #406 the people that make up congress just do what there told and they are more or less controlled and manipulated just like the rest of the masses. So by congress mandating that broadcasting be in digital format by 2009 was nothing but the agenda of the controllers which are as you already know those who clandestinely control the U.S. government. So now that you know this turn them damn T.V. sets off and get in tune with yourself. Because remember the negative forces and there ground crew which are those who clandestinely control the U.S. government will do and are doing anything and everything in their power to keep you stuck in extrovertism.

423. Always remember that ever since you were a child as far back as you can remember you were always taught, trained, and programmed to look everywhere except within, inside yourself for knowledge, help, and strength. So now that you know that you been lied to all your life and know that all the knowledge, help, and strength or whatever that you could ever want or need is in you. Please wait no longer and start the ultimate self-empowered process of getting in tune with yourself.

424. Always remember that the human brain is nothing but a radio receiver that is capable of tuning into the flow of knowledge ever present in the creative flow. And all one has to do to tune into this virtually unlimited source and flow of knowledge is get in tune with his or herself.

425. Now in this thought here I'm going to give you a little bit more information on these new so called high definition digital T.V.'s as you already know I already briefly spoke on them in thought #422. But there were a few things that I didn't get to mention so I'm going to make up for it here. Because I want you too clearly and explicitly understand that these new digital T.V.'s are no joke. For one they have interactive chips in them meaning that these new digital T.V.'s have the inherent ability of watching you while you're watching them. But that's the least of it. The imminent danger that these digital T.V.'s pose is that they have the ability of actually recognizing, remembering, and knowing the people that watch them yes they are endowed with a degree of artificial intelligence and they have the ability of receiving and putting out programmed response systems and as you already know a programmed response system can virtually contain anything. As I explained programmed response systems in thought #412 so if those who clandestinely control the U.S. government or their agents, henchmen, or there Gestapo agencies want to give someone a programmed response

system and that person has a digital T.V. or even if he or she watches one it won't be hard because remember these digital T.V.'s have the ability of recognizing, remembering, and knowing people. And it is said that these digital T.V.'s recognize and know people by picking up on their individual biological field frequencies so they will absolutely make no mistakes. So as soon as you walk in the room or anywhere in there radiance they know who you are. And these T.V.'s are hooked up via satellite to the supercomputers in the underground cities and all the information is interchangeable so you best believe me that they know who you are. And this is the real reason why those who clandestinely control the U.S. government had congress make it imperative that all broadcasting be in the digital format by 2006, delayed because of public pressure to 2-17-09. And it is said that all electronics manufactured after 2003 such as radios, phones, cell phones, pagers, fax-machines, computers of all kinds, video games, microwaves, and many other electronics have chips in them that make them compatible, and able to communicate with these new digital T.V.'s and this isn't paranoia but just reality. And believe me it isn't like the technology to do just that is not available. Please because you best believe me it is. So all I can say for all you gadget aficionados out there is that when you get done using your gadgets pull the plug on them. That way they will be powerless. And I'm not being funny but serious here.

426. Always remember that every man dies. But not every man really lives.

427. Always remember that some might call this book insanity. But remember what's really going on in the world. And what those who clandestinely control the U.S. government are actually doing to the masses of people, America, and the world as a whole is so inordinately sneaky, crafty, malevolent, nefarious, and surreptitious that it stretches the imaginations of the most creative and imaginative and as William A. White put it there is no insanity so devastating in a man's life as utter sanity. Because utter sanity recognizes the complete utter insanity of the world.

428. Now this thought here is for all of you who for whatever reason or reasons do not believe that our government has been completely taken over and subverted by those that clandestinely control it. Alright, the following senate bill Title (VII, S.B. 2834) that I'm going to expose and speak on was passed on August 4, 1990 for the fiscal year 1991 so this bill has been active and on the books for some 20 years now. And 98% of all Americans and most congressmen know little if not absolutely nothing about this bill. And this bill in a nutshell just gives the President of the United States absolute carte blanche in initiating insurgencies or whatever the hell else he wants around the world with virtually no oversight. Now this bill (S.B. 2834) gives the President the absolute power to initiate covert actions, allows the President to use any federal department, agency or entity, without exception to operate or finance a covert operation. And it empowers the President to use any other nation or private contractor or person to fund or operate a covert action. It redefines covert actions and/or operations as measures necessary to support the foreign policy objectives of the United Sates, which is a definition that is so extremely broad and vague that it could virtually mean anything. And this bill for the first time officially claims the right of the United States to secretly interfere in the internal, political, economic, and military affairs of other nations and countries, which is in direct violation of our constitution and of international law. And the bill does require that the President prepare and deliver a written account of the findings to the intelligence committee of congress. But it allows the President to omit extremely sensitive matters and it authorizes the President to claim executive privilege if congress asks too many questions. Now this bill (S.B. 2834) is just one of many, many surreptitiously passed bills that allow and almost make it legal for the President to completely disregard the constitution of the United States. And do whatever he damn well pleases. And check this out (S.B. 2834) was carefully brought to a vote and passed by a small but powerful bipartisan group of senators in the dead of night at 3:30 A.M. Saturday August 4, 1990 when all opposition to the bill would be gone. And you best believe that each and every one of those senators was a member or is in direct alliance with those who clandestinely control the U.S. government. And they

were just doing what they were told to do point blank and uncut. And just like I told you (S.B. 2834) is just one of myriad bills that subverts the United States constitution and allows the President to have absolute carte blanche control with virtually no oversight. Well all I can say is that bills like (S.B. 2834) and ones like it need to be repealed. But they can't and won't be repealed if no one knows they exist and people wonder why the intelligence community and other U.S. agencies, and departments, can do whatever they want it's simply because of bills like this.

429. If you are already rich or wealthy the knowledge in this book will make you all the more rich and/or wealthier and I'll say this that after you get through reading this book and at least half of the books mentioned in this book you will without a doubt know the truth concerning so many things that those who clandestinely control the U.S. government have for so long suppressed and are still right now more than ever relentlessly trying to keep suppressed away from you the people. Meaning that you will be able to watch T.V., the news, read magazines, newspapers, etc., and is able to immediately without a doubt spot all the lies, misleads, and myriad other plausible deceptions contained in them.

430. Always remember that no matter how bad things seem or how bad they may even get. That there always is, always was, and is always going to be goodness in the world and/or universe. But if you believe in goodness and/or consider yourself a good and righteous person then it is your number 1 job to constantly think positive. And therefore put out good and positive energy to assist, help, and most of all strengthen the universal goodness in the universe which is incessantly at war with the negative energies and evil in the universe. And even though you might not think so but each and every thought that we human being put forth and put out on this planet does count and mean something in the universe. Because the war is between good and evil and the negative forces are trying to overcome and completely overtake this planet with negativity so they can have carte blanche completely have their way with us. But we know that will never happen, and that is simply because of good people and I'm speaking about people from all religions,

dogmas, sects, and ideologies that are good people, righteous people that will always no matter what think positive and put out that good and positive energy that's so desperately needed to aid the goodness and the good in the universe that is incessantly at war with the powers of darkness and evil. And like I told you before, religions, dogmas, sects, and ideologies, don't even matter at all. It's all about getting in tune with yourself, believing in all that is, good and incessantly thinking and putting out good and positive energy . . . that's what it's about. And to conclude this thought, well, I sincerely hope that I got my point across to you in this book about how extremely important and pivotal it is in these times for one to constantly think positive no matter what transpires or happens. Because not just the world but the universe is depending on it.

431. Always remember that it is not the U.S. government of itself and by itself that is foul, bad, and evil. But it is those who have surreptitiously usurped and taken control of the U.S. government for their own selfish and ominous agendas that are every bit of foul, bad, and are the epitome of evil. And they are the ones who are making America, it's government, what it stands for, and us (it's people) appear to the rest of the world as foul, bad, and evil. See it works like this those who clandestinely control the U.S. government are having and have been having for a very long time now it the U.S. government do, and perpetrate all kinds of foul, bad, and evil atrocities all over the world such as in the Middle East, and elsewhere in the world and the people that these atrocities are being perpetrated against are not rich or well off such as the Kings, Princes, and aristocrats of the areas but the people that these atrocities are mostly perpetrated against are the poor . . . the people that mostly live in dire poverty and have annual incomes of about 300.00 dollars a year or less. So these people see all these foul, bad, and evil atrocities being done to them by the U.S. military and other arms of the U.S. government. And say hey the U.S. government is representative of the American people so the American people and their nation must be foul, bad, and evil. When it's definitely not like that. Because 90%, if not more, of the American people have no idea what the U.S. military and other arms of the U.S. government are really and actually doing

to the people of the Middle East and of other areas of the world. Because believe me if the masses of American people really did know what was going on and what the U.S. military and U.S. government was really doing to the people of the Middle East and of other parts of the world you best believe me that they wouldn't support it or sanction it in no kind of way. But the masses of American people only know what they know about the Middle East, Saddam Hussein, and other areas of the world because of and through the T.V. and the rest of the outlets of public information in America. And the American people are so naïve especially the biggest segment which is the middle class of which most are college graduates (Please refer to thought #402 – Group A) that they don't know that they have been, and are being manipulated, lied to, and straight deceived by the T.V. and the rest of the outlets of public information. Because the T.V. only shows what the people of the Middle East and of other areas of the world do after they have been bombed, shot and killed ran from their homes, and hunted in the streets like animals for no real reason by the U.S. military and other U.S. forces and factions both overt and covert. Then the T.V. and the other outlets of public information here in America when these people retaliate they then call that acts of terrorism, and insurrection. And then when the people organize and mind you that's only with the help of the CIA and the rest of the U.S. intelligence community giving the people guns, ammunition, bombs, and other supplies which is just to add fuel to the fire and is very much needed to keep the upheavals going. Then, when these groups attack and try to defend what's rightfully their's, the T.V. and the rest of the outlets of public information in America show them trying to kill, assault, and attack the U.S. military and other U.S. forces. So therefore these people are deemed all kinds of extremist and militant terrorist organizations, and groups that need and have to be stopped. But that's where the average American's knowledge of the Middle East and of other parts of the world stops. Because all the average American knows is that the U.S. is suppose to be the good guy and anybody attacking him is the bad guy. But there is so much, much, more to it that's it's a damn shame. There is so much manipulation, intrigue, and deception involved that it's really just unbelievable. With U.S. intelligence groups playing a main part. And I'm going to tell you something and this might shock the average person who is not in the know to how intelligence agencies really work. But all those suicide bombings that kill so many people and everybody just thinks that it's the extremist, and martyrs, dyeing for their cause is mostly a straight lie. Why? Because over 98% of suicide bombers are given programmed response systems by the CIA. So therefore the vast majority of suicide bombers are nothing but mind controlled slaves, and are not in conscious awareness of committing suicide when they commit it. In a nutshell they are basically being used, and involuntarily killed by the CIA. And something like 1% or 2% of suicide bombers are paid by the CIA and it's off-shoots to commit the act, money given to their families. And the very last few voluntary do it for the cause not knowing the cause is a straight contrived up lie. And you already know about programmed response systems because I explained them to you in thought #412. But anyway . . . and the cold thing is that the overt U.S. military and personnel do not even have knowledge and or know of the actions and of what the U.S. intelligence agencies and other intelligence agencies are surreptitiously doing to keep the conflicts, fighting, and upheavals going. But as you already know that right there is the omnipotent unseen hand of those who clandestinely control the U.S. government which is always present but rarely if ever overt of ostensible. So please don't go thinking that this is some giant conspiracy with all of the U.S. military and other personnel acting knowingly together to keep wars and conflicts going on and to try and manipulate the American people otherwise. Because that's what it's not. This is not a conspiracy because with the exception of a few and I say again a few commanding generals the rest of the U.S. military and personnel is in the blind to what's really going on and they the U.S. military ask no questions and only do as they're told. And the few commanding generals in the know are just there to make sure that the orders and wishes of those who clandestinely control the U.S. government are fully executed and carried out. But then yet there's still more because on the other end of the stick the people in the Middle East, and in other parts of the world, after being done so wrong by the U.S. military and other U.S. forces that they come to really believe that the American people really support it and sanction it. So therefore these people in the Middle East and in other parts of the world who are mostly deeply religious people come to condemn America and it's people as foul, bad, and pure evil. But like I said before its definitely not like that. But if only the people of the Middle East and other parts of the world knew that the masses of American people do not know what the U..> military, U.S. government, and a host of other overt and covert U.S. forces are really and actually doing to the people of the Middle East and of other parts of the world. Then the people of the Middle East and of other parts of the world would come to understand that the vast majority of American people are God-fearing, peace-loving, good people. And then and only then would they be able to put the blame where it rightfully belongs with those who clandestinely control the U.S. government who are manipulating the American people as well as all other people of the world to their own advantage. But like I've said before and I've tried to explain in this book to you how those who clandestinely control the U.S. government operate and what they do. But you best believe one thing that everything they do is aimed in one way or another at not only enslaving America but the whole world with and through their new world order. And if you would like to read more about how the CIA runs and operates terrorist training camps around the world, and has since the 1960's. And how it was the CIA who covertly in 1968 put Saddam Hussein and his Baath Party in power in Iraq. And let the truth be told Saddam was nothing but a puppet, and a puppet of those who clandestinely control the U.S. government. Just like Joseph Stalin, Lenin, Hitler, and every other significant dictator of the 20th century were nothing but puppets. And just so you know the Saddam, the U.S. authorities found or captured in a cave, is not, and I say again, is not in no way the real Saddam Hussein. That dude is or was I should say a mind controlled double given a programmed response system by the CIA, and controlled by them. And the real Saddam is and believe this, somewhere on an island living lavishly. And just think about this for a minute, what better way to appease, and neutralize the public's attention on Saddam then to supposedly capture him, try him, and then kill him, pretty ingenious, huh? But anyway, back to what I was saying if you would like to read more about how the CIA, MOSAD, and other intelligence agencies all controlled by those who clandestinely control the

U.S. government are used to engender, facilitate, and keep going myriad conflicts, upheavals, and insurrections, and wars in almost every country in the world then you must get and read the excellent book: Defrauding America, ISBN: 0-932438-08-03, by Rodney stitch. And I personally guarantee that this book will have any true American patriot completely taken aback and aghasted at the corruption committed by the CIA and other government agencies.

432. But anyway if you really want to know and understand how the media, the T.V., and the rest of the outlets of public information deceive, trick manipulate, fool, confuse, brainwash, and keep the masses of people stuck on straight stupid then you must get Dr. John Coelman's excellent book: The Conspirator's Hierarchy which even discloses how those who clandestinely control the U.S. government stared and spread the inner-city street gangs in South Central Los Angeles (i.e., Crips and Bloods). This book is a must read for anybody who really wants to know about and learn about those who clandestinely control the U.S. government and there execrate sinister hierarchy and they're beyond labyrinth operations, connections, and dealings.

433. And this is just so you'll know that one of the best things of getting in tune with yourself is that you will no longer fear, worry, or be scared of nothing. Because you will be strengthen by the most powerful power there is and that's the power of the source of the universe (God) and with this power running through you I mean it's already running through you now, you just aren't in tune with it. But once you get in tune with it you will feel it because this is actual power and you'll actually emit it. People around you will notice something though they might not be able to put their finger on it. They will just enjoy being around you and not know why. But like I said you will absolutely no longer fear, worry, or be scared of nothing. Because you will be strengthen by all that is (God) and therefore you will be happy to take all things how they come. And how ever they come, because you will be like a solid rock and not just any old rock but you will be like pure uncut granite rock. And then and only then will you be able to realize and

achieve your fullest potential in all areas and things that right now you can't even begin to imagine or conceive. And that's simply because fear, and worry, which is nothing but anxiety, stunt and impede human potential. And I'm going to say this and close. In these days and those coming ahead it's more than imperative to be in tune with yourself. But that's only if you choose to stand firm, and stay firm through these days, only you can make the choice.

434. Carefully remembering your past intuitive feelings brings you to the truth now. That you were always aware and are damn sure aware now after reading this book that something nefarious and sinister was present in the U.S. government.

435. Always remember that in the beginning it was meant that humanity meaning each (person) was to be responsible to live rightously with in the personal focus of their lives, attitudes, motives, and actions. And remember that this ubiquitous profit driven motive ideology (I got to win or benefit), which is at the expense of all others, has not lead to utopia and never will. And is the cause or root of a lot of the craftiness, wrong doing, and/or evil. But this is just the way it is in this world or 3rd dimension right now and man in his true expression is a radiant being, meaning created to give outward the expression of the Creator's love not to live as a usurper with the only intent of drawing all toward himself as depicted and taught by the world.

436. Now in this thought here I just want you to know and understand that there are right now myriad groups associations, secret societies, or whatever one chooses to call them. But these syndicates have been around for a long, long, time and the more prominent, and powerful, one's have been and still are nothing but branches, made and or infiltrated and controlled by those who clandestinely control the U.S. government. Now the following is a small list of the more prominent and powerful syndicates created and/or infiltrated through the years and controlled by those who clandestinely control the U.S. government. Now the list is as follows but is not limited to: The Jason Society, The Thule Society, The order of the Quest, Majesty-12, aka The Secret Government, The Qabbala, The Order of Orange, The Illuminati, The Supreme Council of 39,

The Council on Foreign Relations, The Knights of the Garter, The Trilateral Commission, the Club of the Isle, The Bilderberg Group, The Jocobin Clubs, The Vatican and It's hierarchy, the Club of Rome, The Royal Institute on International Affairs, the Round Table, The Skull and Bones Order, The Parlour Club, The Scroll and Key Order, The Carbonari, The Knights Templar, The Knights of Malta, The Knights of Columbus, The Order of Thistle, The Jesuits, The crown Agents, The Masons, The Brotherhood of the Dragon, The City Livery Companies, and the Ancient and Mystical Order of the Rosicrucians. Now some of these syndicates go back hundreds, and hundreds of years like the Jesuits, the Masons, the Rosicrucians, and others and the Black Families (aka The Black Nobility), which are the Knights Templars, The Knights of Malta, and the Knights of Columbus, but have nonetheless all been infiltrated, subverted, and usurped by those who clandestinely control the U.S. government. Now this thought is just so you don't get confused when somebody says it's the Illuminati, the Masons, the Trilateral Commission, The International Jews or Bankers, the Jason Society, the Council on foreign Relations, the Qabbalah, etc., that runs the U.S. government and controls the world. You'll know that there all one and the same because remember confusion is precisely just what those who clandestinely control the U.S. government want. And just like I told you in thought #406 those who clandestinely control the U.S. government have through the years been called many, many different names and things. But don't let that confuse you because like I said confusion is what they thrive on. And whatever you do please, and I say again please, don't take those who clandestinely control the U.S. government lightly because just look at all the extremely prominent and powerful groups, syndicates, and secret societies that they control. And with the exception of the Trilateral Commission, the Council on Foreign Relations and the Royal Institute on international Affairs this is only a short list of the private not public but private groups and associations, that those who clandestinely control the U.S. government control. And a good number of these groups are for the most part covert and inscrutable and the majority of people don't even know they exist. And that's where people got the phrase the secret societies from. And just so you know both George

Bush, sr. and Jr. are both very prominent members of the Trilateral Commission and the Council on Foreign Relations. And every President since Franklin D. Roosevelt with the exception of John F. Kennedy have been members in some capacity of the Council on Foreign Relations or the Trilateral Commission or both. And mostly all the prominent members of Congress and the Senate are members of the Council on Foreign Relations and the Trilateral Commission . . . again, in some capacity. And most government agency heads are too. And the Council on Foreign Relations and the trilateral Commission are the vehicles, or groups, for membership mostly used in America by those who clandestinely control the U.S. government while other groups or syndicates are mostly used in other parts of the world. But like I said it's a known and proven fact that the Council on Foreign Relations and the Trilateral Commission are primarily used in America. And now days one need not be a direct member of the council on Foreign Relations or the Trilateral Commission to be affiliated with those who clandestinely control the U.S. government. Because like I told you in thought #406 the Council on Foreign Relations and the Trilateral Commission have many smaller individual branches with an assortment of various names, titles, some covert and some overt. And the Council on Foreign Relations was started by J.P. Morgan and John D. Rockefeller in 1921 and the Trilateral Commission was started by David Rockefeller in 1972. And if you would like to read about and learn more about all the secret societies that those who clandestinely control the U.S. government control then you must get Steven Sora's book: Secret Societies of America's Elite, ISBN# 0-89281-956-5.

437. It is sincerely hoped that the knowledge in this book enlightens, awakens, and brings to a real understanding the living hell planned for every human being in America, and possibly the world, should those who clandestinely control the U.S. government succeed in implementing there execrate totalitarian new world order.

438. Always remember that the more in tune you get with yourself the more self aware you'll become, until you reach the allowable limits of self awareness in this 3rd dimension. And even that can be transcended for those determined and desiring

to completely transcend the limits of this world and or 3rd dimension.

439. Always remember that the absolute truth is always more times than not an astounding reality that most people are not ready to face.

440. Always remember that it is not America or the lawfully constituted American government that is guilty of imperialism. But it is those who clandestinely control the U.S. government that are guilty of imperialism and imperialism on an immense scale.

441. It is strongly recommended and it is this author's desire that anyone reading any claim made in this book that they doubt in any way, shape, or form, that they themselves take up the task of independently studying, researching, and investigating, any such claim or claims.

442. Always remember that in this life we are all innately endowed with the power of choice, meaning we all have a free will. And we all can personally and independently choose how we want to experience and express ourselves in this life. And we are all personally responsible for our actions or inactions. And when all is said and done you are responsible for absolutely no one but you. And when what you know as judgment is pronounced at the end of this particular experience, and/of life, you and you along will be held accountable what you did or didn't do. And just so you know, judgment will be pronounced in duality, meaning that you will be judged as the doer and the done to, so that you will see and feel both experiences. And that is also the time when all lies, ulterior motives, and hidden agendas one may have had will be made known and clearly revealed.

443. Now in this thought here I'm going to inform you about the truth about T.V. commercials and advertisements. Now did you know that in most all T.V. commercials and advertisements there are subliminal messages, and triggers, and these subliminal messages and triggers completely by pass and are not picked up by the conscious mind. But are designed to embed themselves in your subconscious mind. And the

subliminal triggers contain certain programmed information that can be triggered into effect at a later time by any of various sites or sounds. So, now you can know and understand why when you're driving down the road and you see a Starbucks or you hear over the radio a Starbuck's commercial you suddenly feel an intense, and compelling need, and want, for a Starbuck's cup of coffee. And you don't know any better, so you think it's just you wanting a cup of coffee. But that's just what it's not, it's that trigger in the deep, deep regions of your mind and/or subconscious being triggered into effect by a certain sight or sound. And Pepsi and Coco-Cola and myriad other companies and corporations do this and have been doing this now for well over 3 decades. And you must remember that these big corporations and companies make and design their own commercials and advertisements and then they just buy air time on the T.V. and radio to run them. And like I said, most if not all T.V. commercials and advertisements contain these hidden subliminal messages and triggers. And just so you know they are now getting very creative with the content of these subliminal messages and triggers. And that's why I've belabored you throughout this book on why it's so detrimental for one to constantly watch T.V. and I'm also very well aware of the fact that a good number of people (the average Joe's and Jane's) are going to read a lot of the stuff in this book and say no way. But check this out in 20 or 30 years from now if we're still around a lot of the stuff in this book, underground cities and all will be public knowledge. Just like in the 50's, 60's, and early 70's when then FBI director J. Edgar Hoover was spying on almost a quarter of the American population and had almost a 100,000 dossiers on law abiding citizens just because he J. Edgar Hoover deemed them political dissidents in some capacity. And this is not even to mention all the countless counter-intelligence programs administered by the FBI against law abiding citizens for no just cause during that time. But now just think about it for a minute the average person back than would not in their wildest dreams believed the FBI was capable of perpetrating such atrocities. And just think what if somebody would have had that knowledge at that time and decided to be courageous and write a book and impart that, he or she would have been deemed crazy, a wacko, and probably a communist or something, with a hidden agenda to subvert the established order. But all in all had such a book been written at that time people would not have believed it. But now just look 30, 40 years later all of J. Edgar Hoover's atrocities are public knowledge. So just take what I just said as an example and be smart because history does nothing but repeat itself. And if you would like to read all about Edgar J. Hoover's atrocities in great detail with even copies of the declassified documents and internal FBI memos with Edgar J. Hoover's signature on them. Then you must get the book: The Counter-Intelligence Program Papers, by W. Churchill. And if you would like to read all about subliminal mind control technology and how it is secretly being used against the masses of people by those who clandestinely control the U.S. government, then you must get the following book: The Age of Manipulation, by Bryan W. Key.

444. Always remember and never forget that all of us human beings that live or are living in this 3rd dimension physical world without exception, are all but just one easy slip away from disaster meaning that anything can happen, at anytime, to anyone. So no matter what success you are enjoying in life or have enjoyed or what capacity you are in, in life never think or believe that you are beyond reproach.

445. Always remember, just like all wise people know that one must always be aware, and stay aware of the subtle changes and differences inherent in all things.

446. Always remember that just because something isn't overt and/or conspicuous, does not mean that it isn't there and/or doesn't exist. Just like pain, hurt, suffering, regret, and myriad other things that are not always conspicuous. But are there . . .

447. Always remember that everything and this is without exception that you can think of and even what you haven't thought of, and what you as a human being are incapable of thinking of, exists as mere possibility. And this just means that regardless of whether it manifests or is given form or remains unmanifest and formless it still exist and is there. So this means that all things no matter how absurd, crazy, surreal, or whatever exist. You

just have to know how to make whatever you want manifest into your dimension which would be the 3rd. And you must remember as a human being living in this 3rd dimension you're limited thinking capacity. And now that you know that everything without exception exist as mere possibility or pure potential, you have to learn how to convert that potential into desire. And then that desire into possibility. And then, that possibility ultimately into manifest expression. Because remember all is possible.

448. It is strongly recommended and encouraged by the author of this book that people reading this book and wishing to learn more about the immense, myriad, suppressed truths of the world that they not only educate themselves with this book and the books mentioned in this book. But that they share this greatly emancipating, uplifting, and extremely enlightening, knowledge with as many people as possible and that when time, circumstances, and resources permit that they even hold study groups where this book and the books mentioned in this book are studied and therefore that this knowledge of such importance to the masses of people is imparted to as many as possible.

449. Now in this thought here I'm going to read you a small except from what's known as: "The Protocols of the Learned Elders of Zion." Now the Protocols of the Learned Elders of Zion are nothing but the secret teachings of the predecessors, and forefathers of the executive governing body of those who clandestinely control the U.S. government. Now the 24 documents known as the protocols of the learned elders of Zion were first made available for public scrutiny in America in 1905. And for anybody interested in learning about the history of those who clandestinely control the U.S. government and there execrate plans to manipulate, deceive, and bring the whole world under their totalitarian rule. The reading of The Protocols of the Learned Elders of Zion is imperative and a must. But anyway here is a small excerpt from The Protocols of the Learned Elders of Zion:

When we come into our rule, and are supreme one world government is acknowledged by the entire world, our orators will expose the great problems which have turned humanity upside down in order to bring it to this end. And then who will ever suspect that all these problems, and upheavals, and the people and things that caused them were all stage-managed by us according to a political plan which no one has so much as guessed at in the course of many centuries.

And now like I said if you want to read more about the protocols you must get the book: The Protocols of the Learned Elders of Zion, by Victor E. Marsden.

450. Let me expose and share a truth with you – Now I am well aware of the fact that many and when I say many I am speaking of the majority of the people specifically the people that make up and are part of group A which is 55% of the people. Please refer back to thought #402 for a quick clarification. But anyway the aftermentioned segment of people are going to doubt, and are not going to be inclined to believe this truth that I'm about to expose and share. But the truth is: that a politician with real morals and virtues will get eaten up, digested, and shitted out in the political arena where myriad issues, agendas, both overt and hidden, and beliefs of all kinds contend. So what does this tell you it just tells you that the vast majority of politicians and especially the skilled and prominent ones are more than willing to sacrifice the welfare of all for the sake of securing their own ends. And now just think why do politicians spend millions of their own dollars to try and get a seat or office that pays $135,000 to $200,000 a year tops??? Well that's because there after the seat or office for the privileges that come with it and for their own personal aims at power, not to look out for the best interest of you the public . . . wake up! And this is one of the ways that those who clandestinely control the U.S. government (control it, the U.S. government) because they know all too well that every politician that's in politics for the long haul has a price point blank and uncut. And on how this is done please refer back to thought #406.

451. Let me share with you one of the proverbs of those who clandestinely control the U.S. government: Let us however always keep our attention directed no so much to what is good

and moral, as to what is necessary, and useful, to attain our ends. And this is an excerpt from Protocol #1 of the Protocols of the Learned Elders of Zion.

452. Things are not the way they are in the world by accident but things are the way they are by design.

453. Always remember one must fully and thoroughly understand in a very proficient way the subtleness of deception, duplicity, craftiness, and manipulation to really know and understand how those who clandestinely control the U.S. government operate and function.

454. Now let me if I may elaborate, and expound on what could arguably be one of the, if not the most debated, pondered, and asked question of all time and that is what is the real, and true meaning of life??? And I'm not just talking about the worldly or secular meaning of life which is nothing but transitory, and pretty much trivial. But I'm talking about the immutable real and true meaning of life and why we, human beings are here and why we get to, and must experience this trip in the physical realm. First of all ours is not the only physical realm there are many other physical realms and or planets with intelligent civilizations on them in this 3rd dimension and as by reading thought #412 you pretty much already know that we are not alone. But anyway the real and true meaning of life is not so much categorized by what we attain or get as in wealth or material things as it is in the learning and experience that we get in this journey in the physical. Because every being in the physical realm is in training and/or learning. Meaning let me explain . . . you your physical self is not truly who you really are because your physical self is nothing but a vehicle for you to be able to experience, express, and exist in the physical. And that vehicle your physical body wears and tears and once it is no good any more you will leave and exit that vehicle, your physical body. And you who, and what, you really are is a being or spirit whatever you want to call it an entity and the reason you are here on earth in the physical is for you to learn and to experience what the physical sphere is like because as a being or spirit without ever existing in the physical you would have no idea of what it is to exist in the physical. I mean you

would have no idea of what limitations the physical and a physical body can impose on one. And not only that but you would have no idea of what existing in a physical sphere is like. And of all the things beings in the physical go through and must put up with, and deal with. First of all there is all the physical needs such as eating, sleeping, food, shelter, clothes, and these are just the very rudimentary needs because there are myriad more from love in all it's assortments, and then comes all the cupidity, wants, feelings, and other things we must deal with because we're in the physical such as jealousy, envy, hatred, staying physically healthy, and I haven't even mentioned all the cut-throatness, craftiness, lying, deception, manipulation, and just plain wickedness that we must deal with in the physical. And then last but not least we must deal with our own physical fleshy selves, which like I told you in thought #97 is nothing nice. And then not only that but in the physical sphere which is this 3rd dimension is where we are most tempted, and most susceptible to the negative forces and all there infinite tricks, lies, and deceptions. But you really can't be mad at them because there just doing what they do and that is trying to prove us unworthy at the time we transmigrate (die). And therefore have us barred from ascending to the higher dimensions and essentially try to claim us for themselves because as you already know once we transmigrate, leave this life and/or dimension comes what's known to you as the judgment meaning that everything you ever did, or thought, in this physical sphere will be clearly revealed and made known and you and you alone will be judged and graded on everything you did or didn't do, and all motives, hidden agendas, and thoughts without exception will be judged and graded. And the grade that you get will determine if you are allowed to pass and ascend to the higher dimensions and if you don't get a passing grade you're in danger of getting sent back down here to the 3rd dimension to try it again or maybe even worse if your grade is to low you might get sent somewhere else where it's real, real, hot as you would say if you know what I mean. And if you happen to get sent there where it's like you say real, real hot, also known to you as hell, which is the 1st and 2nd dimensions. And the first being the worst, then you are going to fully, completely, and undoubtly, understand the real and true meaning of hell.

Because the evil, wickedness, distress, agony, hurt, and pain, here in the 3rd dimension is held back to a good degree. But in the 1st and the 2nd dimensions also known as hell it is not held back at all. It's at full and uncut force, which means the evil, wickedness, distress, agony, hurt, and pain in the 1st and 2nd dimensions is completely uncomprehendable to the human mind in the 3rd dimension. And then once you're in the 1st or 2nd dimensions the evil, and wickedness, is to such a degree like I just said, that it's going to be almost or I should say totally impossible for you to even think and/or contemplate, positive, good, or Godly things because the evil, and wickedness, is going to totally, and completely consume you to a degree that your human mind right now cannot even being to comprehend or imagine. And then all the hell, hurt, and pain, that you felt here on earth you're going to wish that you could feel it a 100 times over, and/or worst, if you could only emancipate from the 1st or 2nd dimensions and come back to the 3rd dimension, which is here on earth but then it's going to be too late. And just so you know the flames, and fire in hell are only a metaphor there's none of that in hell only pure wickedness and evil that's it and that's all. That's why I've belabored you in this book on why it's so very pivotal for one to do what's right, be positive, have faith, believe in all that is, (God) conquer your physical fleshy self, get in tune with you real and true self and not be stuck in extrovertism. So that once you leave this physical sphere transmigrate you'll get a passing grade at judgment and therefore be able to continue your ascension to the higher dimensions which is really what it's all about. And you must remember that knowledge like this and the rest of the real, and true knowledge of life, nature, and the universe has been suppressed and hid away from the masses of people and in it's place has been put straight lies, misleads, and throw offs, such as for example religion which is one of the negative forces biggest lies to keep the people confused, thrown-off, mislead, and just completely hindered spiritually. But anyway I hope that you now know and understand that the real and true meaning of life is not categorized so much by how much wealth , recognition, status, or accumulation of material things one has attained, as it is by how one has acted either positively or negatively and how one conducted, his or her self under all of life's experiences, and how much learning and experience one gets in all areas, ways, and things, and on a last note: Just remember that just because a person was a positive, righteous, and maybe even in tune with his or her self doesn't necessarily mean that when they transmigrate there going to automatically be given a passing grade. Because if there lacking in learning or experiences in the physical there very much liable to get sent back down here to the 3rd dimension which is the physical sphere to try it again. And the same is true for people who have vast learning and experiences in the physical if they were not positive, righteous, and in tune with their self, they are very much liable of getting sent back down here to try it again to, or with people like these there even in great danger of getting sent somewhere else much worst. That is which as you already know where it's as you would say very hot. And just so you know it doesn't take money, wealthy, status, or great material possessions to be righteous, positive, in tune with yourself, and learn and just experience much in this physical realm known as life.

455. Always remember that once you really get in tune with yourself you'll also be in total balance and in total harmony with yourself, which is absolutely and undoubtedly one of the greatest feelings one can feel, and/or experience, in this material physical world which is the 3rd dimension.

456. Remember that humanity right now as a whole collectively that is, on this planet at this moment in time is experiencing a degree of utter frustration that is incredible indeed.

457. Well in this thought here I'm going to show you how those who clandestinely control the U.S. government surreptitiously control over 90% of America's radio stations. Well, it's like this and I don't know if you're aware of this or not, but there are 2 corporations which together own and control, over 90% of America's radio stations. And the first is Infinity Broadcasting, which is owned and controlled by the Rockefeller Interests through there media giant VIACOM of whom the CEO, there front man, Sumner Redstone, controls 71% of the company's voting shares. And by now you already know about the Rockefeller's which are very prominent members of those who

clandestinely control the U.S. government. And the other is Clear Channel Communications owned by one Lowry Mays, who is also a member of those who clandestinely control the U.S. government. And he's also a known personal friend and confidant of the Bush family. Now these 2 corporations together like I said own and control, over 90% of America's radio stations. Now if this is not a monopoly then I don't know what a monopoly is. But here is the catch . . . just like I told you previously in this book that myriad legislations is passed that the masses of people or the average person knows nothing about. Well these radio monopolies held by these 2 corporations are legal because of, and under the 1996 telecommunications act which lifted caps on radio station ownership. So now I hope you understand how those who clandestinely control the U.S. government also control your radio. And you know something?! Infinity Broadcasting and Clear Channel Communications aren't happy with their over 90% monopoly of America's radio stations but are aiming for and want a total and complete 100% monopoly of all of America's radio stations and are therefore relentlessly trying to pressure, bully, buy-up, swallow-up, or just shut down out of existence the last few remaining independent radio stations that they don't own and control, of which believe me there is not that many. So all I can say is that now that you pretty much understand and you pretty much know what's really and actually going on here in American and elsewhere. Don't you think something needs to be done before it's too late? And remember knowledge is power. Just like it was said by the rapper Nas: read more, learn more, and change the globe.

458. Always remember that just because of the fact that the nation may be at war, does not mean or impose on citizens a moral or legal obligation for them not to say what they feel, and want, and for them to just shut up, and support the government at any and all costs. Because remember as long as we got a constitution you got a first amendment right to freedom of speech, and all that bullshit that if you don't support a war and or the government you're being unpatriotic is straight bullshit and put out there for one reason, and for one reason only, and that's to manipulate you the people into supporting a war and/or the government. And it's just something that sounds good,

sounds real good. Also known as good talk, talking good, meaning slick. To say if one doesn't support a war and/or the government it's unpatriotic. Now that's nothing but straight manipulation. And if you're into or like being manipulated then keep believing it. Because remember you're an individual and have a God given right and luckily still a constitutional right to feel how you want to feel, and to like or dislike, or believe whatever you wish. And once you let somebody or something steal or manipulate that away from you then at that very second you cease to be an individual and have lost all individuality and are now a product or a thing instead of an individual or person, which is just what those who clandestinely control the U.S. government want, which is to make products out of the people and to have all the people act alike, be alike, and think alike, and anyone who exercises individualism will be looked at as unpatriotic, weird, eccentric, or just plain crazy or maybe even worse. But in short it's nothing but a systematic program implemented and put out there many years ago by the virtually unlimited omnifarious sources of those who clandestinely control the U.S. government. Simply put it's nothing but a system of brainwashing, and control, and of which system I've exposed a good part of throughout this book. So all I can say is be yourself, an individual in the truest, and fullest since of the word. And always stand up for what you believe . . . whatever it maybe.

459. In the organization of the civilization of the future we anticipate that the individualistically-oriented man will become an anachronism. Indeed, he will be viewed as a threat to the group organization as well as to his fellow man.

--Henry Kissinger

460. Now in this thought here you are going to learn the history and the real truth about the Federal Reserve. Yes, the Federal Reserve, the agency that controls all our money here in America. And that most Americans think is a federal agency but in reality it is a private entity. And the real reason that so many wars were fought. Wars like the American Revolution and the Civil War. Yes, these wars were not fought for all the

reasons that most people believe today. These wars had a covert agenda and that covert agenda was the enactment of a central bank in America. And the word conspiracy that will subsequently appear in this thought will refer to those who had surreptitious de-facto control of America at that time. Just like their successors still do right now today. So the thought goes as follows and please read this thought on the Federal Reserve very carefully because it's nothing but the unabridged, and immutable truth and I believe the masses of people should know the truth about the Federal Reserve and about those who clandestinely control the U.S. government and virtually the world. So it goes like this, after their successive failures at convincing the American people that they needed a central bank by forcing them into a series of wars the international bankers connected with and working for those who clandestinely controlled the U.S. government at the time decided to change their methods instead of utilizing wars for this purpose they would convince the unsuspecting American citizen that they needed a central bank through the use of artificially created depressions, recessions, and bank panics. It was easy for those who clandestinely controlled the U.S. government to create a banking panic because of the nature of the banking business; they knew that only a small percentage of the deposits stored in a bank by the depositors are ever called for on any given day. Because of this only a small percentage say twenty percent is kept at the bank at any one time. The other eighty is loaned out at interest to borrowers who in turn reinvest it in capital goods or consumption goods. So therefore it would be easy for those who clandestinely controlled the U.S. government at that time to cause a bank panic also called a run, convincing the depositors of any particular bank that the bank was insolvent and didn't have the money to pay the depositors should they withdraw their cash. This was of course a true statement, and if all of the depositors went to the bank at the same time to withdraw their deposits the individual who had made the statement would prove to be rather prophetic in his analysis of the situation. The news that a particular bank didn't have the deposits belonging to the depositors would cause other depositors at other banks to withdraw their funds as well to make certain that there deposits were safe. What would start as a bank run on a particular bank would end in a full-fledged national bank panic. And the individual or individuals who made the assessment of the banks insolvency would be recognized as prophets of the first order. The banks who would experience a run on their deposits would ask those to whom they loaned the money to return it and there would be a rush to sell properties to pay off the mortgages to the banks and when this happened all at once property values would drop allowing those with extra cash to buy properties at reduced prices. The preplanned panic could work two ways, the bankers who knew it was coming could withdraw their cash prior to the beginning of the panic and then go back into the market to buy capital goods at a reduced price. This became then a powerful tool in the hands of those who clandestinely controlled the U.S. government and wished to change our banking system from one where individual bankers functioned to one where a small group of bankers operated a national bank. The bankers who were connected to those who clandestinely controlled the U.S. government would then blame the current banking system for the troubles in the economy and influence other bankers to do the same. But more importantly those who clandestinely controlled the U.S. government had caused the problem in the first place could offer their desired solution a central bank. So the tactic changed from one of creating wars to one of creating bank panics to influence the American people into the creation of a permanent central bank. One of the prime movers in this movement was J.P. Morgan, one of the individuals who clandestinely controlled the U.S. government at the time. And whose father was a Rothchild agent during the Civil War. But anyway in 1869 J. P. Morgan went to London and reached an agreement to form a company known as Northern Securities that was intended to act as an agent for the N.M. Rothchild Company in the United States. The first major bank panic created by those who clandestinely controlled the U.S. government occurred in 1893 when local bankers around the nation were told to call in their loans. Senator Robert Owen testified before a Congressional Committee that the bank he owned received from the national Bankers Association what came to be known as the panic circular of 1893. It stated: You will at once retire one-third of your circulation and call in one-half of your loans. Congressman Charles A. Lindberg the father of the famous aviator saw the circular that Senator Owen reported on and said that it was intended to cause a stringency a tightness of money and to cause businessmen to appeal to Congress for legislation that would favor enactment of a central bank. Those who clandestinely controlled the U.S. government didn't create the bank panic by advising the American people that the banks were insolvent. They had a circular issued to have the bankers themselves do it because they would hold the former strategy for later panics. This tactic of course is exactly the same as that explained by Jan Kocoak in his book (Not a Shot Is Fired) create the problem and then encourage the people affected to ask Congress for laws favorable to those who created the problem. It was now 1900 and the administration of President William McKinley was prosecuting the Northern Securities Company under the anti-trust laws McKinley changed his Vice President for his 2nd term and less than a year later he was assassinated. His 2nd Vice President Theodore Roosevelt became President and the prosecution of Northern Securities stopped. Roosevelt was later elected in his own right in 1904. Another agent of the British Rothchild banking empire Colonel Edward Mandell House wrote an extremely important book in 1912 it was entitled (Philip Dru Administrator) and contained the personal beliefs of the author in the form of a fiction novel. And the book was written in 1912 and only if the people then would have known how real and true the book was anyhow the plot concerned a meeting in 1925 between John Thor described as the high priest of finance and Senator Selwyn a very prominent Senator. Selwyn had discovered that the U.S. government was secretly run by a few men from behind the scenes and that outside of that circle no one really matter or was of much importance it was Selwyn's intention to break into it if possible and his ambition now leaned so far as to want not only to be part of it but to run and control it. Senator Selwyn was not content with just electing the President of the United States; he also planned to bring under his control the whole world as we know it. It was a fascinating game to Selwyn. He wanted to govern the whole world with an absolute hand and yet not be known as the dictating power. The nation came to know of this conspiracy between these two important individuals by a fluke when Mr. Thor's Secretary played back a tape recording made on a dictograph that had been inadvertently turned on during the meeting. The secretary then gave the recording to the Associated Press which spread the story of the conspiracy across the nation. America read the story and could not believe it and would not believe it. But anyway, after publication of the novel it became known that Colonel House admitted that the book formulated his ethical and political beliefs. And every act in his real life career, every letter, every word of advice that passed from him to President Woodrow Wilson was consistent with the ideas in the book Philip Dru Administrator. Colonel House had very close relations and ties with those who clandestinely controlled the U.S. government and who had put President Woodrow Wilson in power. As a matter of fact President Wilson was the student of Colonel House and as he began to learn the thoughts of his mentor he became so close that Wilson once said that House's thoughts and mine are one. And President Wilson was a very confusing person a sort of enigma in the events of that day. He admitted that there was a group of people who clandestinely controlled the U.S. government from behind the scenes. But yet he was involved with it. He wrote: There is a power somewhere so organized, so subtle, so watchful, so interlocked, so complete, so pervasive that they better not speak above their breath when they speak in condemnation of it. Mr. Wilson never identified the people who make up this power he had become aware of. But Colonel Edward Mandell House was an extremely important person during the Wilson years as he once told biographer Charles Seymour: During the last 15 years I have been close to the center of things although few people ever suspected it. No important foreigner has come to America without talking to me. I was close to the movement and/or power that made Roosevelt president. So not only did House control Woodrow Wilson he was also involved in making Franklin Roosevelt President of the United States. So House was a part of the secret power that was behind both Wilson and Roosevelt, exactly like his fictional character Senator Selwyn had hoped to become. And you must also remember that people only write about what they know. But anyway, like I said, another agent of the Rothchild interests was J.P. Morgan who was preparing for the next scheduled event in the creation of America's central bank. Morgan during the early months of 1907 was in Europe for 5 ½ months shuttling back and forth between London and Paris, homes of two branches of the Rothchild banking family. Apparently the reason J.P. Morgan was in Europe was because the decision was being made to have Morgan precipitate a bank panic in America. When he returned he started rumors that the Knickerbocker Bank in New York was insolvent. The banks depositors became frightened because they thought that Morgan being one of the best known bankers of the day might very well be right. There panic started a run on the bank. Morgan was right and the panic at the Knickerbocker Bank also caused runs on other banks, and the panic of 1907 was complete. The propaganda that J.P. Morgan and others spread almost immediately after the panic stated that the State Charted Banks couldn't be trusted anymore with the banking affairs of the nation. The need for a central bank had become apparent by the bank panic of 1907 or at least this is how the bankers connected with those who clandestinely controlled the U.S. government argued. Historian Frederick Lewis Allen writing in life magazine became aware of the plot. He wrote: Certain chroniclers have arrived at the ingenious conclusion that the Morgan interests took advantage of the unsettled conditions during the autumn of 1907 to precipitate the panic guiding it shrewdly as it progressed so that it would kill off rival banks and consolidate the pre-eminence of the banks with in the Morgan orbit. Woodrow Wilson was President of Princeton University in 1907 when he spoke to the American people attempting to remove whatever blame might be placed upon the Morgan shoulders. He said: All this trouble could be averted if we appointed a committee of 6 or 7 public spirited men like J.P. Morgan to handle the affairs of our country. So Wilson wanted to hand over the banking affairs of the nation to the very person who had caused all of the trouble, J.P. Morgan! But the main thrust of the explanations about the causes of the 1907 bank panic was that the American people needed a strong central bank to prevent the abuses of the Wall Street Bankers. But what finally convinced the American people of the need for better control over the nation's banking was the one stark event. The bank panic of 1907. The panic subsided and public agitation grew for an effective national banking system. So the American people who had suffered through the American Revolution, the War of 1812, the battles between Andrew

Jackson and the bank of the United States, the Civil War, the previous bank panics of 1873, and 1893, and now the bank panic of 1907 were finally conditioned to the point of accepting the solution offered by those who clandestinely controlled the U.S. government who had caused all of these events to happen. And there solution was a central bank so they could monopolize all the money in America. And look at this but keep in mind that John D. Rockefeller was one of those who clandestinely controlled the U.S. government at the time. But the individual that those who clandestinely controlled the U.S. government used to introduce the legislation that created the central bank better known today as the Federal Reserve was a senator from Rhode Island, a mason, and the maternal grandfather of the Rockefeller Brothers, David, Laurence, Winthorp, Nelson, and John D. the 3rd. By the name of Nelson Aldrich he was and is the maternal grandfather of the Rockefeller Brothers. But anyway, he was appointed as chairman of a National Monetary Commission and charged to make a thorough study of financial practices before formulating banking and currency reform legislation. So for 2 years this Commission toured the banking houses of Europe. Supposedly learning the secrets of the central banking systems of Europe. But as we all know they already knew the banking secrets of the central banking systems of Europe. Upon Aldrich's return in November 1910 he boarded a train in Hoboken New Jersey for a ride to Jerkyll Island Georgia. His destination was the Jerkyll Island Hunt Country Club owned by J.P. Morgan. It was there that the legislation that would give America its central bank or better known today as the Federal Reserve was written. And aboard the train with Senator Aldrich and headed for the Jerkyll Island Hunt country Club were the following individuals: A. Piatt Andrew, Assistant Secretary of the Treasury; frank Vanderlip, President of the Rockefeller's national City Bank of new York; Henry Davidson senior partner of J.P. Morgan; Charles Norton, President of J.P. Morgan's First National Bank of New York; the legendary Paul Warburg of the Banking House of Kuhn and Loebs; and Benjamin Strong, President of J.P. Morgan's Banker's Trust Company; Now check this out one of those Mr. Frank Vanderlip later went on to reveal his role in the writing of the bill that created the Federal Reserve system, he wrote in the

Saturday Evening Post: In 1910 when I was as secretive indeed as furtive as any conspirator I do not feel it is any exaggeration to speak of our secret expedition to Jerkyll Island as the occasion of the actual conception of what eventually became the Federal Reserve system we were told to leave our last names behind us. We were told further that we should avoid dining together on the night of our departure. We were instructed to come one at a time and as unobtrusively as possible to the terminal of the New Jersey Littoral of the Hudson where Senator Aldrich's private car would be in readiness attached to the rear end of the train for the south. Once aboard the private car we began to observe the taboo that had been fixed on last names. Discovery we knew simply must not happen or else all our time and effort would be wasted.

Notice that those who clandestinely controlled the U.S. government did not want the American people to know what they had in store for them. A central bank. The legislation was written not by a group of legislators but by a group of bankers that were all connected to those who clandestinely controlled the U.S. government. And they also had one additional problem . . . they had to avoid the name central bank and for that reason they came up with the designation of Federal Reserve system it would be privately owned by them of course. And they would draw profit from the ownership of the shares and they would control the entire nation's issuance of money. Now that's power, and now look at this, the method those who clandestinely controlled the U.S. government used to defraud the American people was to divide the Federal Reserve system into 12 districts so that the American people could not call the bank a central bank. The fact that the 12 districts have one director called a Federal Reserve chairman apparently was not to be considered relevant. And the only non-banker at Jerkyll Island was Senator Nelson Aldrich but he certainly could have qualified as a wealthy man capable of staring his own bank when he entered the senate in 1881 he was worth $50,000. When he left the Senate in 1911 he was worth $30,000,000. Now let's see what the American people got from the Federal Reserve System. Well the system itself published a paperback textbook entitled (The Federal Reserve System, Purposes and Functions) that is used in colleges to explain the activities of the system to college students, especially in a class entitled money and banking. This booklet explains the functions of the Federal Reserve: An efficient monetary mechanism is indispensible to the nation the function of the Federal Reserve is to foster a flow of money and credit that will facilitate orderly economic growth, a stable dollar, and a long run balance in our international payments. Now isn't it a fair question to ask the Federal Reserve System why us in America haven't had orderly economic growth, a stable dollar and a long run balance in our international payments which has been the Federal Reserves so called aim since it's creation and why is it allowed to continue? Now it would seem to me or any other rational thinking human being that a system with such a dismal record for about 100 years would have been abolished a long time ago without delay. But now could it be that the system was really created to ensure that America didn't have orderly economic growth, a stable dollar, and a long run balance in our international payments? In other words the system was created to do exactly the opposite of what it tells the American people. SO the system is working, working for those who created it. There were those who opposed the creation of the system at the time and made that opposition public. One such individual was Congressman Charles Lindbergh Sr. Congressman Lindbergh warned the American people that the Federal Reserve act . . . established the most gigantic trust on earth. When the President signs this act the invisible government by the money power will be legitimized. The new law will create inflation whenever the trust wants inflation. From now on depressions will be scientifically crated. The wise old Congressman had put his finger on exactly what was about the happen. And had figured out that the Federal Reserve was created by those and for those who clandestinely controlled the U.S> government. But anyway the staffing of the systems key positions with those who created and supported it followed. The first Governor of the New York Federal Reserve branch was Benjamin Strong of J.P. Morgans Bankers Trust & Company and a participant in the Jerkyll Island writing of the bill. The first Governor of the board of directors was the legendary Paul Warburg of the Banking House of Kuhn-Loeb and Company also a participant at Jerkyll Island. What had those who called the system federal created? Was it really federal? No! It is private and when I say private I mean it's totally private. It's a private corporation and not a government entity as the masses of people have been lead to believe. Since the 12 member banks own all of the stock on which they receive tax-free dividends. And it must pay postage like any other private corporation. It's employees are not government employees. And it's physical property held under private deeds is subjected to local taxation. As a matter of fact America' elected officials know that the Federal Reserve System isn't federal at all. In speeches to the American people former Presidents Richard Nixon, Gerald Ford, and Jimmy Carter have stated to the Associated Press in a primer on the system that the system is independent. And not directly controlled by the U.S. government. Now what does that tell you??? Now other Congressmen more recent than Congressman Lindberg have also warned the American people about the dangers of the non-federal Federal Reserve System. Congressman Wright Patman, the chairman of the House Banking and Currency Committee said:

In the United States today we have in effect 2 governments. We have the duly constituted government, and then we have an independent uncontrolled and unconstitutional government in the Federal Reserve System operating the money powers which are reserved to congress by the constitution.

But anyway the privately owned Federal Reserve System is in complete control of the money supply in these United States. And has the ability to create inflation and deflation at will. So remember that those who clandestinely control the U.S. government and that own the Federal Reserve have the power to create inflation and deflation at will. The money supply per capita in 1913 when the reserve system was created was about 1.48$. By 1978 it stood at 3.69$. The value of the 1913 dollar taken as a base of 1.00$ had shrunk to approximately 12 cents by 1978 and is probably lower then that by now. But I guess this is what the Federal Reserve calls a stable dollar. The quality of money in January 1968 stood at 351 billion and in February 1980 it was 976 billion a 278 percent increase. In fact the quality of money doubles approximately every 10 years. But strangely this increase in money supply or so the American people are told does not cause inflation. Even though the dictionary definition of inflation states that an increase in the money supply always causes inflation. And check this out the Federal Reserve has admitted that the ability to cause inflation and deflation rest with their agency. So in other words the ultimate capability for expanding or reducing the economy's supply of money rests with the Federal Reserve. And anyway not all of the banks in American however were interested in the creation of the Federal Reserve some were concerned about their membership in the system and were withdrawing. And in fact William Miller a former chairman of the Federal Reserve in 1978 warned that the flight of the member banks out of the system was weakening the financial system of the United States. A total of 430 memberships had left the Federal Reserve in an 8 year span including 15 major banks in 1977 with deposits of more than 10 billion and another 39 banks left in 1978. As a result of this attrition twenty five percent of all commercial bank deposits and sixty percent of all banks were now outside of the system. Miller continued: The ability of the system to influence the nation's money and credit became weaker. The trend away from the Federal Reserve system continued and in December 1979 then Federal Reserve chairman Paul Volcker informed the House Banking Committee that some 300 banks with deposits of 18.4 billion have quit the Federal Reserve system within the past 4 ½ years. And he said another 745 of the remaining 5,480 member banks with deposits of more than 70 billion have given us some indications of their intent the withdraw. And in February 1980 it was reported that in the last 4 month 69 banks had withdrawn from the Federal Reserve System taking with them 7 billion dollars in deposits. Another 670 banks holding 71 billion in deposits have expressed a desire to leave the system. So now with their Federal Reserve, well, so called Federal Reserve, because you now know that there is nothing federal about it. But anyway with their Federal Reserve System now in serious jeopardy those who clandestinely control the U.S. government got congress to pass the monetary control act which gave the Federal Reserve System control of all depository institutions whether or not the banks were previously members of the system itself. (Now that's cold) But anyway, in addition to the

Federal Reserve's ability to create interest bearing debt the system also has the ability to create economic cycles through the expansion and contraction of the quantity of money and credit. There first major opportunity to create a depression by this method occurred in 1920 when the Federal Reserve created what has become known as the panic of 1920 one of those who say how this was the result of prior economic planning was Congressman Lindberg who in 1921 wrote in his book (economic pinch) the following: Under the Federal Reserve act panics are scientifically created the present panic is the first scientifically created one worked out as we figure a mathematical problem. The process works in the following manner. The system increased the money supply from 1914 to 1919 the quantity of money in the United States nearly doubled then the media which is controlled by the same people encourages the masses of people to borrow large quantities of money on credit, and once the current amount of money that they desire to be out on loan is out on loan the Federal Reserve has the banks contract the money supply by calling in their outstanding loans. The entire process was laid out by Senator Robert L. Owen a former chairman of the senate banking and currency committee and a banker himself he wrote: in the early part of 1920 the farmers were exceedingly prosperous. They were paying off their mortgages and buying a lot of land at the insistence of the government they had borrowed money to do it and then they were bankrupted by a sudden contraction of credit which took place in 1920 what took place in 1920 was just the reverse of what should have been taking place. Instead of liquidating the excess of credits created by the war through a period of years the Federal Reserve board met in a meeting which was not disclosed to the public. They met on the 16th of May 1920 and it was a secret meeting. Only the big bankers were there and the work of that day resulted in contraction of credit by ordering banks to call in outstanding loans which had the effect the next year of reducing the national income by 15 billion dollars, throwing millions of people out of employment and reducing the value of lands and ranches by 20 billion dollars. Not only did those who clandestinely control the U.S. government transfer large quantities of land from the famers to themselves by this contraction but the process also transferred large numbers of banks from the hands of those bankers who could not meet the demands of the Federal Reserve and had to sell their banking assets for a reduced price to those who had the money to buy bankrupt banks the panic of 1920 bankrupted 5,400 banks. And one of the major non-banking targets of this panic was Henry Ford Sr., the automobiles manufacturer. But despite inflation Henry Ford ordered a price cut for his automobiles but demand was still insufficient and a number of ford plants had to be shut down. Rumor had it that a huge loan was being negotiated. But Ford who thought New York bankers were nothing short of vultures was determined not to fall into their hands. Bankers lined up to offer their help in return for his surrender of his company. One representative of a J.P. Morgan owned and controlled bank in New York came forward with a plan to save Ford but Ford declined. Ford saved his own company by turning to his dealers to whom he now shipped his cars on consignment in spite of the slowness of the market. And demand eventually grew and the Ford plants that had to be shut down re-opened. So Ford had out smarted those who clandestinely controlled the U.S. government who had planned the panic in part to destroy him. He did not need to borrow large quantities of money and surrender control of his company to those who clandestinely controlled the U.S. government who would certainly wish to control that which they subsidized. But anyway the panic of 1920 was a success and this success lead to those who clandestinely controlled the U.S. government to plan another . . . the stock market crash of 1929. The first step was once again to increase the money supply and this was done from 1921 to 1929. The Federal Reserve expanded the money supply from a low of 31.7 billion in 1921 to a high of 45.7 billion in 1929 an increase of approximately 144 percent. To move this increase in the money supply into the economy from the Federal Reserve and reloan it to the buying public. The money was borrowed at 5% interest and reloaned at 12%. And contributing to the increase in the money supply or the money being made available by the Federal Reserve was money being made available by the large corporations that were owned or controlled by those who clandestinely controlled the U.S. government they were loaning there surplus funds to buyers on wall street. And these loans from these un-banking sources were approximately equal to those from the banking system. For instance look at the total loans to Wall Street brokers in 1929 made by some corporations were as follows. (American and foreign power total amount loaned 30,321,000$ J.P. Morgan owned) (Standard Oil of New Jersey total amount loaned 97,824,000$ Rockefeller owned) in addition J.P. Morgan and company had another $110,000,000 in the call-loan market. This expansion in the money supply brought prosperity to the country and the American people were encouraged by the media to buy into the stock market. They were told that those who did were making large quantities of money. The stock brokers who were handling the influx of buyers coming to make a fortune in the stock market were using a new tool to induce them into buying more shares of stock than they had anticipated. This new tool was called buying on margin and it enabled the stock buyers to borrow money and use it to buy stock. The buyer was encouraged to buy stock with only 10% down borrowing the remaining 90% from the stock broker who had arranged for the buyer to borrow from either a bank or one of the corporations. The following will show you how this method worked. A share of stock sells for 100$ a purchaser could borrow 900$ using the stock as collateral for the loan and therefore buy 10 shares for the same investment of 100$. Now for this example presume that one share of stock went up 10% in the stock market or to 110$. This would increase the profits made by the stock buyer. The investor could now sell the shares of stock and make a 100% profit with only a 10% increase in his stocks value the buyer could double his investment after paying off the loan to the lender. There was one catch however as the money was loaned to the buyer on what was called a 24-hour broker call loan. This meant that the broker could exercise his option and require that the borrower sell his stock and return the loan amount 24-hours after the lender had asked for it. The buyer had 24-hours to repay the loan and had to either sell the stock or come up with the loan amount to pay off the lender of the money. This meant that whenever the brokers wanted to they could require all of the stock buyers to sell at the same time by calling in all of the loans at the same time. This activity would precipitate a panic on the stock market. When all of the stock owners went to sell their stock at the same time the price drops rapidly. The whole process was detailed by one author who wrote: When everything was ready the New York financiers started calling 24-hour broker call loans. This meant that the stock brokers and the customers had to dump their stock on the market in order to pay the loans. This naturally collapsed the stock market and brought a banking collapse all over the country because the banks not owned by the oligarchy were heavily involved in broker call loans at this time and bank runs soon exhausted their coin and currency and they had to close. The Federal Reserve system would not come to their aid although they were instructed under law to maintain an elastic currency.

The Federal Reserve would not come to their aid even though they were required by law to do so and many banks and individuals went bankrupt. Notice that those banks owned by the oligarchy had already gotten out and therefore missed any damage whatsoever and those who didn't went bankrupt. So after the stock market crash of 1929 even a casual observer had to notice that the ownership of the banking system had changed. In fact today 20 out of 15,000 banks less than 1% control 75% of the nation's banking assets. But anyway the stock market crashes and the masses of people did not have the slightest idea why. And check this out one of the spectators of the stock market crash was Sir Winston Churchill who was brought to the stock market on October 24, 1929 by Bernard Baruch who was one of the one's who clandestinely controlled the U.S. government at that time. And some sage historians have put it together and are convinced that Churchill was brought to witness the crash first hand because it was desired that he see the power of those who clandestinely controlled the U.S. government first hand. And even though many stockholders had to sell their stock it is not commonly said or asked who was buying all of the stock being sold. The history books generally discuss all of the selling of stocks and bonds that went on during the crash but fail to discuss who was doing all of the buying. But we already know why that is. That's because those who clandestinely control the U.S. government control all the outlets of information, i.e. media, public school system, public libraries, etc. etc. And therefore all information in those entities is censured because they are not going to expose themselves in any kind of way. Because there agents were the one's doing all the buying. John

Kenneth Galbraith in his book (the Great Crash of 1929) said this: Nothing could have been more ingeniously designed to maximize the suffering and also insure that as few as possible escaped the common misfortune the fortunate speculator who had funds to answer the first margin call presently got another and equally urgent one and if he met that there would still be another and another, in the end all the money he had was extracted from him and lost.

And some of the stockholders went to their banks to withdraw whatever cash they had in the bank to pay whatever they could of their stock call in cash. This caused a nearly nationwide bank run. To end this panic President Franklin D. Roosevelt 2 days after his inauguration in March of 1933 shut down all the banks for a holiday. There weren't many who saw what was happening to the American people by these machinations of those who clandestinely controlled the U.S. government. But one who did was Congressman Louis McFadden who was quoted as saying:

When the Federal Reserve act was passed the people of these United States did not perceive that a world banking system was being set up here. A super State controlled by a secret government and international industrialists acting together to enslave the world for their own pleasure. Every effort has been made by the Federal Reserve to conceal it's powers but the truth is the Federal Reserve has usurped the U.S. government. It controls everything here and it controls all our foreign relations. It can make and break governments at will.

After the stock market crash had run it's course Congressman McFadden charged that: "The money credit resources of the Unite States were now in the complete control of the bankers alliance between J.P. Morgan's first National Bank Group and the Rockefeller's National City Bank." On May 23, 1933 McFadden brought impeachment charges against the Federal Reserve Board, the agency he thought had caused the stock market crash of 1929 with these charges amongst others he is quoted as saying:

I charge them with having taken over 80 billion dollars from the United States government in the year 1929. I charge them with having arbitrarily and unlawfully raised and lowered the rates on money increased and diminished the volume of currency in circulation for the benefit of private interests. I charge them with having conspired to transfer to foreigners and international money lenders title to and control of the financial resources of the United States. It was a carefully contrived occurrence the secret government and the international bankers sought to be about a condition of despair here so that they might emerge as the rulers of us all . . .

And don't think that Congressman McFadden didn't have a price to pay for his attempts to expose those who clandestinely controlled the U.S. government and explain the causes of the stock market crash. On 2 occasions assassins attempted to kill McFadden with gunfire but he escaped each time virtually unharmed. But they eventually got him because a few hours after attending a banquet he dropped dead and it was later found out that he was poisoned. But anyway now that the stock market had crashed the Federal Reserve took steps to reduce the nation's quantity of money. The quantity of money went from a high of nearly 46 billion in June of 1929 to a low of 30 billion in June of 1933 just 4 years. This action of the Federal Reserve rippled throughout the entire business world to the point where production at the county's factories, mines, and utilities fell by more than 31 1/2. The total output of goods and services dropped by one-third. And check this out in spite of all of the cumulative evidence to the contrary there are still those who don't know who or what caused the stock market crash of 1929. One of these is economist John Kenneth Galbraith, who in his book (The Great Crash of 1929) wrote that: the causes of the great depression are still far from known or certain. In fact Galbraith knows that people did not cause the crash and the resulting depression he is quoted as saying:

No one was responsible for the great Wall Street crash. No one engineered the speculation that preceded it. Hundreds of thousands of individuals were not led to the slaughter. There were impelled by the lunacy which has always seized people who are seized in turn with the notion that they can become very rich. There were many Wall Streeters who helped foster this insanity. But there was none who caused it.

And then you know the surreptitiously controlled media had to do their job, they now entered the fray by proclaiming that the free enterprise system had failed and that government was needed to solve the economic problems caused by the lack of wisdom inherent in the system. The solution was of course new government measures and controls. And you guessed it; the powers of the Federal Reserve were enhanced and strengthened. But anyway, more recently a Congressman attempted to investigate the Federal Reserve, Congressman Wright Patman introduced a bill which would have authorized a full and independent audit of the system by the general accounting office. Patman claimed that the audit was essential to give the public's elected representatives complete and accurate information on the internal operations of the system since they had never been audited since their inception in 1913. But Congressman Patman wasn't aware of the fact that there are people who clandestinely control the U.S. government from behind the scenes. He wrote: Although I had anticipated that officials of the Federal Reserve System would vigorously oppose my bill I am frankly amazed by the massive lobbying campaign now underway to prevent enactment of this measure. But Congressman Patman did score a small victory however. Congress passed his bill but attached an amendment that will limit the audit to administrative expenditures "only." Meaning the expense accounts of the executives of the system the numbers of pens and pencils purchased per employee, etc., hardly what Patman had in mind. And then look at what happen to Congressman Patman he was removed from his chairmanship as chairman of the house banking finance committee. And we all know by whom by those who clandestinely control the U.S. government because Congressman Patman was a thorn in their side and they always have and always will, get rid of meaning eradicate all problems, thorns, and anything else to that effect. So now you know the truth about the Federal Reserve. And check this out, there have been myriad books written about the truth about the Federal Reserve. And a good book to check out on this is: the Creature

From Jerkyll Island by G. Edward Griffin. And also in this great book is how those who clandestinely control the U.S. government created the World Bank and the international monetary fund for the sole purpose of keeping the 3rd world nations in poverty through the guise of helping them. That whole story is in the chapter called: Nearer To the Heart's Desire. And you'll see and learn in meticulous detail how those who clandestinely control the U.S. government through their world bank, and international monetary fund, and other international bodies, not only keep the 3rd world nations in a state of perpetual poverty through highly sophisticated trickery. But finance famine and genocide in those nations. And there's been no shortage of whole books written on this particular topic such as: Lords of Poverty, the Power, Prestige, and Corruption of the International Aid Business, by Graham Hancock; and more recently in 2004, Confessions of An Economic Hitman, by John Perkins.

461. Always remember that the central intelligence agency (CIA) and the federal Bureau of investigation (FBI) and myriad other government agencies and institutions that are supposed to be for the security and service of the public are nothing but the black hands of those who clandestinely control the U.S. government. But don't start thinking that everybody who works for these agencies or is involved with these agencies is corrupt, sinister, or evil. Because they're not, it's only some but the some are running and controlling these agencies just like Oliver North said when he was testifying in 1989 that there's a secret (FBI) with in the (FBI) you better believe it there was then, and there still is right now today a secret (FBI) with in the (FBI) just like there a secret CIA within the CIA. And that's how it works.

462. Always remember that to really be smart and intelligent means to be able to use your mind and your creative imagination to see endless options, and opportunities. In everything and anything because you best believe me the options and opportunities are there it's just do you have the ability to see them or not.

463. Always remember that some people are naturally suited and inclined to higher learning, self betterment, and the

endeavorment to perfection then others may be. And that is because they possess the virtue of motivation, the patience of effort, and the vision to see pass their front gate.

464. Always remember that the science of life is the supreme science of all sciences. And the art of living meaningfully the finest of all the arts.

465. Always remember that everything in the material physical world and this is without exception is subject and susceptible to corruption.

466. Always remember that by you taking the time to read this book and to really understand it, and comprehend it you are now consciously beginning the task of liberating yourself from the bondage of ignorance, and lies. Because whether you know it or not you have been lied to all your life by the media, the press, the T.V., magazines, the public school system, the public libraries, and by many other outlets and sources of information in mainstream society. And you know what the cold thing is? The cold things is that these sources and outlets of information might not even be conscious or aware of the fact that they have been and are putting out disinformation, misleads, and sometimes straight lies. Because you know how it goes everything is controlled from the top and only those at the top the very top that is know what's really going on and the rest of the personnel, hierarchy, or chain of command knows little or nothing of what's really being done or going on.

467. Do you know what's wrong with the modern educational system in America today? The universities, and public schools they're not only surreptitiously controlled teach the curriculums, and program people to believe and think as those who clandestinely control the U.S. government want, but they do not teach people real truth or real knowledge like the true knowledge of life, nature, and the universe. I mean they teach people worldly or secular knowledge but they do not teach universal knowledge or the real knowledge of self and the real knowledge of self is the greatest knowledge of all because anything and everything that you would ever want to know is in you, and starts with you. You just must learn how to unlock

this infinite knowledge. And that the modern education system and universities and public schools do not teach and I'll say it again they do not teach that in no kind of way. See the knowledge of self is hidden and recondite knowledge. It's the knowledge that the modern educational system of learning knows little if anything about. And that's where they go wrong at. But you also must understand that the modern educational system has unspoken rules that it goes by and one of those unspoken rules is that they don't teach or like to teach nothing that they cannot back up by their own facts or evidence. And so being that the knowledge of self cannot be fully backed up 100% by their tangible facts and evidence so they don't like, or should I say they don't know how to teach people about it. But all the tangible and worldly evidence is there always has been and always will be. What do you think telepathy, déjà vu, intuition, clairvoyance, remote viewing, and telekinesis is and every single one of us and this is without exception has experienced at least one of these as they would say phenomenons. And at the time chances are you probably didn't know what you were experiencing. And therefore didn't know how to define it. But what you were experiencing was the indefinite power of you. It's all in there, anything and everything that you would ever want to know you just have to know how to unlock this infinite and unlimited knowledge and power that each and every one of us human being has at our own personal disposal. What do you think real self mastery and genius is?! That's when one has learned how to unlock and tune into this infinite and unlimited knowledge and power, and use it at will. That's when one has really reached the state of real self mastery and/or genius. And how to unlock and use this knowledge and your real innate powers is what the modern educational system of learning does not teach or I should say does not know how to teach. Because remember the more stuff they put into your conscious mind like teaching you economics, history, philosophy, business, liberal arts, whatever, this is all good of course. It's all good to learn these subjects. But you must remember the more they put things into your conscious mind the further you can get away from your real self which is your infinite knowledge and innate powers if you're not careful. Has this happened to you? But that's what modern education does, they fill your conscious mind with all kinds of plausible practical knowledge and leave your infinite innate powers virtually undeveloped. And that's sad, very sad! But it's true, and that's because like I said modern education and learning has really no knowledge of this infinite and unlimited power within you. So therefore they can't teach what they don't know. So stop just filling and developing your conscious mind and start learning how to unlock and develop you're innately given infinite power. Because just think if you had never developed your conscious mind you would not know how to read or write, right now. So start to get in tune with yourself, and therefore, start to unlock and develop your mind which is your God given infinite power source. And if you would like to learn about the true knowledge of life, nature, and the universe and have the secrets of the ages disclosed to you. Then you must get the book: The Secret teachings of All Ages, by Mannly P. Hall.

468. Always remember to always, but always, keep your mind ever expanding because once you stop expanding your mind right then and there, at that very moment is when you stop learning and growing. Because remember you can never ever know it all because the universe is much to vast, it's so infinitely vast that you can never know it all in 30, 40, or 50 lifetimes with all the knowledge that you gained each lifetime running successively. So remember keep you mind ever expanding because the universe and everything in it moves forward and so should your mind.

469. Always remember that time spent to yourself and by yourself in total seclusion and solitude is precious, priceless, and damn near without equal. Because it's the only way for one to be able to get in tune with his or herself. And therefore be able to tap into his or her infinite power. And it's nothing but an exercise because the more you do it the better you'll get at it. And then after so long of doing it eventually you will be able to tap or use your infinite power at will and then you will be on the level of what's called or known as genius. Because meditation has been used since the beginning of time it was used by the ancient Egyptians who built the pyramids and were alchemists and they were the ones who said that the last part of the super secret, alchemical formula was within oneself. And you know

something??? They had it right, because like I've said before everything and anything that you would like to know is within you. One just has to know how to have access to it. And the ancient Egyptians, if you know anything about Egyptology, were transcending in knowledge wisdom, and understanding and they attainted that by being in tune with themselves. And once in tune with themselves they had all access to their infinite power. And they were known to have some astonishing, incomprehensible, and inconceivable knowledge. They had knowledge of self, life, and the universe that is still not known to modern learning or education today. Like I said the ancient Egyptians and not all of them . . . I don't want you to get it wrong, and to think that it was the whole ancient Egyptian population. Because that what it wasn't, it was only the learned Egyptians. The ones known or called adepts. They were the ones transcending in all knowledge and were even alchemist. And alchemy is the practice of turning base and regular metals into pure gold. And alchemy is also the science of creating an elixir, a substance that if taken orally will cure all human ailments without exception and if you keep taking the elixir it will keep you from aging and prolong your life considerably. And check this out . . . alchemy is one of the oldest sciences known to man it dates back into the obscurity of prehistoric times and modern learning and education knows little if anything about alchemy. And they damn sure don't know the super secret alchemical formula. So therefore, they modern learning and educational calls alchemy, a speculative art or science. But believe me there's nothing speculative about alchemy. It's real, very real and the learned ancient Egyptians had figured out the super secret formula to alchemy. And you can to because half of the formula to alchemy is in you. Because the knowledge that lies in you is so inconceivable to your conscious mind that you cannot even begin to conceive with the conscious mind the knowledge and power that's available to you though your mind, and thoughts. I mean intuition, telekinesis, clairvoyance, déjà vu, and the formula to alchemy are but the tip and I say again the very tip of the iceberg of knowledge that is available to you through your infinite innate power. And the only way for one to gain access to his or her innate power is for one to be in tune with his or her self and the only way for one to get in tune with his or her self is through meditation . . . positive focused concentrated thought, positivity, and faith. Always remember that once you get in tune with yourself you'll not only have access to you your infinite power but you superconscious which is your soul will be in contact with all that is (GOD) and God knows exactly who you are by your individual soul frequency which is yours and yours along because no 2 human beings or entities in the universe have the same individual soul frequency. So if you have ever wondered how God knows who you are when you pray well that's how. That's why when you pray your suppose to pray with faith, and emotion, and positive emotion that is. Because when God picks up on you individual soul frequency He knows exactly what you're thinking and feeling and if you're thinking or feeling any deception and or thinking or feeling you are a victim that is negativity your soul frequency will lose contact with all that is (God). So like I said once you get in tune with yourself you'll not only have access to your infinite power, but your super conscious which is your soul will be in contact with (God) and therefore you will feel a peace that surpasses all human understanding. And whether you believe it or not you will be in actual contact with the Supreme Master, all that is (GOD) because God talks to you through your super conscious, your soul, and your soul relates to your subconscious, and your subconscious then relates to your conscious. It's nothing but a chain of command. So if a person is not in tune with theirself then they will most likely not hear God when he talks to them. So people please get in tune with yourselves. And the only way to get in tune with yourself is through meditation, positive focused concentrated thought and faith.

470. Always remember that everything and anything that you want is within you. And this is without exception you just must call it into material physical existence through thought projection just like I've said previously you are a creator and you are no more than what you create for yourself through you mind and thoughts. And the truth is, whether you believe it or not, that the material physical world is subject to you and not the other way around which is the way that you have always been taught, that you are subject to the material physical world that is a

straight lie. Because if you remember when God made man He made man supreme over all the beast and animals of the air, water, and land. And also He crowned man supreme over all the land, and physical world. So whether people know it or not they have been endowed with power over the material physical world by God Most High and that right there is immutable. But the thing is, are people right now aware of that?! Probably not because the majority of people are not in tune with theirselves. Because if they were in tune with themselves they would most definitely be aware of that. But by people not being aware that they have power and are supreme over the material physical world the negative forces of the universe capitalize off the 100% and use that to their ultimate advantage. And therefore keep the people thinking that they are completely subject to the material physical world which is a straight lie. And that right there keeps people trying to conquer the physical world when all they got to do is conquer self, because remember you are whatever you create for yourself through your thoughts, subconscious and your super conscious, which is your soul. And through these channels you may call into existence into the material physical world whatever you may wish. And this is without exception as long as it is capable of existing in the physical sphere. So therefore, people need to stop going about the process of trying to acquire material things backwards because it's just not going to be too effective. People need to stop looking to the world for things that they want and start looking within themselves for whatever things they desire and going about the proper channels I just mentioned. Because these were the channels ordained by God for man to go by and once man goes by them believe me they will have whatever they may wish. So I do hope and pray that all people who are blessed to read this book get in tune with themselves and start their regeneration.

471. Always remember there are a lot of secrets, and mysteries, in nature, the world, and the universe. But believe me, once you get in tune with yourself and stay in tune with yourself they can and/or will be made known to you if you so wish to know these things.

472. Always remember that one must first conquer his or her fleshly physical self before he or she can ever get in tune or in contact with his or her real or higher self.

473. Do you know the real meaning of faith? I mean the real, actual definition and meaning of what faith really is? Well I'm going to quickly brief you on what faith really is and how it actually works. Faith is a power that emits from you or better said for your super conscious (your soul) and goes directly into the universe and does your bidding, advocates your cause, and fights and works for you. But you must keep your faith strong because remember it's out there in the universe fighting for you against other energies, specifically, the bad, evil, and negative energies of the universe which are trying to tear it down. That's why it is so pivotal that one keep his or her faith strong at all times. Because your faith is always out there in the universe doing your bidding and this is whether you are aware of it or not and this is why I always tell people that they should ceaselessly believe in themselves god, and what they're doing or trying to do. Because like I just told you your faith is out there in the universe bidding, advocating, and fighting your cause against other very powerful malevolent energies and powers that are like I said trying to destroy your faith. And therefore destroy you. So now that you know what faith really is and how it actually works you should have no logical reason to not want to keep it strong.

474. The public does not have a clue where money comes from. They just have some vague idea that the government prints it or something . . .

--David Icke

475. It is well enough that the people of the nation do not understand our banking and monetary system, for if they did I believe there would be a revolution before tomorrow morning . . .

--Henry Ford Sr.

476. Always remember that a lot of things in life have effects on people freudianly, meaning it's happening or taking place so deep in their minds that there not even conscious of it happening, or having an effect on them. Some things, to name a few like what people see on T.V., what they read in books, newspapers, or magazines, and what they see and hear every day . . . things like that and many others have real Freudian effects on people. And they don't even know it or recognize it. And the effects can be positive or negative. It just depends on what you're feeding into your mind via the T.V., books, newspapers, magazines, etc., etc. And via whatever you see and experience, and hear every day. So the next time you're looking at, reading or listening, to something negative watch out because it might just be having an effect on you, and you won't even consciously know it. And then you wonder why you're angry, made, stressed out or just plain not being yourself. And then you blame it on "you're just having a bad day." It's not that it's the effects of that negativity that you had picked up, and you weren't even aware that you had picked it up, and now you're experiencing the effects of it. And remember things that are Freudian work both ways you can pick up positive things and not be aware of it either, because you're picking them up subconsciously. And therefore you won't be conscious of them or of you picking them up, you'll just wonder why am I feeling like this and you won't know why. And like I said it could be positive or negative, good or bad, because a lot of things in life do have effects on people that are Freudian and people don't even know it or are even aware of this. And this is a very common happening.

477. Always remember that life, sometimes it's sweet, and sometimes it's sour, sometimes it's good, and sometimes it's bad. Sometimes it makes you happy, and sometimes it makes you sad. And sometimes you like it, and sometimes you hate it. Life, who can fully decipher, understand, and completely comprehend it nobody but God, the one who ordained it. So therefore don't worry yourself about it just live your life, be happy, believe, think positive, project the thoughts of what you're trying to create for yourself, love yourself, treat others right, seek and speak the truth, and thank God everyday for

what He's done for you, what He's doing for you right now and what He's going to do for you. And always remember that you're not the first nor are you going to be the last to experience chaos in your life.

478. Once you get done reading this book you will feel replenished in many ways. And you might just want to keep this book close on hand so whenever you need replenishing in any kind of way you can just grab it. And go right to the thought or thoughts that you need to read at that time for replenishing because this book will replenish you time after time, over and over, and over again.

479. Always remember that believing and faith are just so very powerful that it's just really indescribable really. But here is the thing; believing and faith tend to run out in people. They get all used up in us. And therefore they need to constantly be replenished. So don't ever let your believing or your faith get low because they will if you don't constantly replenish them meaning fill them back up. So always, but always keep your believing and faith full, because they will run low and out if you don't.

480. May God bless us all.

481. Always remember that all kinds of supernatural and spiritual beings travel, and flock the earth day and night, night and day, incessantly.

482. Always remember that us human beings are such infinitely complex creatures that it often takes us most of our lives just to come to a basic understanding of ourselves, and/or who we are, meaning to figure out who we as individuals really are, and what our real individual meanings, and purposes are in life.

483. Sometimes the thing you don't want maybe the best thing for you.

484. It was once said that physical exercise was a personal responsibility of great magnitude.

485. Always remember that physical exercise and eating right are the hallmarks of physical health.

486. Remember they say that the darkest hour is just before the dawn. And more times than not in life at our darkest hour is just when God pours out his blessings on us the most. And in my experiences that has proven so true. So never abandon your faith or cease projecting the thoughts of what you want to create. And stay positive, because remember the power of thought is just inconceivably incredible.

487. Remember to always stand up for yourself and for what's rightfully yours. And never let anybody misuse you in any kind of way. And remember that lying is a very nasty and very progressive addiction because once you start lying and not telling the truth. You can't stop. Lying is an addiction and it's very nasty and wrong. But most people lie anyway. They lie according to their personality. But the person who doesn't lie and always tries his or her very best to tell the truth, and nothing but the truth he or she is to be highly commended.

488. Now for a word on drugs and alcohol addictions, because the overall rate of drug and alcohol abuse and addictions is at an all time high right now and I'm not just talking about the usages of illicit street drugs either. But what I'm talking about is the constant rise in the usage, abuse and addiction of alcohol and over-the-counter and prescription medications and the number of people these days that are addicted to these legal drugs is extremely disproportionate. And the people themselves don't even know that they have a problem. They just think they need them or that they just got to have them and that's the drugs for whatever the reason or reasons may be. But in reality these poor people are heavily addicted and dependent on these drugs just because they think that they need them. And let the truth be told most of the people addicted and dependent on these drugs don't really need them for no medical reason they just think that they need them for medical reasons. But in reality they're using these drugs for crutches because they don't want to deal with their problems, their life, and just their plain reality. But what their failing to realize is that all human beings have problems

from the richest person in the world all the way down to the poorest person we all have problems. Our problems may vary, but you best believe me that we all got problems. And rational thinking people don't run to drugs to deal with their problems, if anything, drugs are just going to make matters worse not better. And furthermore drugs are nothing but temporary fake relief from your problems, your life, and your reality. Deal with your problems, your life and your reality without the fake temporary relief of drugs. Because the relief drugs give you is just so fake it's as fake as a 4 dollar bill. Because as soon as the effect of the drug wears off, you're right back in your problems, your life, and your reality. So people, if you want to get it right, you need to deal with your reality, your problems, and your life head up like decent rational thinking human beings. And remember that you're not the only person in the world who has problems because we all got problems if we're alive. But we deal with them and face them in a rational thinking way not running from them or hiding from them behind drugs of alcohol. And you know the thing that gets me the most is the fact that people can deal with their problems if they really wanted to. Because people are very powerful creatures they have all the power they're ever going to need right inside of them, in their mind that is. And all they got to do is believe and really want to do something and you best believe me they can, if they stop being so weak and giving into temptations and instant gratification. But anyway what I want to say is that being addicted and/or depended on alcohol or drugs will bring a lot of unnecessary negativity in to your life that you don't want or even need in no kind of way. Things like worries, anxieties, fear, and depression and everything else to that effect. And that right there you really don't need or want in your life or do you??? So if you have a problem with alcohol and/or drugs and not just illicit street drugs but any kind of drugs whether it's legal over-the-counter medications or prescription medications or even all of the above please rectify your problem and/or addiction(s) and if you can't rectify it on your own seek professional help. Remember, the first step rectifying any problem is knowing that you have one.

489. And now for a word on cigarettes and tobacco . . . and everybody knows about cigarettes and tobacco . . . everybody

knows that cigarettes and tobacco are extremely carcinogenic things . . . and everybody knows that cigarettes and tobacco are extremely bad and no good in no kind of way for one's health. And we all know about the fake temporary relaxation rush that cigarettes and tobacco give. And I'm sure you already know that cigarettes and tobacco are extremely addictive and extremely detrimental in many ways to ones overall health. But I bet what you didn't know was that the tobacco companies were, and you can bet your last dollar, more times than not still are surreptitiously spiking and adding all kinds of additives and other unknown substances to tobacco. Because check this out during the 1980's a major tobacco company grew a genetically engineered tobacco leaf with 4 to 5 times the level of nicotine in it. They code named the leaf Y-1. In 1994 the tobacco companies swore to congress that they had never actually used Y-1 that it was just a prototype. Then an internal tobacco company memorandum leaked out stating that ever since the tobacco companies had started using Y-1 in 1986 there sales had almost quadrupled. And this was early in 1997 when this memo leaked out. And this memo was one of the key pieces of evidence used against the tobacco companies in 1998 when they were found guilty of deceit fraud, and of wrongful doing, and ordered to pay an unprecedented 144 billion $ in actual and punitive damages. And did you know that 60% of people with ailments such as emphysema, lung cancer, asthma, and other smoking related illnesses still smoke? Why? Because they just can't stop. And why do you think that is???

490. Remember that the power of faith and believing is just like the power and the force of gravity you can't see it or physically touch it, but you damn sure most definitely know that it exist . . . it's real and it's there.

491. Always remember that in life you will always have challenges. You will always be tested and you will always have to stand up for yourself and for what you believe in.

492. Always remember this that we are now living in the age of deception. People are now more than ever before always trying to fool someone, manipulate someone, or are just plain

deceivers naturally. So don't be too trusting of people or what you see of people these days, even the Bible speaks on this and tells you about deceivers in (2 Timothy 3:13). So be on your guard, and stay on your guard against people.

493. Always remember that anger can cause and/or bring one to ruin and/or a wreck in his or her life. Because feelings of hostility can control us and therefore cause us to do things that we would never do while thinking rationally and or clearly. And something else, anger that's left lingering or unresolved in a person can be like a ticking time bomb that's in them, and can explode at any time. Because once one has lost his or her temper they have also lost their ability to reason as well.

494. Always remember that patience has been the key and the main ingredient in many a great accomplishments and successes.

495. Always remember to be yourself, don't be, or try to be anyone else because you are a unique person and human being. And there's only one you in the entire world and in all of God's great creation. So remember that you as an individual are great and special for the simple reason that before you there were none and after you there will be no more . . . you, that is.

496. Always remember that in life you got people that watch things happen and you got people that make things happen, and that's the group that you want to be a part of. The ones that make things happen.

497. One of the most common causes of blindness is greed, because once one get greedy he or she can't see nothing but what he or she wants.

498. Always remember that there's a difference between intelligence and confidence, just because someone possesses one does not necessarily mean that they possess the other. Someone can be extremely intelligent and still be fearful and scared. Just like someone can be extremely confident and have no intelligence.

499. Always remember that knowledge is nothing but power and if you can attain it, organize it, and apply it, it will be your

number one confident and you're most valued, trusted, and best servant.

500. Always remember that if you want more from life, you got to ask more of life, which therefore life will ask more of you . . . which will therefore, elevate you to new heights.

501. Always remember to appreciate friends, family, and loved ones, because there are no guarantees that they're always be around.

502. Always remember that the human heart is one of the most stubbornness things known to man because it doesn't give a damn what you tell it or what anybody tells it for that matter because it's going to do what it wants to do . . . it's going to love who it wants to love and it's going to hate who it wants to hate. And so on and so forth.

503. Remember anything at it's inception is going to be hard in trying at first. But once you get it going and started or get things rolling, things will wind down. And then once you pay your dues and if you stay determined and focused after that you will most definitely progress and prosper.

504. Now remember always be confident and have confidence in yourself and in all things that you do. And I don't care what it is be confident, and believe in yourself. I don't care if you're going out on a date . . . something that simple, be confident, have confidence, and believe in yourself. And the reason that I'm telling you this is because you would be completely amazed, and incredulous at the number of people that the negative forces have suffering from secret fears. And I mean all kinds of different and irrational fears that the negative forces of the universes have put in people's heads. And these people don't know they don't know any better so they believe these dumb and foundationless fears, which in reality are just lies and plain untruths. And these people think that it's just them suffering from these fears, and that nobody else suffers from such fears, which is another lie and untruth. And this lie the negative forces put in their heads so they won't talk about their fears to nobody else. For yet another fear, the fear of being

looked at like they're silly, stupid, or crazy. So what do these people do? These people suffer in silence, just what the negative forces want them to do. But it doesn't have to be like that no more. If you're one of these people that have been suffering in silence from secrete fears you can speak out, and I strongly suggest you do. Because let me tell you from my years of experience, of watching, studying, and observing the masses of people something like 5 or 6 out of every 10 people suffer from self imposed secret irrational fears of various and different kinds. And it's sad real sad, because most of these people that suffer from these fears are everyday functioning people - people who have jobs, wives, husbands, and families. And even in the Bible it says over 360 times to fear not. Because why should you fear . . . you're just like everybody else they hurt, cut, feel, bleed, and think just like you do . . . believe that. So always be confident, have confidence, and believe in yourself because it is so very important that I can't stress it enough to you, I just can't. And don't never doubt, not even a little bit. Because once you doubt that's all the leverage that the negative forces need and they're in there. And that will be all she wrote, and your confidence, faith, and your courage will start to weaken and will soon be gone out the window. And let me tell you a little secret when you say audibly I will not be scared, I'm not scared, I will be confident, I am confident, I believe in myself, I believe in what I'm doing. And that's just the way it is period. And there's nothing that nobody, nothing or anything, can do about it. And the second when you say that to yourself audibly in your mind you drop, reject, and eradicate all negative and adverse thoughts of fear that are trying to hinder your confidence, courage, and/or faith. And like I said when you say audibly that you're not scared, that you will be confident and that you do believe in yourself, and/or what you're doing and will fear not when you say these things audibly. The sound vibrations of these very powerful words, literally let off energies that can be felt by you if you're in tune with yourself. And by other's in a very real way. And do you know what those energies are? Them energies are coming from and are the power that's in you. Like I've said previously in this book, human beings are very powerfull creatures, you have power at your disposal and are capable of unleashing it whether you know it or not. Now one of the things that separates us and makes different from one another is whether we utilize this God given power that's innately in us.

505. Always remember to never be insecure about anything, because insecurity is a very negative thought and a form of fear.

506. Alright! There are very few people in the world right now who know truth such as I. I mean aside from those that clandestinely control the U.S. government the number of people who actually know the truth. And what's really going on in the world is negligible, but is growing. And what I'm writing in this book is very concise. I just wanted to share a few facts of reality with you people. But what I'm getting at is that people since the inception of the world have not really changed, they're still the same. How people acted back in antiquity they still act the same way today. The only thing that's changed is the means by which people are able to do things by or with (technology). But other than that human nature is still the same. And let the truth be told, even the ancients had advanced technology because there have been many technologically advanced civilizations in the history of the world but you're not told that. That part of history is suppressed and kept away from you. But the remnants of these past technologically advanced civilizations are everywhere. Like for example all over the planet are fantastic structures built thousands of years ago which could only have been created with technology as good or better than what we got today. Like for example at Baalbek, northeast of Beirut in the Lebanon, 3 massive chunks of stone, each weighing 800 tons were moved at least a 3rd of a mile and positioned high up in a wall. So cars, airplanes, spacecrafts, computers, satellites, and some things that mainstream society still doesn't even have today, like free energy technology and anti-gravity technology, not saying these things don't exist today because they most definitely do. But right now at the present time they are being withheld and kept from mainstream society but all these things that I just mentioned are not new but have been around for eons. And the most commonly asked questions is what then happen to these technologically advanced past civilizations? Well it's like this and what I'm about to say has been well documented and supported by vast geological and

biological evidence, but it has all be suppressed from mainstream society. And that's that the earth has suffered from a number of enormous cataclysmic events of which almost wiped out all existing life each time. And therefore each time destroyed the technologically advanced civilizations. And I'm not just talking about one cataclysmic event, but there have been many, there have been at least 10 recorded from 11,000 to 1,500 BC. And if you don't believe me then please research this subject for yourself . . . hit the internet, read some books. Here are a few great books on the subject: when the earth nearly died, by D.S. Allen and J.B. Dealer; and Atlantis the Eighth Continent, by Charles Berletz. And these are just 2 that I just gave you off the top of my head. Because believe me there are many more. And like I just said the evidence and remnants of these past technologically advanced civilizations is all over the planet. Like in Peru where the mysterious Nazca Lines are . . . the ancient's scored away the top surface of land to reveal the white subsurface and through this method were created incredible depictions of animals, fish, insects, and birds . . . some of them so large they can only be seen in their entirety from 1,000 feet in the air. The technology which allowed wonders like Nazca, Baalbek, The Great Pyramid at Giza, and other amazing creations to be built with such precision and scale, could only come from a technologically advanced civilization. I mean forget for a minute all the programming, conditioning, pseudo-teachings, and bullshit taught to you and put in your head by the modern educational school system and mainstream society, and use your common sense. How else without advanced technology were those structures and many others around the world built? I mean you have got to understand people. 85% of the world's true history and ineffable amounts of knowledge have been suppressed away from you. And it's time you wake up and understand this!

507. I just want to say here that whatever you can think of, believe me it's been thought of before, good or bad. And whatever you've been through or are going through, it's been went through before. So when I hear people say you just don't know what I've been through or what I'm going through, I just shake my head and I tell myself, what do they think they're the first person to ever go through whatever they're going through?!

And then I tell myself if they only knew, if they only knew . . . if they only had a little tiny bit, just a little tiny bit of a glimpse of the knowledge of all ages they would not ever so much as even utter the words of what they're going through again. Just try this for a second, try to imagine all the pain, hurt, suffering, and injustices that people have endured throughout all of the ages since the inception of the world. And you can't, and I know that you can't. You know why you can't imagine it??? Because you don't have enough knowledge to . . . that's why! And 2nd you can't even begin to imagine it because you don't have the mental ability to conceive such a thought of such proportion. But just sit back and try. And try to go about it slowly. And to the best of your knowledge and ability and see what you can come up with. And when you get done doing that I want you to think about what you been through . . . and then thank God for what you've been through or are going through. Because you now know that it can be a whole lot worse or it could have been a whole lot worse. And I hope you now know and understand that innumerable people have been in much worse, through much worse. So be thankful to god for what you went through or are going through. And for what you haven't gone through, be thankful.

508. Always remember that the very few people in this world who do know things such as I am not at liberty to disclose a lot of what they know.

509. Always remember that power is very intoxicating and too much power will more times than not make the best of people arrogant.

510. Remember that when you believe and are confident you give off energy that can be felt by other people. And the same is true when you're scared and fearful you give off that scared and fearful energy that people can pick up and feel too. And remember some people are more sensitive to picking up energies than others.

511. Always remember that you don't never want to look for love because if you do look for love, you best believe me that you

want find it. All you'll find is a whole lot of unwanted hurt, pain, and heartache. Because you don't look for love, you position and open yourself to love. Then love looks for you, and will find you.

512. Always remember that human beings are to complex of creatures for us to be labeled either all good or all bad, because we all each and every one of us has good and bad in us just some of us have more of one or the other in us. And it's also up to us individually to choose which we want to exercise in our lives.

513. Always remember that there's something very magical and special about being 4, 5, 6, 7, or even 8 years old. Just take a second and think back to when you was that age. Just think . . . now, wasn't life just wonderful back then no bills, no problems, no real life concerns, no stress, no worries, and so on and so forth. Life was just fun and wonderful. And now if you have kids and they're in the aftermentioned age range make sure that you let them know how very special it is to be that age. And how that once it's gone they will never ever be able to be that age again. And how very important it is that when they're that age for them to really be that age, because they can never be that age again.

514. Always remember that time eats away at everything no matter how great or of what significance a person or thing may be or have been, time is going to eat way at them or it. Because time eats away at everything no matter what it is just as long as it's worldly, you best believe me time is going to eat away at it and eventually deteriorate it. And as human beings with our finite minds we cannot and will not ever be able to fully comprehend the real meaning of eternity, because to fully comprehend eternity is to put a limit on it and eternity has no limit. Because just think what is 50, 100, 200, or even 500 or 1000 years compared with eternity??? Nothing, absolutely nothing! But to us 5, 10, or 20 years is a long time, and don't let it be 50 or 100 years. Because that's so long for us that our understanding just completely stops right there. But just think of god . . . time does not apply to god. He's always been and He will always be. Because time only applies to worldly things, that is things that

are transitory. And remember you as a human being only have so much time here on earth and then it's time for you to go and you best believe me you will not leave a minute late or a minute to soon. So just remember time is life and your time is your life. Because once you've exhausted all your time you're out of here. And there's nothing nobody or anything can do about that. So don't let anybody lie to you about it. So while you're here don't waste your time frivolously . . . be smart.

515. Always remember not to let anything stress you out . . . not your job, not your family, nothing. Because stress is everywhere these days and more than ever before. And do you know why? Because the negative forces of the universe have turned up the volume on us all. And it's going to get worse, must worse. And if you can't handle it now I sure hate to see you in 2, 3, or 5 years from now because then it's going to be bad . . . real bad. And I'm not being pretentious and cynical about this either . . . I'm just being truthful and real. Like I told you in the preface of this book I'm going to give it to you raw . . . uncut. Just the way it is. Nothing but pure reality . . . 150%. But if stress is getting to you like it's getting to everybody else these days, you must do things to alleviate it and don't ignore it because it can be very detrimental to you physically, mentally, and emotionally. And can lead to various types of disorders and depression from mild to serious, if not rectified. So don't just think that it's nothing and you can handle it because stress if not alleviated can be very progressive. So don't be afraid to have you a drink every now and then or to take time out of your day to just relax or to just sit back and listen to some slow relaxing music of your choice like for instance, jazz is very relaxing or whatever a good physical workout is a great stress reliever. Everybody is different. Whatever works for you, because if you don't it will build up and then you will be in trouble. Because stress is nothing but the offspring of the negative forces of the universe. And stress gives them enormous leverage in your life and if it is not alleviated on a daily basis. Like I said, it can and will lead to many other very negative, detrimental, and perverse things.

516. Always remember that it is extremely pivotal for one to find an effective way of alleviating stress on a daily basis and for one to make some quality solitary time for oneself on a daily basis. So one can gather one's thoughts, replenish, think, and most important of all, remain focused on what's pivotal to you and your life such as your spiritual goals and keeping your mind clean and free of all bad and negative thoughts. Because you best believe me if you don't take time out for yourself on a daily basis to do the aftermentioned, chances are that you will began to stress and some people stress and don't even know that there stressing. And that's call stressing silently and there going around blaming their problems on everything and everybody else. And that's why I said that it's so very pivotal for you to find a way to alleviate stress on a daily basis and for you to take time for yourself on a daily basis. Because you must not forget that the negative forces are now working beyond overtime and are turning the volume up on us all daily and that's no lie. God! If you only had in-depth knowledge of what is actually going on right now in the universe, you would not be taking what I'm saying here so lightly. People better wake up because nothing is getting any easier or better for that matter it is only going to get harder . . . and that is so real! Because the negative forces of the universe now have in this day and age so many myriad things. Technology, the internet, T.V., etc. etc., to keep us thrown off, confused, distracted, unstable, preoccupied and just away from what's pivotal to us and our life. Such as getting in tune with ourselves, and most of all away from the truth. Because like I said previously one of the most important things to the negative forces and I mean this is extremely, extremely pivotal to them is to keep the people ignorant to how the universe really works and to what's really and actually going on in the world and the universe right now. Because the negative forces don't want the people to know or have knowledge of any of this. And as long as they can keep technology incessantly advancing they're able to keep people worried and caught up in the worldly and material things and concerns it will be contingent that the people will stay ignorant to what they the negative forces are doing and to what's really going on in the world and the universe right now.

517. Always remember that one of the main hidden agendas of the negative forces of the universe is to try to completely ruin your mind by all and any means possible, and have you unable to control your thoughts, and have you fearful, stressed out, paranoid, worried, depressed, and/or just plain crazy.

518. Always remember that there are 4 basic powers in the material physical world and that's money, influence, knowledge, and politics or political power. And the greatest of these powers is money.

519. Always remember that just like you go and get a physical check up once or twice a year to make sure that nothing in wrong with your physical body, one must also go and get a mental check up once or twice a year to make sure one is O.K. mentally. Because people have been known to be stressing or in a state of depression and to not have even known it themselves . . . also called stressing silently and/or to have been experiencing depression silently and to have not have known it. So it is very important that one gets mental checkups once or twice a year right along with his or her regular physical checkups . . .

520. Always remember that some things in life you just have to ignore them in their entirely. So that they cannot and will not be able to hurt you. Because if you pay attention to them, believe in them, or feed into them in any kind of way, they can and will hurt you emotionally or mentally. So you have to know how to ignore things that are or can be detrimental, negative, or adverse to you or your life, and/or your emotional or mental well being. And this right here is nothing but an old ancient Chinese technique. Because you just can't let everything and anything get to you. Because if you do you will become a prime target of those of negative intent for stress, depression, anxiety, and just all kinds of negativity that you don't need or want in your life.

521. Always remember that influence is one of the most powerful things in life. And that a lot of people shape and form their

lives after those that they respect, like, and admire most. And that might not necessarily be a good or wise thing.

522. One of the world's coldest but realest ironies is when genuinely good and honest people are wrongfully accused of being selfish, evil, and having ulterior motives.

523. Always remember that inspiration is one of the most powerful things in the world . . . get inspired and there's no limit to the things that you can do or accomplish. And then once you get inspired it is pivotal that you find a way to stay inspired. Because inspiration is real power. And always remember that people are inspired in different ways and by different things. Because we're such complex creatures, what inspires you may not inspire me and vice-versa. So remember inspiration is real power to anyone who can attain it, utilize it, and keep it.

524. Always remember to think big because if you don't think big then you will never be able to accomplish anything big. Because remember before you can do anything you must first be able to cogitate, and/or conceive it. And if you can conceive it then you best believe me if you can believe long and hard enough then you can achieve it. So don't be no small minded person, and don't never be afraid to think big and/or grandiose, and to put some power behind your thought or thoughts by believing. Because having faith and being able to believe is a form of intelligence and believing and projecting positive thought will not only set you free, but will take you to new heights in all areas of your life. So always remember to think big and to project those thoughts, and the only limits you have are the ones you set for yourself. Because the world can be yours if you want it to be, and if you can think it to be. So think big, as big as you wish, and believe and put those thoughts out. And there's really no limit or telling to what you can do. But I do guarantee you one thing you'll surprise yourself beyond all belief.

525. Always remember that the more you know the more you'll be able to do. And it's a very beautiful thing for one to be proficient in various branches or forms of knowledge.

526. Always remember that there's no limit to what one can attain or do through knowing and confidence.

527. Always remember that in life one can never appreciate or really understand the real meaning and significance of something until one has experienced the negative or the opposite of it. I'll give you a few examples, one can never appreciate wealth unless one has been poor and broke, one doesn't really appreciate his or her freedom until one has been locked up or in jail, one doesn't really appreciate their good health until they're sick, debilitated or in the hospital, one doesn't never appreciate their youth until they're old, and one can never really appreciate joy and happiness unless one has experienced pain, sorrow, hurt, and misfortune. And this goes for and applies to everything in life. Because like I said one can never really appreciate or really understand the real meaning and significance of something until one has experienced the negative or the opposite of it.

528. Now for a real quick word on power and authority. Did you know that power and authority are extremely addictive? They're like a drug and a very powerful and insidious drug that people get hooked on real quick, and then need and want more of. And then the war inside of them will start they will try to control the power and authority that has been given to them. But sad to say more times than not the power and authority will control them. And do you know why? Because power and authority especially over other people feeds the ego of the one or ones exerting it, and feels so good that it's really indescribable and will corrupt the best of people.

529. Always remember that love, jealousy, and hate are all very closely related. Because when you're involved or dealing with one of these the others are not too far behind.

530. This book that you're reading right now is for you in life just like a breath of fresh air. It's like a drink of ice cold water while you're walking in 115 degree heat.

531. Always remember that your mind is one of the greatest tools that you can possess or will ever possess. So it's all on you how effectively you use it.

532. Always remember that out of anything bad or adverse, good can come out if you stay thinking positive and projecting and putting out positive thought . . . believe that!

533. Always remember that life is to serious not to be taken one day at a time. So please take your life seriously and one day at a time.

534. Always remember that everybody in life needs self-esteem to be happy and productive because self-esteem is extremely pivotal to ones mental and emotional health, well-being, and stability. And self-esteem not only drives out fear and depression but produces confidence in oneself. So remember in order for one to stay confident in his or her self and healthy mentally and emotionally one must keep his or her self esteem up.

535. Always remember that the biggest mistake or failure one can make in life is not trying or doing at all. That is the biggest mistake or failure that one can make in life. Because remember that you're always a winner just as long as you tried and in the depths of your soul you know that you did the very best that you could.

536. Always remember that life is very serious so please don't underestimate, misjudge, or take life for granted because if you do it can be of immeasurable misfortune to you. And all it takes in life is the simplest, littlest, slip or mishap for one to suffer immense catastrophes in his or her life. So please take life seriously and for what it is. And don't ever think or say what can't or won't happen to you, because if you do you'll just be setting yourself up for a very rude awakening.

537. Always remember that one of the best things in life is to be able to vigorously physically exercise, be fit and stay physically active on a daily basis which is really one of life's greatest joys.

538. Human beings age each and every single day, but we just don't really know it and we really can't see it. But we are . . . we're all getting older, aging and slowly deteriorating more and more each and every single day until one day we'll be old and almost

completely gone and of no good physically to nobody not even our selves so please don't waste or take your life and your youth for granted because you only have your life and your youth for a time and then there gone first your youth, and then your life. And the time will go by so fast that you won't even know what happened. And remember that it is a blessing from God for one to be able to live into old age. And it is a great sin for one to abuse, mistreat, look down on, hurt, ignore, or to bring miscontent in any kind of way to an elder or older person that's up in his or her age.

539. Always remember that more times than not people will say one thing but do another.

540. Always remember that the best physical exercise that one can do in the world is weight train and that's with free-weights. Because weight training will keep you young, energetic, looking good, and the best of all physically strong, believe me.

541. Always remember that there are some things that money or wealth just can't buy. No matter how much money or wealth one has and those things are things such as: real and true love, a good physical workout, keep disaster and misfortune from striking you, blessings from god and good fortune, a real true and gunuine friendship with another human being, happy, smart, healthy, and beautiful children, real and true confidence, in yourself, the ability to believe and have faith in God, yourself and whatever you're doing or trying to do, real and true peace of mind, guanine trust and loyalty from your friends and associates, being liked for who you really are as a person even if you didn't even have a pot to piss in, a fast metabolism, good health and genetics, a good heart, and love for other people, to really and actually be a fun and good person to be around even if you didn't have a dime to your name, real good laugh from the depths of your soul, patience, experience, your youth, time, meaning time that you already wasted because money can't buy none of that back, motivation determination, perseverance, keep you from thinking bad, negative, or adverse thoughts, keep the negative forces of the universe from missing with and/or getting a hold of your mind. A real and true sense of meaning in life,

fill the void in your life that only God can fill with His divine love, a sound mind and a real understanding of yourself, life, nature, and the universe, discipline, to be in tune with yourself, and what one learns as he or she goes through life. So there you have it a small list of some of the things that money, no matter how much of it you have, cannot buy.

542. Well did you know that right now the U.S. government is overtly and surreptitiously building huge immense networks of databases of personal and private information on every man, woman, and child. And that in the last 15 to 20 years congress have been vastly approving such legislation to build these databases and to add to already existing ones. And this has mostly been at the behest of the president both (Clinton and Bush Jr.) because remember that the U.S. government always nine times out of ten has a hidden agenda behind what they do, and it will always more times than not have some kind of covert adverse effect on the people. And I'm going to give you a brief and quick sound bite of some of the legislation that I'm talking about that has been passed and approved by Congress in the last 15-20 years. And remember that this is just a sound bite because there are copious amounts of legislation that the government has passed and is passing to surreptitiously use to build their immense data bases of personal and private information. The mandate to create a unique health identifier the key to keeping tabs on each of us medially was buried in the health insurance portability and accountability act of 1996. The provision creating a directory of new hires and electronic collection of personal employment profiles was packed into the personal responsibility and work opportunity reconciliation act of 1996. It dovetails nicely with the tracking and certification called for in the school to work opportunities act of 1994. The provision inaugurating the requirement that employers check with the government before hiring anyone was included in the illegal immigration reform and immigrant responsibility act of 1996. And you see all this innocent sounding legislation has hidden agendas to it. But you see most members of congress don't know what's burred deep, deep, in the legislation itself or the real purpose of the legislation all they know is about as much as you or I would know if we were to be present at the voting of such legislation. And I bet you didn't know that some

laws when they are written are the size of city phone books?! And if you don't believe me, well there's a great book on just this topic by: California State Senator, Bill Richardson, titled: What Makes You Think we Read the Bills. And remember the only ones that know the real agendas of such legislation are those members of Congress that are working covertly and subversively for and/or with those who clandestinely control the U.S. government. And you have got to remember that those who clandestinely control the U.S. government have some of the most ingenious and clever social engineers masterminding all of this. And this is all nothing but pure subversiveness of our government. And remember that those who clandestinely control the U.S. government and their affiliates and henchmen surreptitiously control the U.S. government by strategically placing individuals in seats of power throughout the government's infrastructure and hierarchy. Now when you look at all this in its totality what the government is surreptitiously doing collecting personal and private information on every man, woman, and child in America. Then you factor in their systematic surveillance of the people on more than one level of which I've spoke on in great detail in thought #412. And so much other shit that there doing that you'll read about in subsequent thoughts in this book that the U.S. government is surreptitiously doing. And that the masses of people are not in no way aware of then you'll begin to understand what's really going on and how sinister and execrate it has become. But don't get me wrong now it isn't the whole government that has malevolent hidden agendas for the people. It's just a few or I'll just says it's the individuals working behind the scenes to sinisterly subvert the U.S. government and our democracy so that they can implement their law and the agendas of their master's, better known as the new world order. And you already know who their masters are there those who clandestinely control the U.S. government. But the masses of people don't know this, they have no idea what's really going on. And do you know what's really sad . . . and that's that the vast majority or run of the mill government workers, those people that are part of the government and work in government sometimes all of their lives don't know or have any idea that the government has been subverted and completely infiltrated and all but overthrown out of actual operation. So with that said do you think that the average everyday person is going to know of course not. Because I'm going to tell you like it is uncut right now these sinisterly evil individuals actually and do clandestinely control our government from behind the scenes.

543. Now in this thought I'm going to speak on marriage . . . and if America is a free country like they claim it to be, then not the government, the state, or anybody else should have the authority to define marriage for the people that should be left up to the individual to define for themselves. If a person wants to marry his cat, his car, or his dog, that should be his own personal business and something between him and God and nobody else. But sad to say the masses of people have been programmed, conditioned, and literally brainwashed through public education, the mass media, and all the other outlets of public information that are all virtually owned and controlled by those who clandestinely control the U.S. government to accept such totalitarian dictates in their life's. And that's why those who clandestinely control the U.S. government do not want you the people reading books like this because if the masses of people ever wake up from their mental slumber that has been stealthily and surreptitiously induced upon them, then those who clandestinely control the U.S. government would have a real problem, and would not be able to control the masses of people as they do now. Because the thing is to be truly free, and be yourself and remember you owe account to nobody but to God and the universal laws that He put in place to govern us, that's it and that's all. And once you come to a real realization of that you'll understand that you don't owe an account of your life or of what you do to no church which come a dime a dozen, no religion which come a dime a dozen, no dogma which come a dime a dozen or no government or state which come a dime a dozen. Then and only then will you start to truly and really be free. But anyway let me go ahead and finish my monograph on marriage because people these days get married and then divorce so frequently that it's just plain sad. Then they go through these long legal battles in divorce court. So I got a bit of advice for you here. When one gets formally married there married in the eyes of God and in the eyes of the state. Alright! The eyes of God are the only ones that matter here. The eyes of

the state do not matter and mean nothing here understand me??? Remember the state is just going to give you problems, like making you pay more taxes because you're married and a bunch of other legal ramifications so what you want to do is exclude and delete the eyes of the state from your marriage completely. And you're not wrong for doing this because the eyes of God are the only eyes that mater in your marriage. Because like I just said the state is only going to cause you trouble and problems, in more ways than one. And plus, who are they? You owe no account of what you do to them as long as you're not bothering or harming nobody. And also you don't need no state to sanction your marriage who are they, they aren't God, there man just like you and I. So please believe me, to have a real honorable and good long lasting marriage in the eyes of God you do not need the state. And on a last note how you go about making your commitment to your significant other is strictly your business.

544. This book is full of truth, positivity, and love. And emits just that and if you're reading it you most definitely can feel it.

545. Always remember that some of the world's best and greatest inventions ever invented were invented under adverse conditions. And that's because adverse conditions produce innovativeness and creativity in an unusually profound way.

546. Always remember to be good to yourself everyday because if you don't who will.

547. Always remember that money and wealth is nothing without peace of mind and real knowledge and understanding.

548. Always remember that a very important aspect and part of being smart and intelligent is being able to keep your mouth shut and not talking too much, especially about your business because like I previously told you in this book that the less that people know about you the better off you'll be . . . is so true, please believe me.

549. This book, because of the blessing of God only, came together like a miracle.

550. Well chick this out if you think that you're doing bad or that you're at a low point in your life or that things are just so bad in your life that they just couldn't possibly get any worse you better think again. Because you best believe me things can always get worse. And whatever you're going through right now, nine times out of ten is probably nothing compared to what you're about to read. And please consider the following with caution and prudent forethought to minimize risk to your emotion and feelings. (Please)

On Wednesday, August 23, 2000, in Merced California at about 7:30 A.M. a deranged possessed man by the name of Jonathon David Bruce, 27 years old, broke into the Carpenter Family Farmhouse and stabbed to death with a pitchfork twp completely helpless innocent little children, and terrorized three other helpless innocent children whom he tried unsuccessfully to murder. Now the two helpless innocent children whom he murdered were John William Carpenter, seven years old, and Ashley Carpenter, nine years old. And the other three whom he so desperately but unsuccessfully tried to murder, were Anna Carpenter, 13 years old, Vanessa Carpenter, 11 years old and Jessica Carpenter, 14 years old. Now at about 8:00 a.m. Jessica saw a naked man in the living room of her home pulling up his pants and she saw that he had the furniture of the living room pushed against the walls and doors of the house to barricade himself and the children inside. Jessica then ran and locked herself in her room after seeing the strange man. And he then ran after her and began to bang on her room door she then picked up the phone and tried to call 911 for help but the line was dead. So she then jumped out her window and ran to a neighbor's house for help. But while still inside the house Bruce stormed into the bedroom that Anna and Vanessa shared and began to ferociously jab at them with a pitchfork as they helplessly cuddled in each other's arms trying to fend off their attacker. Then at the same time there youngest sister Ashley came in from another room and yelled at the deranged man ... stop it ... don't hurt my sisters. Then Bruch with one jab of the pitchfork, he pitch forked her to the wall, her tiny body stuck to the wall with a pitchfork going through it. You got to remember that she was so small she was only a nine year old. And at that time Anna and Vanessa ran screaming down the hallway pushing a bookshelf out of their way to get into laundry room and they locked themselves in and then Bruce came knocking on door saying let me in . . . I'll be nice to you. Bleeding Anna and Vanessa fled through a window in the laundry room and joined up with their sister Jessica at the neighbor's house to wait for help. But while still in the house Bruce went into their parent's bedroom and mercilessly pitch forked to death there brother, seven year old John William Carpenter as he lay in his parents bed asleep. But there is a lease one somewhat; good thing about this story and that is when the police arrived on the scene they shot Johnathan David Bruce 13 times killing him dead on the spot. Because he allegedly came at them with the pitchfork. But some of you might think that Johnathan David Bruce got the easy way out. But the truth is we do not need in any kind of way, shape, or form, scum like Johnathan David Bruce on the face of this earth. So the point of this inordinately sad story is that whatever you're going through right now, nine times out of ten it isn't as bad as what happened here. So please be thankful and grateful, because like I've told you in previous thoughts God does not condone negativity in no kind of way. So if you're going around feeling sorry and sad for yourself and putting yourself and/or others down, swaying how bad things are for you. You better watch out . . . you had better stop. Because you best believe me that things can get worse. And remember that whatever you put out in thought, deed, or action, good or bad, will come back to you. That is the universal immutable law of compensation which was ordained by God before the beginning of time as you know it and does not and will not fail. So all I'm saying here is do not feel sorry or sad for yourself in no kind of way or go around worrying or saying how bad things are for you. Because all that is nothing but negativity. And if you put it out you best believe me that you'll get it back and like I told you in previous thoughts that you must break that negative cycle. And remember that there's always somebody out there that's worse off then you. And if you continue to feed into the negativity, things most definitely can and will get worse for you. So please if for nobody else but for yourself, break that negative cycle. And I ask one or more thing that when you pray say a prayer for the Carpenter Family because they lost their two youngest children, Ashley and John, to an immensely horrible act. Something that Mr. and Mrs. Carpenter, John and little Ashley parents and their siblings Anna, Vanessa, and Jessica will never ever be able to get fully over. I mean that these poor people will have to live with this immense pain the rest of their lives. It's just that there's no word or words for how sad it is. So please remember these people in your prayers when you pray because god is the only one who can make good come out of anything . . . believe that. Even something like this. And why it happened I couldn't even begin to tell you but I can tell you one thing that the universe makes no mistakes.

551. Always remember that you don't have to be an Ivy League graduate to be successful and have a great life.

552. Always remember that one of the greatest joys in life is to be able to give love, and to receive love. And that is most definitely one of the greatest joys in life.

553. Always remember that thinking especially going into deep thought produces ideas, and ideas produce motivation, and motivation produce action.

554. Always remember that mainstream society will always encourage you to strive for you goals, to go to school, and to work hard for what you want. But whatever you do just don't think outside the box. And the box is the mental prison that they got you in, because once you start to think outside the box then mainstream society will ridicule you, call you crazy, a nut, and an extremist. And probably even say that you're guilty of sedition and why is this. Because once you start to think outside the box you're a threat. And again, why is that? Because once you start to think outside the box they can no longer control you. And not only that, but now you are completely unpredictable and who knows what you might morph into or who you might start to tell and/or wake up also. So you're like a disease now to them those who clandestinely control the U.S. government. That is and with a strong possibility of spreading. Now as long as you stay in the box, you're okay. Why because they can and do control you and you're probably going to ask how they control you. Well very

simple they control you by having programmed, conditioned, and indoctrinated you through public education, the media, and the rest of mainstream society on what to believe and what not to believe. So therefore you are pretty predictable and you are only going to believe and therefore get the mass majority of your information from the aftermentioned sources and who owns and controls the aftermentioned sources of information. Yes, they do, those who clandestinely control the U.S. government. So therefore there controlling you, as long as you think inside the box, which is the mental prison they created for you and got you in. And they been having you in it ever since you can remember since you were about 5 years old. And you had no idea, shit and some people will never know. They will stay in it until the day they die. And nine times out of ten your parents and grandparents were in it, and more times than not even your great grandparents were in it. Because this is not something that just started, this mind control or social conditioning or engineering has been going on at least for the last 100 or so years. Now just think for a minute a person that's inside the box, in the mental prison, anything outside that box is surreal and/or not real or true to him like for example the stuff in this book. He'll say it's not real and/or true . . . why? Simple. Because he has never been taught or has heard, or has ever came in contact with too much or anything outside the box and/or information such as this. So therefore his mind is going to naturally reject it. And you best believe me that this is well known to those who clandestinely control the U.S. government. But the minute you start to think outside the box, it's like you're an outcast all of the sudden. And mainstream society will turn on you like a Doberman pincher. Because it's like this people who think outside the box, are not in a mental prison and therefore are not controlled mentally, that is by those who clandestinely control the U.S. government. And I'm going to tell you like this there is a mass awakening going on right now amongst the people. People for whatever reason or reasons are starting to wake up and starting to think outside the box and they are not caring what anybody says or thinks. And that right there in itself and of itself is just a beautiful thing. And that is also one of the reasons that I wrote this book, and that's to help the people start thinking outside the box. And I could go on forever telling you how much knowledge and information has been kept and suppressed away from you the masses of people. If this book had a million pages times 10, which is 10 million it would not be enough to hold even a small fraction of all the knowledge and information that has been suppressed and kept away from you the people. And please believe me this is not hyperbole. Now once you start to think outside the box you'll start to learn some of the secrets that those who clandestinely control the U.S. government do not want you to know. Such as that they do really exist and have been controlling America since like 1850, even before that, and other things such as the corruption orchestrated and controlled by them in virtually all of the high echelons of government and industry in America. And how this corruption is hid and extremely insidious, and how the manipulation, craftiness, and deception is carried out on a daily basis. But it is so masterfully disguised and camouflaged that you would only recognize and know it if you were thinking completely outside the box, and were completely alert and in tune with yourself. And for those of you who know what I'm talking about, my hat is off to you. And in closing this thought I'm going to say this if you doubt that the kind of subtle and insidious, corruption that I just spoke on exist at the highest levels of government and industry in America, then I recommend that you get this book and this book was written by a person who spent 35 years working in many different capacities in the U.S. government and has meticulously documented in 750 pages just the kind of corruption that I speak on. And most of the things he exposes and says come from his direct experience and/or public record. And if one takes the time he or she can check them out, the book is just phenomenal there's no other way to put it. It's called: Defrauding America, by Rodney Stich, ISBN# 0-932438-08-03.

555. Always remember that there's nothing wrong with being down and out in life. Because it's all in how you take it, and how you look at it . . . either positive or negative. Now being down and out is naturally going to look negative and bad on the surface, but one must look deep and beyond the surface of one's situation and circumstance. Because believe me the biggest blessings a lot of the time come in disguise. Because being down and out just could be the best thing that ever happens to

you. If you look beyond the surface of things and keep projecting and putting out positive thought and stay believing (stay positive) and you're probably be on the verge and susceptible to receiving one of the biggest blessings of your life and that's no lie. Like for instance this book that you're reading right now I wrote this book at a time in my life when I was very, and have to say it again, totally down and out at that time and that turned out to be one of the biggest blessings of my life. And that's no lie; this book was one of the fruits of me being down and out. And do you know why? Because I looked beyond my situation and circumstances, and kept my faith, stayed positive and believing in myself, and putting out thoughts of what I wanted to create, that's why! And I'm going to disclose one of the secrets that has been suppressed away from you. And that's when one chooses to ignore all the negativity in one's life, situation, and circumstances. And therefore place their thoughts and energy into the positive meaning into the creation of a new experience and or situation. Then you're withdrawing your consent and support of the present experience in which you no longer wish to participate. You are using the 2nd law of the universe which is the law of attraction. By you incessantly putting out positive thoughts of a new experience you're attracting that experience to you. Because like I've told you before thoughts are real and exist in a world of their own, and as you put them out they do come back and manifest themselves. So when I say being down and out could just be one of the biggest blessings of your life I know what I'm talking about because I'm talking from experience. So don't be no fool and miss what could be the biggest blessing of your natural born life . . . by being ignorant to how the universe really works and by being negative which is just what the negative forces want you to be, ignorant and negative.

556. Always remember that a lot of the time people will only say what sounds good or is appropriate for the moment instead of what's necessarily true or real.

557. Always remember that you as a human being are obligated to yourself, and to the ones that love you to keep going, keep trying, and to keep doing no matter what.

558. Did you know that people in this day and age are now more than ever before in our history more keen, aware, and sensitive to spiritual energy, good and bad, than ever before. And this awareness, keenness, and sensitivity that people now have for spiritual energy is only going to increase as time goes on. Why? Because we are nearing the great shift of the cycles in 2012. But the pivotal thing is which one of those energies either the positive or the negative are people going to yield themselves to, because you best believe that they are going to yield to one or the other, whether they want to or not. Whether they're conscious of it or not. So all I can say is think positive thoughts. Put out positive energy and yield yourself to the good and positive one.

559. Always remember that your body, soul, and mind need and crave relaxation. And it is extremely pivotal to your health and well being that you get it on a regular basis if not every day. Because if you don't find some time everyday or at least every other day to just cool out, unwind, and just relax and when I say relax I mean relax, no beepers, phones, fax machines, computers or anything of the like around you. Just you somewhere in total solitude unwinding, cooling out, and just relaxing. And once you start to do this every day or at least on a regular basis you'll be amazed at how it alleviates stress out of your life and puts you so much more in tune with yourself. For example try listening to some smooth jazz and sipping some light wine while you're relaxing. People just don't know or even understand how pivotal it is for them to attain some form of peace of mind and relaxation in their daily lives.

560. The thoughts or certain parts of the thoughts in this book that really inspire and motivate you it is recommended that you photo copy them, maybe even blow them up and hang them in your office or somewhere you can visually see them every day.

561. Always remember that there are many ways to start being positive like for example instead of talking behind someone's back don't say anything at all. Instead of putting someone down give them a compliment. And just start being positive in your daily and mundane actions and interactions with people. And you best believe me that after you start to do this on a

regular and constant basis you'll see how much of a difference it has and makes in your life as a whole, because all the positivity that you put out in thought, deed, or action will come back to you it's inevitable, it's the universal immutable law of compensation at work here. You call it karma, so all I can say is strive to be positive in life and in your dealings with people, because if you don't negativity will only take you down, and if not abated will eventually after so long totally consume you.

562. Always remember that you can always come up with a thousand reasons of why something won't work, but by the same token you can always if you want to and if you think about it come up with a thousand reasons of why something will work. It just all depends on you which position or stand you choose to take. Remember that thinking positive and having faith are the keys.

563. This right here is a direct quote from former President Woodrow Wilson concerning the unseen powers that control our government here in the United States:

We have come to be one of the worst ruled one of the most completely controlled and dominated governments in the civilized world no longer a government by conviction and the free vote of the majority but a government by the opinion and duress of a small group of dominant men. That is actually what modern so-called democracy really means.

And this was a quote on quote from President Woodrow Wilson in 1916. It just goes to show that those who clandestinely control the U.S. government have been around a long time.

564. I just want to let the masses of people know that right now we as a people must stand together like never before, because right now as your reading this there are very evil and powerful forces both supernatural and worldly, inordinately at work to corrupt, enslave, and just totally neutralize us the people. And you already know who the worldly evil forces are who want to enslave, and neutralize us. Yes, those who clandestinely control the U.S. government. And the world from behind the scenes. And you most definitely already know who the supernatural evil

force or forces are; it's those malevolent spiritual entities that I call the negative forces of the universe. And these two immensely powerful, and evil forces are working in concert, and in confluence to bring about the full and complete implementation of the new world order, which will without a doubt enslave and neutralize us all.

565. Did you know that gold, and yes, I said gold . . . the gold that you have and now own is really and actually not yours. Did you know that the U.S. government has the power to confiscate and take all gold away from the American people and what I just said is based on a little known law and provision of the Federal Reserve act that reads:

Whenever in the judgment of the secretary of the treasury such action is necessary to protect the currency system of the United States, the Secretary in his discretion may require any and all individuals to deliver forth-with to the treasurer of the United States any and all gold, including but not limited to gold coins, gold bullion, and gold certificates owned by any and all individuals.

So if and when the U.S. government wants to recall and take away the gold of the American people it the U.S. government most definitely can. And without even giving the people a sufficient and prior notice. And the only options left to the American citizen that owns gold of sentimental value or not is for them to surrender their gold over to the government or face the penalties of the penal and judicial system. And if you doubt or disbelieve what I just said, well it's not like this hasn't happened before. Let me give you a little history on this in April of 1933 President Franklin D. Roosevelt without giving the people any kind of prior notice what so ever ordered any and all individuals owning gold without exception to turn it in to the banking system and the banks would buy it at 20.67$ an ounce. Later to be raised to $35.00 an ounce. And the American people were told to turn in their gold before April 31, 1933 or suffer a penalty of fine of $10,000 or imprisonment of not more than 10 years or both. And the records show that not all of America's gold was turned in because more than 165 million dollars worth of gold went unaccounted for and went into hiding.

566. Here is a quote about the government from Barry Seal, former CIA covert operative, international drug runner and DEA informant:

The most crafty, deceptive manipulative and odious schemes that you can possibly conjure up with your mental faculties, have already been conjured up and are for the most part carried out on a daily basis by those in the highest echelons of government.

--Barry Seal

1939 to 1986

567. Remember that it's very much true that you never know what you got until it's gone.

568. Remember hell is a place in which the soul neither dies nor lives . . . you're just there.

569. In this world you can't always, all of the time do everything right, because you'll kill yourself trying to. You can only honestly try to do the very best that you can.

570. The people in the upper echelons of the U.S. government are some of the biggest liars the world knows. Believe that!

571. Let me tell you something that you might or might not already know, and that's that those who clandestinely control the U.S. government via there tool, the U.S. government are even endeavoring to control your kids. Because it's like this if you spank or even yell too loud at your kids it could be considered child abuse. So you tell me what control are the parents left with over their own children???

572. Remember motivation is so powerful that it's really ineffable and all motivation is a state of one's mind. A thought, a thought that if fed properly can linger and stay in one's mind. And the way you give a thought power is by constantly feeding it; by constantly thinking about it.

573. The U.S. government, corruption, lying, cheating, politics, manipulation, organized crime, craftiness, and deception are all very close siblings in the world we now live in.

574. Do you know a good time to do some real thinking is when you're eating, as long as you're alone and it's quite and you're hungry, is a very good time to go into deep thought. And you'll be amazed at how thoughts get to popping into your mind while you're eating.

575. Remember that you had better cherish every minute of your life, because you can never ever get even a second of it back. And let me tell you something, it is not going to be fun being old. Believe that!

576. The world now is becoming to be all about political and social correctness which is bad and all wrong because you should be yourself no matter what. Be what you want to be, not what someone else or the crowd wants you to do. Speak when and what you think you should speak. Because listen up it's not good to hold your breath or stuff in because if you do you'll just feel bad later on. So you had better let it out. And remember that you only have one life to live. And you don't want to have a bunch of dumb regrets when you get old. Because it'll just make you feel bad. So be yourself and not who they, the crowd or establishment wants you to be. And do what you yourself need to do for you.

577. Remember no amount of money is worth your youth. So don't kill yourself working while you're young. Enjoy some of your youth, because if you don't enjoy it now you never will. And remember money will always come and go, but your youth only comes once, and if you miss it you can best believe me, it'll never come back around again.

578. Remember don't never be afraid of what people think because people been thinking things from the beginning of time, and they'll be thinking things till the end of time. So it's nothing new! And remember you're not going to be the first person that people talk about, and you are damn sure not going to be the last. And people are always talking about somebody behind

their back. So what makes you think they're not talking about you behind your back? It's like this . . . just like water is always going to be wet; people are always going to talk behind somebody's back. So never be afraid of what people think or say, because it means nothing.

579. Remember time spent alone in solitude and in total quietness is said to have no equal and thinking and going into deep thought is not only good for the body, mind, and soul. But is an education with in itself. And time to yourself and spent with only yourself feels so good that it can even be like a drug . . . and can be intoxicating.

580. Remember the 3 things you always want to keep pure no matter what are your mind, heart, and soul.

581. Remember love yourself and be good to your family and friends, treat other people right, and do the right thing, and you'll be much a happier person.

582. Two of the deadliest things on earth . . . and these two things will break up families and friendships . . . and they are sex and money.

583. Now for a word on infomercials, those paid advertisements that come on T.V. mostly in the wee hours of the morning, but are starting to come on at more respectable times now are fallacious, and very plausible, but are nothing but deception and trickery to say the least. Because check this out, most of the devices they peddle and sell 80% of the claims that they attach to them are misleads or straight deceptions. And the schemes they peddle like there so called get rich quick schemes based on real estate or whatever. Now just use your God given common sense here for a minute. And think, if somebody really had a get rich quick scheme that actually worked would they be advertising it on national T.V.? For God's sake I think not . . . something like that if it really worked would be kept so secret that it would be unbelievable. Honestly, because something like that would be damn near priceless and let me put something else in your ear, the people who you see on those infomercials who get up and say well yes it worked well for me and/or I made this

much money in this amount of time, they are paid very well for their statements . . . believe that. And then you have the other kind of infomercials that prey and try to take advantage of people who are overweight or obese. And they try to sell them a hope and a dream, i.e. some kind of miracle diet or device. And they tell them poor people just what they want to hear. I mean all I'm saying is why don't they just be truthful and tell them folks the truth. And that's that there is no easy or miracle way to lose weight or look like a supermodel. Tell them what it takes, which is lots of strenuous exercise, real determination, a low fat diet, and a whole lot of hard work. And then you can have the kind of body that you desire or wish, because the truth about it is there's no easy or miracle way about it and that's just the uncut and unabridged truth. But they the infomercials don't tell you that. They just tell you what they know you want to hear. So you will stay tuned in and won't change the channel and hopefully by the end of the infomercial they got you convinced and if they got you convinced, they got your money because you will have purchased something. So people please wake up.

584. Now this thought here is for those of you suffering from anorexia-nervosa, which is a very bad and sad eating disorder. But really it's a mental disorder that keeps its victims in a constant state of denial. Because for one it keeps it's victims believing and thinking that they can never be skinny or slim enough which is a straight lie. Because there is a point where one can get to thin or skinny where one is not healthy anymore. For two no matter how slim or skinny they get for some reason they still think that they're too fat which is another straight lie. And for three, and this is probably the worst one of all they think that every single piece of food that they eat is going to automatically make them gain weight which is another lie and totally crazy. They think that however many ounces or pounds the food weighs they're going to automatically gain. That's just totally crazy. But I would just like to say this for those suffering from anorexia-nervosa that you have powerful acids in your stomach that almost completely disintegrate your food after you eat it, the acids brake it all the way down to almost nothing. And then your body distributes what's left throughout your body according to your body's needs. And what your

body doesn't want or need, it makes into waste. And remember food produces energy, and energy produces strength. So please don't starve yourself because your body was made for food and you need nourishment to stay alive and healthy to say the least. And anorexia –nervosa is nothing but a mental disorder, it's nothing but a mind thing. Believe me; it's all in the head. It's a pathological fear of weight gain. And if you suffer from anorexia-nervosa or any other eating disorder you need to take your life back from that ugly demon that has took control of your mind, G.N.C. health food stores sell what's known as weight gainer that you can drink in the form of shakes and they have protein in the form of shakes too. And my advice to you if you suffer from anorexia-nervosa is that you go to G.N.C. and get yourself a nice weight gainer and some protein and drink them together in one shake 3 times a day one in the morning, one at noon, and one for dinner. And if you do that I guarantee you that you'll be well on your way to recovery. And it'll just be 3 shakes a day that's all. And you parents had better watch your kids, because anorexia-nervosa and many other eating disorders are nothing but a mind thing, a thought. But remember the power of thought is powerful and that's for good or for bad. And just remember the extremely sad story of Terri Schiavo who in 1990 suffered severe brain damage after collapsing from an eating disorder. And to this day, and is this 2004, she is still on life support. This is an addition Terri Schiavo subsequently died in 2005 from her condition.

585. Remember that it's not good to entertain bad, negative, irrational, or counter-productive thoughts of any kind. Why? Because they can and will take control of your life. Again, why? Because thought of any kind is powerful, very powerful! And is not to be misused or abused. But the sad thing is that most or a lot of people inadvertently entertain bad, negative, irrational, or counterproductive thoughts which are bad and very pernicious to them.

586. Now for a word on junk T.V. Jerry Springer I must say is the epitome of junk T.V. Because the nationally syndicated Jerry Springer show consist of nothing but negativity, promiscuous sex, infidelity, ignorance, and violence. And you know what

the saddest thing is . . . and that's that it sells. And that right there gives you a glimpse of what kind of world we now live in. And just keeping it real and being uncut with you, Jerry Springer puts out nothing but garbage, ignorance, and junk. And the ones who like it and watch it, might not know better. Because like attracts like. And remember what you put into your mind is what you're going to get out of your mind. Junk in, junk out . . . it's invariable.

587. Now remember, and I want you to know that people have all kinds of weird, and sick, sexual fetishes. But the thing is, you'll never know it. Because people keep their fetishes and other sick sexual agendas hid . . . and hid well. But believe me they exist and people got them . . . more than you think.

588. You will be amazed at what you can learn by trial and error.

589. Remember there's a power in deep thought because you're building though, upon thought. And then as your building and projecting thought you're creating.

590. Always remember in life every single human being fights there own war or wars with life.

591. Always be careful and keep your guard up when you show kindness and generosity to others. Because people tend to and will take advantage, and take your kindness and generosity for weakness. They might not even be conscious of it. It could even be Freudian, but they will so don't be a fool.

592. Always remember we all go through things and got things that we must battle with and fight with, within ourselves. That's why I previously said that in this life we all must fight our own war or wars. Now what I meant is that we all have problems, fears, addictions and maybe even refractory fetishes that we don't like to talk about or even let anybody know that we suffer from. But let me tell you something, don't feel bad. Because you best believe me you're not the only one in the world with these secret problems. We all got them. It's just how you deal with them. And some of us have them worse than others, because they vary just like everything else in life varies. So like

I said we all must fight our own war or wars. So stop feeling like a lone soldier. Because you're not the only one. People just don't overtly talk about these things for various reasons and one reason is there scared. They don't want people to think there weak, vulnerable or just plain crazy, which in reality is very true. So everybody keeps these problems, fears, addictions, and/or whatever else that's inside of them, that they're fighting with or going through, to themselves. And that's simply because people have images to uphold so you can't really blame them. But this is just to let you know you're not the only that has to fight your own war or wars. Because we all got to fight our own wars. So all I can tell you is to get in tune with yourself and stay thinking right, good, rational, and positive thoughts, because like you should already know there's power in thought, and a whole lot of it. And remember you are your thoughts, and if you can't control your thoughts, you damn sure can't control your life. Because life is a mind thing, everything originates as thought first no matter what it is. And on a last note I'm just going to say this . . . that it absolutely makes no sense for intelligent, smart, rational thinking people to suffer from their own thoughts.

593. Don't ever forget that the U.S. government has many sides, both overt and covert. And it only shows the side that it wants to the people. In other words the U.S. government only lets the masses of people see and know what it wants them to see and know.

594. Always remember the more you think and go into the deep thought the more you'll be able to see things that you didn't see before. Things will just begin to pop into your mind while you are in deep thought. And then, and only then will you be able to make the smartest and best moves. And believe me . . . you'll be absolutely amazed at how smart, and efficacious you really can be if you'll only take the time out to think.

595. Always remember that eight or nine times out of ten what you see of people is a façade, and fake, it's nothing but an image or an illusion that there portraying, but you got to watch out to because some people are so proficient, and adept, and

inconspicuous at portraying facades that it's very hard to tell and spot them. So you got to be careful, and just to be safe don't believe what you see of people too much, because just like I said eight or nine times out of ten what you see of people is going to be fake and/or some kind of façade.

596. Always remember that some things you just can't understand, you can't even imagine them until you experience them.

597. Now remember you can sit around all your life and do nothing. Because if so you best believe me, when you get old you'll have nothing. Because if you do nothing then you'll get and have nothing. And there's absolutely no way around that, because there's no free lunch in this life. Hard work is what it's going to take to get anything worth anything. So don't sit around on your ass wasting your time doing nothing. Get up and do something worthwhile with your time and life so that time will work with you and not against you. Because the clock never stops and it takes time to build or accumulate anything that's worth anything. That's why I'm belaboring you with this.

598. Did you know that laughing, just plain old laughing is one of the best natural antidepressants known to man? But people don't know that laughing is the best antidepressant that there is. And this has been scientifically proven that laughing releases endorphins. And that a good long hard laugh can rearrange the chemical compositions in your body. So if you're depressed or stressed out try laughing. And not just regular laughing, but some good deep long laughing. And I bet you'll not only notice the difference but you'll feel the difference.

599. Remember . . . believing, faith, determination, and motivation are nothing but thoughts and they all work together in harmony.

600. Remember you're never too old to learn and to feel good about yourself.

601. Remember the older you get the more you'll start to appreciate life.

602. And don't ever forget that life really is beautiful. But in order to appreciate and love life you have to love and appreciate yourself first.

603. Remember in life you can't make it and you won't be able to make it without courage, patience, discipline, and faith.

604. Always remember that just because you haven't heard of somebody doing something or ever seen somebody else do something doesn't mean that it can't be done or it doesn't happen whatever it may be. It just means that you have to learn more about the world and/or whatever you're trying to do. And this calls for more learning and knowledge.

605. Remember everybody wants muscles and a nice body. But nobody wants or likes to work out. Lest we forget muscles and nice bodies like so many other worthwhile things in life take hard work and lots of it. So I'm sorry but there's no free lunch in this life. So wake up, smell the coffee, get real, and face reality for what it is. And don't lie or kid yourself about nothing.

606. Remember in the real world and in life the truth and peoples real motives are always more times than not hidden and seldom if ever exposed, because people keep their real agendas, motives, and their real selves hid.

607. Remember in life more times than not without a struggle there's no progress . . .

608. Remember people, everybody lies. But only according to their personality, that's the only difference between people's lies. Because every single human being is a liar and has lied at some point in time in their life. And as you're sitting here reading this book you cannot honestly sit there and tell yourself that you have never lied. And if you do, you're lying to yourself right now. But like I said everybody lies, but everybody lies differently . . . people lie according to their personality. Some people have a personality where they lie compulsively and almost everything they say or comes out of their mouth is a straight lie. And some people have a personality where they

might just exaggerate or like to put a lot on it. And other people might have the kind of personality where they might just lie when they need to. But the point is everybody lies, and there are no exceptions to it.

609. Always remember and don't ever forget that thinking is an education with in itself.

610. In life you got to roll with the punches and blows that come at you and just keep going.

611. Remember always keep your eyes on what you want and where you're trying to go and never lose sight of your goals.

612. Education sharpens and enlightens your mind. But thinking and going into deep thought grows your mind.

613. Alright . . . you already know that the U.S. government only shows and lets the masses of people know what it wants them to know. And that's it and that's all! But check this out . . . did you know that the U.S. government has right now and has been having for like the last 30 years or so all kinds of secret armies, militaries, and armed forces ready to go into action at the drop of a dime. That you the people did not even know or could even believe existed. And these covert armies and militaries are highly and proficiently trained in genocide, chemical and biological warfare, psychological warfare and in the destabilization, containment, control, and suppression of societies and populations and the reason the government has these covert armies and military forces is so they could get rid of, eliminate and eradicate masses of people, and whole societies, and populations, if and when they need to. And these secret militaries and armies are nothing to be played with or are they to be taken lightly in any kind of way. Because the weapons and technology they have at their disposal are so lethal that it's really inconceivable for the average person to understand. I mean everything from acoustic sound weapons to laser ray guns to chemical and biological weaponry on down. And you could not even began to conceive how lethal and destructive there technology and weapons are. And they're already tested their capabilities in April 1984 with RX84A.

And that was designed to test the readiness and capabilities of the secret armies and militaries. And these tests were carried out under the guise of the federal emergency management agency (FEMA), which is one of the fronts for the secret armies and militaries. Now I'm going to impart something else to you and that's that the Department of Defense in collusion with FEMA has been building and maintaining surreptitiously a massive concentration camp or detention camp program in above ground and underground locations. The above ground locations are mostly in extremely remote areas such as the Appalachian Mountains of Central Pennsylvania, El Reno Oklahoma, Florence Arizona, Tule Lake in California, Mill Point West Virginia, Alderson West Virginia, Lewisburg West Virginia, Greenville South Carolina, and Avon Park Florida. Now these are just a few of the above ground facilities. And if you're not a diligent researcher you will not find these facilities, because most of these locations on maps don't show that they have concentration camps or detention facilities of any kind but if you personally go to these areas you will most definitely see the prisons. Because that's just what they are . . . uncut, complete with 10-foot barb-wire fences, cells, and gun towers. And it's rumored that the government now has ready and built underground and above ground over 180 facilities capable of holding millions of people. Now the authority for these concentration camps / prisons comes under the old 1950 emergency detention act that was supposed to have been repealed in 1971, but if you research as I did you'll learn that even though the act was repealed there are 17 other bits of law that provide for the same thing. And the coldest thing is that the U.S. government doesn't even tell the people there constituents that these secret armies, militaries and concentration camps / prisons they have, even exist. And I think that you as a tax payer and a constituent have a de-jure right to know about these things. And these covert armies, militaries, and prisons are for one thing and for one thing only . . . and that's to facilitate their new world order and the imminent eradication of you the people if and when needed. So don't never think that those who clandestinely control the U.S. government aren't serious about implementing there new world order. Because there more serious then serious is about that. There more serious than 15 heart attacks happening at once and that's serious. And believe me there more than willing to go to any length that they got to go to, to get there new world order implemented. And when I say any I mean any and all . . . genocide and the elimination, and eradication of the masses of people. So now that you know that there preparing and getting ready with these covert armies, militaries, and prisons that they got. So just in case the people don't want to comply with their new law, which is their new world order because people will comply with it or be eradicated by the masses if need be. And for more on the new world order please read on.

614. If you think that all that is necessary is to pay your house notes, to pay your car notes, to go vote when there is an election, and to stand back during the rest of the year and watch as your country and way of life are replaced by a system in which you will be a slave in a concentration camp . . . you, not the conspirator, are to blame and are guilty. Because you by silent acquiescence, invite tyranny and oppression. And when you have to steal food to eat because our production is for foreign use because the Department of Commerce through executive order #11490 and it's predecessors is responsible for international distribution of our commodities, don't sit in a culvert hiding and sobbing and wondering what happened because you made it all possible. And when your family is split up and spread across the United States to do slave labor and you never see your loved ones again, it will be all your fault because you did nothing to prevent it. And once we lose our freedom, we are never going to regain it. That is why we must stand together to prevent the loss of our freedom as citizens of the United States.

That is an except taken from a lawsuit filed in U.S. District Court #75-H-667 in the Southern District of Texas, Houston Division in April of 1979 against the concentration camp program of the U.S. Department of Defense. By one Mr. William R. Pabst.

615. Now in this thought here I'm going to speak on something called the new world order. And I don't know if you have ever heard of it before or not, but it's something that those who clandestinely control the U.S. government have been planning

and plotting for a very long time now. And many books by a vast assortment of assiduous authors who have perused the new world order and it's architects which are those who clandestinely control the U.S. government have been written and published through the years. But sad to say like most other things that those who clandestinely control the U.S. government don't want the masses of people to know or find out about have been suppressed for many years by those who clandestinely control the U.S. government. It's starting to leak out now as more and more people start to wake up to the truth which is by any standard a beautiful thing. So it would not be right if I didn't at least briefly speak on the new world order in this book. So hopefully using brevity I'm going to give you a summary of what the new world order is. And what it means to all human beings living on the planet at this time. And especially living in America. Because of the degree of freedom that we so call enjoy at this time in America, but is being exponentially atrophied. But anyway the new world order is nothing but the draconian restructuring of society, our way of life, and the world as we know it. And I know that you're going to ask how? And in what way? Well, I'll tell you how and in what way . . . by you losing all your rights and your freedom. And if you think that this is not so or can't happen in America. Then you better wake up and think again. Like I Said the knowledge of this has been around for a long time but has been and still is to a good degree being suppressed by those who clandestinely control the U.S. government. But I'm going to tell you this, the laws and the legal foundation for the new world order was laid down a long time ago via and through presidential executive orders, which are legal laws that are made by a sitting president with the stroke of his pen, with little if any oversight. So that way no matter how outrageous or way-out the law there will be none if any opposition to it. And this was the vehicle that was used by those who clandestinely control the U.S. government to lay the laws and legal foundation for their socialistic totalitarian new world order and these laws exist and are operating law right now as we speak. And I'm talking about laws that will actually strip you of all your rights, personal, and real property, and freedom, and for a reference of these laws, please go to thought #619, where I list some of these laws. Now the new world orders implementation as we speak is in inchoate and incipient stages and is picking up momentum and progressing at an exponential pace. And I know that you're probably wondering how the new world order is going to be brought from it's covert existence, which it's in now to the ostensible, and to over existence. Well, I'll tell you if, well I won't say if, because it's just a question of when. Because it's inevitable . . . it's going to happen when the President of the United States declares a state of national emergency in America. In that second all those laws that I just told you about that strip every American of all their rights, personal and real property, and freedoms will go into effect and that right there is also law. But the mass majority of people don't know this and when that happens and the President declares a state of national emergency there's laws right now on the books that provide for the suspension of the U.S. constitution and with that all of your former liberties and rights will be gone and you can't say I have a right or you can't do that I'll call the police there will be none of that because when the constitution is suspended all of your rights you once had will be gone. Then martial law will be implemented to so called keep the peace, but that will be a lie that will just be the excuse so they can bring in their secret armies which have been trained for the last 40 years or so for just this day and for more on the secret armies and detention centers or prisons that they have all over America above ground and underground ready and waiting for this faithful hour then you must read thought #613. And now this state of national emergency I discuss that in thought #620 and don't worry because all of these thoughts follow one another. And now you must understand that when all this comes about and it will be in the not too distant future society. Your way of life and the world will be like I previously said restructured in a way that you cannot even began to imagine right now. All of you former liberties, rights, and freedoms will be gone, nonexistence, a thing of the past. There will be strict control; uncut totalitarianism will be the order of the day. And almost a 3rd of all America will be thrown into work bridges to work for the state, which are nothing but detention centers / prisons which are already built and ready and waiting right now. And the rest of the people will be virtually confined to their homes under martial/totalitarian law living under and in a complete and absolute police state where such mundane things like child-bearing is going to be controlled by the state. Child-bearing and having children is going to be a criminal offense unless the parents are licensed and certified by the state to have children and then only ones who are going to be granted child-bearing licenses are those who pass certain genetic testing and scanning to make sure the babies that they produce meet certain state mandates and criteria. In other words the only people who are going to be allowed to legally have children are those that are damn near genetically perfect. So that they will produce only damn near genetically perfect babies . . . eugenics is going to be the law. Because they want complete control and in their eyes that will be a utopian society. And all new born infants even those of licensed child-bearing parents will have to undergo certain tests regarding their genetic code to make absolutely sure that they meet certain state mandates and criteria and if the newborn infant fails or doesn't pass these tests then it forfeits it's right to live and they will kill it declaring it genetically defective. And everything will be global; there will be a new global credit card and monetary system. In other words a one world currency. There will be a global food system meaning a one world food authority that will control and administer all of the world's food. There will be a global one world legal system, meaning a one world constitution and repealing and indefinitely suspending are original American constitution and all others like it. And all laws will be under a system of unified world courts and euthanasia will be mandatory and the law for any person 60 years of age or older because they will be deemed useless eaters, unless you're associated with or part of those who clandestinely control the U.S. government. And each and every person shall be fully indoctrinated that he or she is a member and/or creature of the one world community. And if you refuse this indoctrination and programming you will be sent away for psychological testing and evaluation and probably never heard or seen from again. And every man, woman, and child will be chipped without exception of which chips will contain virtually all your information, medically, financially, and otherwise and not only that but these microchips are said to be able to control a person's thoughts (mind), emotions, and physical health via the chip. And check this out it's a known fact in the intelligence community that these microchips that I'm speaking on have been and are being covertly put in people all over America and the world by doctors, surgeons, and dentists who are either under contract, for the intelligence agencies or are intelligence agency operatives who work for the CIA and other intelligence agencies and networks. And this has been going on at least since the late 1980's and these chips being implanted in the unsuspecting populace are so small that they cannot be seen with the naked eye and chips the size of rice grains are virtually obsolete now. And did you know that congress under the 1990 safety medical devices act mandated that all medical devices, such as artificial limbs, dentures, all prosthetic apparatuses, and all internal prosthetic apparatuses like, pace-makers that are manufactured in America and those imported for use in America must be equipped with passive or electronic RF-receiver which are radio frequency receivers which are capable of receiving and emitting signals. And this is for the so-called purpose of them making and keeping a database of all medical devices and knowing where there at at all times and the coldest thing is that the patients who use these medical devices and apparatuses are not even told or warned that these devices are equipped and fitted with RF-receivers. And these RF-receivers some of them are so small that you cannot see them with the naked eye. And like I told you some are passive and some are electronic. Passive means it does not need electricity or power to work or the electricity or power is sent to it via a signal from an outside source. Most external medical devices are fitted with passive RF-receivers. Electronic RF-receivers means it has its own electricity or power source or is directly hooked up to one. Most internal; medical devices are fitted with electronic RF-receivers meaning they get there power probably from the body's own electromagnetism. And these signals that these RF-receivers receive and emit are like cellular and wireless phone signals. Matter of fact they work on the same networks. And if you don't believe me or you think that this is too far out, then I suggest that you do some research and look up on the internet the 1990 safety medical devices act and read it for yourself because it's there. It's just that people don't know that it's there and that's what this book is for to wake people up and lead them to knowledge. And damn near everything I say or mention in this book can be researched or studied in a phalanx of books, the internet, or in official or government records. So please don't take my word for it because my only objective is to get the word out about those who clandestinely control the U.S. government and there odious agendas. And while I'm on the subject of RF-receivers let me drop something else on you that I know that you're going to be incredulous to. But it's very much true and absolute fact. And that's that about 1000 companies and corporations have collogued and are in collusion and this includes some of the biggest corporations, retailers, and manufactures on the face of the earth. Such as Kraft, Coca-cola, Kellogg's, Microsoft, Sony, Procter and Gamble, IBM, Wal-mart, Nestle, Gillette. And many others have come into collusion to actually tag or implement a RF-receiver on every single manufactured item, product, or good on earth. I'm talking about soda cans, clothes, toothpaste; even your draws will be chipped. Now like I said this might sound crazy, or impossible or whatever, but I absolutely guarantee you it's true! And this nefarious scheme has been in the making for the last 10 to 15 years and has been funded to the tune of billions of dollars by the multi-national conglomerates of which all are unequivocally owned and controlled by those who clandestinely control the U.S. government. Because as you already know their ultimate plan is to chip absolutely everything and everybody. Now as always if you don't believe me, please, and I say again, please, check it out for yourself. There's a website and an excellent book by two inclusive researchers who have studied and perused for many years this malevolent plan of these multi-national conglomerates to chip every item, product, or good on earth. The website is www.spychip.com or www.antichips.com. And I strongly suggest that if you're interested you stop reading this book right now and go to it. It's at www.spychips.com or www.antichips.com and the book by the same name is: Spychips, How Major Corporations and Government Plan to Track Your Every Move with RF ID by, Katherine Albrecht and Liz Mackintyer. And just so you know the U.S. State Department starting January 01, 2006 is going to start putting in all U.S. Passports RF-receivers. And before I leave the topic of RF-receivers and chips let me just say this and that's that starting in the beginning of 2008 all the major credit cards such as Visa, Master Card, Discover, and American Express will start putting and implementing RF-receivers in all of their credit cards. So if in the middle of 2008 your credit card company out of the clear blue sends you a new credit card for no reason, well, now you'll know why and that's because that new card is fitted with an RF-receiver. And check this out if you call the credit card company and ask them why did they just replace your perfectly good credit card with a new one they will tell you that the new one has got for your protection against theft an added or enhanced security feature and if you ask about RF-receivers, they are strictly prohibited from using the term or phrase RF-receivers or RF-ID they will either 1) not answer you, 2) tell you that they don't know or, 3) straight out lie. But they are strictly prohibited from using the term or phrase RF-receivers or RF-ID. So what you ask them is whether they are prohibited from using the term or phrase RF-receiver or RF-ID with you? That's how you get them. Now I'm not saying that RF-receivers or RF-ID on every credit card is a bad thing . . . shit, some people might want that on their credit cards. All I'm saying is that the credit card companies should let people know what they're doing and give them a choice about RF-receivers or RF-ID being put on their credit cards and fully disclose to people everything that RF-receivers and RF-ID can and can't do. Then with people fully informed about RF-receivers and RF-ID let them choose if they want or desire such a feature on their credit cards. But that's too much like right. And you need to know that certain U.S. corporations specifically in the defense industry and in other industries as well. And certain government agencies are right now and have been for a number of years now requiring and making it mandatory that there employees take chips. And if the employee refuses then they are demoted and if they continue to refuse they are eventually laid-off and/or terminated. And just so you know some major corporations in league with the U.S. government are right now in the process on unveiling a major program that offers monetary incentives to people if they voluntary take chips such as tax cuts, cheaper insurance premiums or whatever. The monetary incentives are vast and of many assortments. So don't be fooled. And they'll tell you that the chip is nothing and absolutely harmless and is somehow for your benefit, well-being, and best interest. And all RF-receivers and/or chips are comparable with and can be indefinitely tracked by the global positioning system (GPS). And did you know that on 12-20-04 or 12-21-04 President George W. Bush signed the national ID and/or driver's license act into law. Also called the federal ID card act. So your local and state ID's and driver licenses that you have right now might only be good for the next few years. And after that, here in America there might be a national federal ID. Now, how many of you knew that? And laws like these are passed everyday herein America. And these laws effect every American, but are given little if any attention in the mainstream media. Why? Because that's just the way that those who clandestinely control the U.S. government want it and the mainstream is unequivocally owned and controlled by them. And the mass-mainstream media has been one of the main tools used by those who clandestinely control the U.S. government for brain-washing, conditioning, and controlling the unsuspecting docile and extremely acquiescent masses of people. And check this out . . . there was an in depth study done a few years ago of the mainstream media and it's power to condition, control, form and mold the opinions, dogmas, and tenets, and beliefs of it's viewers and the findings are something all media aficionados should know or be aware of. But like always the findings of this very pivotal and objective study were suppressed by and through the very vehicle (the media) which was the object of the study. But anyway the study was carried out by the research staff of National Vanguard INC. And the findings were succinctly as follows:

Who rules America? There power . . . reaches into every home in America. It works it's will during nearly every waking hour. It is the power which shapes and molds the mind of virtually every citizen. Young or old, rich or poor, simple or sophisticated. The mass media form for us our image of the world and then tell us what to think about that image. Essentially everything we know or think we know about the events outside of our neighborhood or circle of acquaintances comes to us via our daily newspaper, our weekly news magazine, our radio, or our television . . . employing carefully developed psychological techniques . . . they guide our thoughts and opinions. Most Americans fail to realize that they are being manipulated even the citizen who complains about managed news falls into the trap of thinking that because he is presented with the apparent spectrum of opinion he can escape the thought controllers influence by believing the editor or commentator of his choice. Every point on the permissible spectrum of public opinion is acceptable to the media masters and no impermissible fact or viewpoint is allowed any exposure at all, if they can prevent it.

Now like I said in the foregoing what you just read was the findings succinctly put of the National Vanguard INC. study of the mainstream media and it's power and impact on it's viewers. But anyway like I said previously the new world order is nothing new it's been in the making for many, many, years. But for the most part has been kept suppressed, but just because the new world order has been successfully suppressed by the controllers does not mean that it's not real or does not exist. Because, please believe me it is very real, and very much does exist and there have been and are right now myriad organizations, movements, publications, and programs that overtly and covertly advocate, stand for, promote, and support the new world order that are managed, and controlled behind the scenes by those who clandestinely control the U.S. government. And some of the most innocent sounding groups or some apparently ineffective body whose avowed purpose seem totally non-political, maybe one of the more sinister, corrupt and dangerous tentacles of those who clandestinely control the U.S. government. For instance, the new age movement that has been gaining momentum since the 1980's with all it's love, peace, and positiveness, which is all good if it was from sincere motives. But like I done told you before the degree of craftiness, deception, and manipulation that those who clandestinely control the U.S. government are capable of is completely beyond the comprehension and understanding of the average person. And if you're a newager or have read their literature then you know that a lot of it teaches one world or global ideology. Now I know that a lot of people are going to say that I'm crazy and that the new age movement is nothing but love, peace, and positiveness. But all I'm saying is that whatever you're into new age, spiritual ascension, channeling, religion, whatever, that you research and study it from every possible point and angle. And I'm going to tell you unequivocally that the new age movement was started in the mid 1970's by those who clandestinely control the U.S. government when it became known and apparent that people were becoming dissatisfied with church and religion. So they had to give the people something else, and that's when they came up with the new age. Now don't get it mixed up here I know and believe that the mass majority of new age followers are good people with genuine intentions, but I'm talking about the controllers of the new age, the high echelon of the new age is what is corrupt and foul. And again, don't take my word for it because many books have been written by new age insiders and former new agers about the truth of the new age movement and who really controls the new age agenda. And again, if you're a new ager or into new age, I think you should know that these points of views, opinions, and books exist, books such as: Inside The New Age Nightmare, by Randal Baer; The Demonic Roots of Globalism, by Gary Kha; The Hidden Dangers of the Rainbow, by Constance E. Cumbey; and Satanization of Society, by Robert Rosio. And these are just a few, because there are many more. And in my opinion the most comprehensive and informative of these books that I just listed about the truth of the new age movement is, "Inside the New Age Nightmare," by Randal Baer. And just so you know Randal Baer was with the new age movement from it's inception and was part of the high echelon of the new age. Now I'm going to speak on channeling for a minute, because it's considered part of the new age for those of you that are channels and into channeling. And as we all know channeling is the ability to be talked to or to pick up communication from other realms or dimensions. And I just think that it's fair that you know that the CIA has been running and operating since the early 1980's something called project Bluebeam, which has the ability to broadcast a vast assortment of myriad messages via extremely low frequency (ELF), very low frequency (VLF), and many microwave bands which can and are picked up by the human brain. And this technology is highly sophisticated and many people will believe that God or their savior is talking to them in their head when it's really the CIA manipulating them. And like I said Project Bluebeam has been in operation since the early 1980's and it's a known fact in the intelligence community and among serious researchers like myself and others that it Project Bluebeam has been the source of much channeled information here in the United States for the last 25 years or so. But I just thought you should know that. But anyway concerning the tentacles of those who clandestinely control the U.S. government to promote, advocate, and eventually brings into actual manifestation the new World order. You must understand and appreciate the long standing interlinking of power in business, academics, banking, politics, and the media that allows those who clandestinely control the U.S. government to promote the same ideas, agendas, and policies through a host of apparently unconnected institutions and organizations. And when the new world order is fully implemented society is going to be divided into the rulers and the ruled with an administrative bureaucracy in between. Private automobiles and things of the like are only going to be used by the ruling elite and those that are part of the upper bureaucracy or those who hold government positions of authority such as those that are part of or belong to the secret armies that are going to enforce the new totalitarian laws. But everybody else will be reduced to the level of serfs and will be indefinitely stuck in a state of perpetual servitude to the rulers. And check this out if the new world order is successful it will not just have extremely draconian implications for us incarcerated beings now living on the planet. But it would severely affect even those yet to be born because when there born they will be born into an absolute socialistic totalitarian police state, oppressively controlled by the plutocracy and oligarchy aka those who clandestinely control the U.S. government. Then after about 20 or 30 years into the new world order everyone will just accept it as natural and nothing out of the ordinary. Why? Because then a whole new generation will be in place that has no memory of another way of life. And many of the older folks will have all but forgotten the ways and details of their previous existence. And of course many of them especially the dissenters of the new world order will have been eliminated and neutralized. Schools and textbooks will speak of the bygone era as one of terrorism, world wars, unabated corruption, competition, selfishness, and rampant lawlessness and injustice. And of course all of these things will no longer exist, but the people will be serfs living in complete and absolute totalitarianism. And previously commonplace things such as cars, private homes, 3 or 4 pairs of shoes, and things of the like will be hardly mentioned. And when they are, they will be derided as wasteful artifacts of a decadent society that fortunately has ceased to exist. And the people will no longer be concerned or worried about terrorism, world wars, famines, or depressions or any of the like, because there will be none of that. Because if the truth be told over 90% of the worlds ills, calamities, upheavals, world wars, famines, depressions, civil wars, violent revolutions, coup d'états, and copious other human miseries, and distresses, have all be artificially designed, created, and put out on the world by those who clandestinely control the U.S. government and if you don't believe me, well, the secret teachings or papers of those who clandestinely control the U.S. government know as the protocols of the learned elders of Zion which are the secret teachings of the predecessors and forefathers of those who clandestinely control the U.S. government tell the story . . . check this small excerpt out from the protocols of the learned elders of Zion:

When we come into our rule and our supreme one world government is acknowledged by the entire world, our orators will expose the great problems which have turned humanity upside down in order to bring it to this end. And then who will ever suspect that all these problems and upheavals, and the people and things, that caused them were all stage managed by us according to a political plan which none has so much as guessed at in the course of many centuries.

Now the excerpt that you just read is from the 24 documents known as The Protocols of the Learned Elders of Zion, which were first made available for public scrutiny in American in 1905. Now remember 1905 is just when they were first made available for public scrutiny but they were around years before that. And remember like I told you previously that the new world order is nothing new, but has been in the making for many, many years. And for anybody interested in learning about the history of those who clandestinely control the U.S. government and there execrate plans to manipulate, deceive, and bring the whole world under their totalitarian rule. The reading of The Protocols of the Learned Elders of Zion is imperative and a must. And you can get the book: The Protocols of the Learned Elders of Zion, by Victor E. Marsden, available from global insights at 1-800-729-4131. And as I start to bring this thought to a close all I can say is that to resolve from the depths of your soul to incessantly think positive, be positive, and to put out positive energy is the one and only key that will open the lock to end the planned immense human suffering and misery, and total imprisonment of America and the world that those who clandestinely control the U.S. government have planned for us all. And remember that thoughts are real, very real, and much more real than you think. And did you know that the whole basis of the physical world is made up of what's known as proto or first matter. And this is nonphysical energy which you can not physically see or touch. But yet this is the basis of the entire physical world. And guess what, did you know that it's a known fact among mystics, shamans, adepts and all those that practice and study the Arcanum and esoteric that proto or first matter is the stuff that makes up thoughts. So what does that tell you? That thoughts are the basics of all that we see in the physical world. Now I hope that you understand how real and powerful thoughts are. And that those who clandestinely control the U.S. government are endeavoring to create a total and completely negative planet. How? By using their immense resources to engender all kinds of catastrophes, upheavals, disorders, chaos, human suffering and misery. But the thing is, and this is so pivotal that you understand this, that they can create all the catastrophes, upheavals, disorders, chaos, human suffering, and misery that they want, but if we the people do not acquiesce and comply and react as they want us to. Then all their evil doings will be just that, evil doings. And there overall plans which are to bring about a total and complete negative planet will fail. Why? Because, and I want you to hear me, and hear me good, they need our conscious consent to create a total and complete negative planet. Again, why? Because that's just the way God set up the universe. And how are those that clandestinely control the U.S. government going about getting our conscious consent to create a total and complete negative planet? Simple, they are manipulating, tricking, and deceiving us into giving our conscious consent. And how are they manipulating and deceiving us to do this? Again, simple! They create all these catastrophes, upheavals, disorders, chaos, human suffering, and misery, and sit back and wait for you the people to react. And react how? By being scared, worried, fearful and pessimistic. Which in turn is nothing but negativity and negative energy. And as you the masses of people become negative and start thinking negative thoughts. And therefore putting out negative energy whether you know it or not are giving your full unabridged and uncut conscious consent to creating a total and complete negative planet. And the process by how this works I explained in meticulous detail in thought #380. But please believe me by you thinking negative thoughts. And therefore putting out negative energy you are unknowingly giving your full and uncut conscious consent for these people to create a total and complete negative planet. And this is why I say and belabor you so much throughout this book to be positive, think positive. And therefore put out positive energy, no matter what, because if not you're not just hurting yourself when your negativity comes back to you and manifests in your life. But you're helping to keep and spread negativity. But I'm just going to tell you like this that one has to make a conscious decision to either be part of the solution or part of the problem. And for all those that are or feel indifferent to this there is absolutely no in between you are either part of the problem or part of the solution . . . point blank. And I'm not going to waste no more time here on those that are indifferent or desire to be part of the problem, because all I can say for them is that they'll eventually wake up. But now for those that are wanting and endeavoring to be part of the solution one must make a deep willful, resolve , and commitment, from the depths of one soul to not under any and all circumstances to succumb to the negativity. Because you best believe me as I say this, that those who clandestinely control the U.S. government are now and in the coming future starting with 2005 hurricane Katrina going to cause catastrophes, upheavals, disorders, chaos, financial and other collapses, and human suffering and misery to a degree that the world of this age has not yet seen. And I'm not trying to be or am I a doom and gloomier, but I'm just being real and telling it like it is. And if you want to label me a doom and gloomer for that then so be it. But all I can say is that, like I said, they need your conscious consent to create a total and complete negative planet. And they're going to endeavor to get that consent by any and all means. And let me tell you something . . . do you know how serious those who clandestinely control the U.S. government are about spreading negativity, and therefore stealthily getting your conscious consent? Well remember Project Bluebeam that I just mentioned well one and another of it's many functions and abilities is it's ability to transmit and broadcast via extremely low frequencies (ELF), very low frequencies (VLF), and various microwave bands negativity, such as abject and despondent energy waves, suicidal energy waves, energy waves of hopelessness, anxiety, despair, and fear, and many other energy waves of nothing but negativity that can and are picked up by the brains of the unsuspecting populace as their own thoughts. And like I said previously, this technology is highly sophisticated and highly advanced and it can be aimed virtually anywhere on the planet or at a specific geographical area or region. And again if you don't believe me, many books have been written about this technology such as: Controlling the Human Mind, by Nick Begich, ISBN# 1-890693; Psychic Dictatorship in the U.S.A., by Alex Constantine, ISBN# 0-922915-28-8; and Mind Control, World Control, by Jim Keith ISBN# 0-932813-45-3. And these are some of the best books on this subject and once you read these books they will lead you to a perpetual stream of material on this subject. But anyway it's just very important, matter of fact it's beyond important. It's extremely imperative that you know and understand that those who clandestinely control the U.S. government are in a very real way using any and all means to spread negativity around the planet and therefore without you knowing it gain and get your conscious consent to create a total and complete negative planet. So the next time you have bad or negative thoughts that you just can't seem to shake it's probably not you. You're probably maybe, and remember all things are possible being bombarded and attacked with Project Bluebeam or one of it's many offshoots. And this is real talk, and something everybody should know, and beware of, when there having, experiencing, or going through otherwise unexplainable negative or despondent thinking. And I'm not trying to make anybody a paranoid. But remember we are all under real attack, and being attacked from many different angles, and in many more ways than one, so it's ones individual responsibility to pray and ask god most high for protection, and to keep one strong, so one won't succumb to the vast amounts of negativity that is being permeated through and around are planet because if not one will surely succumb to the negativity and surely degenerate with it. So all I can say is that one through the exercise of his will must choose to stay strong, choose to think positive thoughts, and choose to incessantly project in his thoughts the good and positive experiences he wishes to have and enjoy. And remember its all in your hands because humanity acting as a collective can change its own destiny by changing its thoughts. And for all you religious fanatics you must do more than just claim to be a Christian, Muslim, Catholic, or whatever or think that you can just pray to God and ask him to do all the work for you, no I'm sorry but it does not work like that or in that way, you must use your will and like I just said will yourself to be strong, will yourself to think positive thoughts, and will yourself to constantly think and project the thoughts that you want to experience, and to will means to make a conscious choice then once you make a conscious choice to be positive, and to put out positive thoughts, and energy, and to stand up against this abominable negativity being permeated through and around our planet, then the spirit of God will naturally be with you. But like I said you must take the initiative that is the only way and be willing to work, because you best believe that this is no easy task. And I'm going to say this the information in this book is not going to be too much of a surprise to a lot of people why? Because these people knew intuitively, and in the depths of their hearts, and soul, that something was wrong, and that something extremely sinister was present and imminent but didn't know what, or how to articulate it, but now thanks to this book they do . . . and I know that there's a lot of information in this book, that's why it is my suggestion, and recommendation, that you not only read this book once but that you read and reread this book at least 3 or 4 times, so that you can fully understand and comprehend, what this book is truly conveying. And while you're reading this book I want you to pray to God and ask him to give you discernment, and understanding, and to let you know if what this book is conveying is truth. Because listen to me, you the average person have got to understand that there is so much, much, manipulation, false propaganda, deception, and disinformation out there that its just ineffable and even that right there is an understatement. And just thinking about all of the manipulation, deception, and disinformation out there is literally overwhelming me right now, why? Because I'm not sure how I can do you justice and adequately convey this to you. I mean the lies, manipulation, deception, disinformation is absolutely and literally everywhere and believe me its masterfully crafted, and dispensed, and if one is not adept in the subtleties of manipulation, deception, and craftiness then one is not likely to see it, and that is what I don't like, and that's what gets to me because I know that the average person is not proficient in such odious arts, but none the less that's how those who clandestinely control the U.S. government are playing the game and people need to know that. Like I said we are being attacked in every way imaginable are TVs, and radios, are full of subliminal messages, and if you don't believe me chick this out. A Dr. Hal C. Becker, patented a black box in the 1960's to pipe audio subliminal messages on top of other music it was used in department stores to plant the messages don't steal you'll get caught and theft dropped by some 60% and that was in the 1960's. Now that same technology and method only way, way, more advanced, and sophisticated, is used today with such subliminal messages mostly negative pouring from our TV's, CDs and the media in general in myriad forms. And even most people involved with the media have no idea that this is going on. And did you know that the music that comes on with your nightly news is designed to convey to your conscious mind in a very powerful way that the news is important, truthful, and imperative, and on a subconscious, and through a subliminal format conveys more of the same. So next time you watch your nightly news pay particular attention to the music and you'll see what I'm talking about. And if you would like more information on subliminal messages, and programming, then you must hit the excellent web site www.subliminalworld.com and or get the excellent book: The Age of Manipulation by Wilson Bryan Key . . . and just so you know the U.S. Federal Communications Commission currently has no regulation against or barring subliminal messages in advertising yet in its own literature considers it deceptive. And then we are being attacked in our food, and water, monosodium glutamate, (MSG), aspartame, in Equal and in NutraSweet and similar substances in the sodas and in the food we eat now days can and do cause harm to our brains and are nervous systems and their relationship to neurodegenerative diseases such as Alzheimer's, Lou Gehrig's, and others is well documented. These substances when added to foods and beverages (sodas) literally stimulate neurons to death causing brain damage, strokes, and other debilitating conditions of the body. And we are fed these artificial stimulants, and taste enhancers to slowly kill us. And once again if you don't believe me there have been many books written on this and a good one is: Excitotoxins, the Taste That Kills by Russell L. Blaylock M.D. Now I bet you didn't know that those who clandestinely control the U.S. government have a diet plan for all of us and this plan has been in motion for at least the last 20 years. And that plan is to put all of us on genetically modified food, better known as GM-Food. Now let me enlighten you a little bit on GM-Food. Dr. Arpad Pusztai is considered the world's foremost expert on GM-Food with more than 270 published studies on the subject and on August 10, 1998 he was interviewed for a World in Action TV documentary program on the subject, GM-Food. And Dr. Pusztai told the program that rats fed on GM-Food had suffered stunted growth, damage to their immune systems, and that there livers, hearts, and other major organs had gotten smaller. Then he said of GM-Food I would certainly never eat it. And what I just said was published in its entirety in the daily mail of July 7, 2003 pages 16 and 17, now GM-food is a world plan by those who clandestinely control the U.S. government like I just told you, because for 1. It will create the health and genetic changes in humans that they want to introduce. 2. It will undermine the human immune system, 3. It will make every grower on the planet, no matter how poor dependent on the seeds of the multinationals, corporations which are all owned and controlled by those who clandestinely control the U.S. government. And one of the main corporations behind GM-Food is the truly appalling Monsanto Corporation in St. Louis Missouri that has been exposed in many books, and by many researchers, as corrupt to its fingertips. And it is owned and controlled by those who clandestinely control the U.S. government. And just so you know the Bush administration was awash with its personnel. And once again there's been many books written on this topic such as: Genetically Engineered Food, Changing the Nature of Nature by Martin Teitel Ph.D., and Kim A. Wilson. But now let me tell you a little bit about are water supplies here in America are drinking water that is, and how its at a exponential rate being polluted with fluoride, now you're probably going to say what polluted with fluoride?? What do you mean? Fluoride is suppose to be good for your teeth and essential for strong and healthy teeth nope all a lie, straight disinformation, even dentist who were trained and schooled by mainstream schooling don't know the truth about fluoride they been lied to just like everybody else. But the suppressed truth about fluoride is starting to come out now believe that! Even though the establishment has there paid dentist experts, Ph.D.'s, and others all over the media saying that fluoride is good for you and essential for strong healthy teeth and that all those saying that fluoride is no good for you and dose absolutely nothing to keep your teeth strong or healthy and is a mind suppressant are crazy and quacks . . . let me tell you something folks don't believe it, its all disinformation. Those people that are pushing, and advocating, fluoride are either being paid to do so, or honestly don't know the truth about fluoride. And like I said before the reason that I'm writing this book is to awaken, and inform, the masses of people to the almost infinite amount of knowledge, and information, that has been suppressed away from them. And the truths in this book believe me are truths, these truths will still be around 10, 20, or 50 years from now. And in years to come when these truths become ostensible you will be able to say that you read them fist in thoughts on life. But anyway back to fluoride let me give you a little history on fluoride and like I always say don't take my word for it, please do your own research and investigation. But anyway fluoride comes from fluorine which is a flammable irritating toxic diatomic gas. And Hitler in Nazi Germany was one of the first to use fluoride as a mind suppressant when he put fluoride in the drinking water of the concentration camps to make the inmates dumb, stupid, and docile, and this is all documented. And you best believe me that the U.S. government knows the truth about fluoride but like always they aren't telling or saying nothing . . . they know that fluoride is a toxin, and when consumed by humans makes them dumb, forgetful, and docile, and docile means easy to control, passive, and fluoride or fluorine is a waste by product of aluminum. And fluorine where fluoride comes from is categorized and is designated as a poison. And to think that they been putting that shit in our toothpaste, and are drinking water for all these years is mind numbing. But moving on ward as always and if you're interested in the suppression of other things like inventions, technologies, and other phenomenal discoveries that have been systematically suppressed for at least the last 100 years by those who clandestinely control the U.S. government then I'm about to lead you to a phenomenal book that speaks on and excellently documents the suppression of such things as the cures for cancer, free energy machines, (of which 5,000 patents exist right now but are classified for so called national security reasons) and other alternative energy sources, the suppression of anti-gravity, and other propulsion systems that you could not even believe existed, the suppression of the transmutation of elements, and physical rejuvenation technology. And not only that but the suppression of irrefutable evidence of highly sophisticated ancient civilizations such as fossilized tangible artifacts like batteries, and remnants of ancient computers, and satellites, and even pictographs showing ancient astronauts which have all been systematically suppressed so they those who clandestinely control the U.S. government can keep you believing there bullshit and lies. And the book is: Suppressed Inventions, and other Discoveries, by Jonathan Eisen 550 pages packed with diagrams, patents, and photos. And its available by calling 1-800-729-4131 or where ever books are sold. And if you're specifically interested in the rise and fall of ancient highly sophisticated civilizations then you must get the excellent books: Technology of the Gods by David H. Childress. Fingerprints of the gods by Graham Hancock. And forbidden Archeology by Michael Cremo & Richard Thompson. And all of these books are available by calling the (800) number I just gave you . . . and like I always say don't knock any of this until you have investigated, and researched it for yourself . . . and before I leave the topic of suppression those who clandestinely control the U.S. government have been suppressing cancer cures, and real cures in medicine for decades. Believe me they own all the pharmaceutical conglomerates and if you're into this or got an interest in the suppression of real cures in medicine then there is two great books you need to read: Racketeering in Medicine the Suppression of Alternatives by James p. Carter M.D. and the Medical Mafia by Guylaine Lanctoto. And I'm just going to say this as I slowly bring this thought a close that those who clandestinely control the U.S. government cannot do what they're doing to us without our consent meaning us putting out negative thoughts, and energy, and even though that there doing everything in their power to engender an environment of fear, uncertainty, and instability we don't have to be acquiescent and think negative thoughts such as being scared, or fearful or any other negative thought or thoughts. But we can think positive thoughts and there for put out positive energy. And I'm not saying that this is going to be easy, but remember that nothing worth having comes easy. This is why we must be resolute, and like I said earlier make a conscious and absolute decision not to succumb to the environment of negativity, fear, uncertainty, and instability, that is being engendered for us. And as you have read throughout this book you have seen that one of the main themes of this book is to believe, have faith, and to think and put out positive thoughts, and energy, no matter what. And I know and I'm well area that the average person who has to get up and go to work every day and has a wife, or a husband, and a family and life to maintain really does not have the time to read and research, and therefore, know what's really going on. Because their trying to make it, and survey, I'm well area of that. But what I'm saying here is that the average working person, or the working, and middle class segment of the American population is the biggest segment of the American people and that's the segment of the population that I sincerely hope that this book reaches. And I know from experience that working class people really don't have too much time to think about too much of nothing but their work and their family, so therefore they are very susceptible and this is consciously, and maybe inadvertently, to think negative thoughts and therefore add to, feed, and entertain those highly negative thoughts of fear in myriad forms, uncertainty, and instability that are so ubiquitous now days. And that is why I sincerely hope that this book reaches them because here in America they make up the critical mass of the people and its pivotal that the critical mass of the people be reached and woke up. And once the critical mass of the American people is reached that will be the stepping stone to reaching the critical mass of the people of the world. And all those terror alerts that constantly come from the White House, the pentagon, and elsewhere are designed to produce one thing and one thing only and that's perpetual fear in the people. And check this out do you know what Amnesty International's 2003 annual report said about the war on terrorism it said:

The war on terrorism, far from making the world a safer place, has made it much more dangerous by curtailing human rights, undermining the rule of international law and shielding governments from scrutiny. The report accused governments of trampling over human rights in the name of fighting terrorism. And Amnesty's secretary general, Irene Khan, said what would have been completely unacceptable on September 10, 2001, is now the norm . . .

And its sad, so sad, but is so very true that the abridgement of our rights, and liberties, that is now accepted and the norm would have been an outrage, and totally unacceptable on September 10, 2001 and I'm talking about such unnatural, and travesties of justice like detention without trial which would of been completely and totally unacceptable on September 10, 2001 is now accepted and the norm. And I'm going to tell you something the agenda is not to just detain foreigners without trial or charge but to detain U.S. citizens without trial, or charge, and again if you don't believe me, well let me give you the actual facts the U.S. Justice Department produced a law with in the Domestic Security Enhancement act of 2003 to allow the government to strip American citizenship from anyone giving support, aid, or advocating, or promoting, any group designated as terrorists. Now that right there is so dam vague and broad that it's a god damn shame. And then how can they take away somebody's U.S. citizenship when that is specifically forbidden by the constitution? And section 501 of the act says that Americans can voluntarily give up their rights to citizenship purely by their behavior. And to quote and give it to you verbatim the act says:

And intent to relinquish nationality need not be manifested in words but can be inferred from conduct . . .

So what does that tell you, that they can just say you are giving support, aid, or advocating, or promoting, terrorism and they can then strip you or your citizenship . . . so first they pass anti-terrorism laws to do what they want with foreigners like holding them, and detaining them without charge, or trial . . . then they pass laws like the 2003 Domestic Security Enhancement Act to strip American citizens of their natural born citizenship so therefore they can hold them and detain them without charge or trials. And much more recently on New Year's Day 2012 President Obama signed the National Defense Authorization Act. (NDAA) which provides more of the same . . . but is so much more draconian . . . and if you would like to learn more about this then just go to www.pandaaunite.org which stands for People Against NDAA . . . And as I bring this thought to a close for the 3rd time because there is just so, so much to say that I could literally write ad-infinitu. But I just want you to fully understand, be aware, and know that there is so much going on right now that is being systematically suppressed and being kept away from you the masses of people that its just ineffable period and that's the best that I can articulate what's going on. Like for instance this is the end of 2012 and for the last 10 years at least there's been and still is a systematic media blackout of some major geophysical upheavals, and earth changes, that those who clandestinely control the U.S. government do not want the masses of people to know about. And right now and for like the last 15 years there's been a massive global spiritual awakening that has been, and is, picking up momentum by the day believe that I'm not talking about no religion, or manmade dogma, ideology awakening either. Because people from all religions, creeds, dogmas, and ideologies around the globe are feeling this massive spiritual awakening. And just so you know what is going on now with the implementation of the new world order, and the totalitarian, socialistic, police state was all uncannily told, prophesied, and written about with stunning accuracy in 1947 by George Orwell when he wrote his now classic novel 1984 which told of a coming big brother totalitarian state . . . now if you go read that novel now you will be utterly shocked at how accurate George Orwell described the future, and the coming of the new world order, and the big brother totalitarian, socialistic, police state. Now in this thought I know that I spoke on a number of different topics, and subjects, but I'll tell you one thing they are all part of, or related, to the new world order. And I didn't intend to be this prolix but it just happened I do apologize. Now like I've said many times previous that my only intention is to awaken, enlighten, and inform, the people of what's going on and happening. And I want you to know and fully understand that this thought and this book is nothing but a grain of sand of what's going on, and has been going on. Now I'm going to lead you to a researcher who has been meticulously studying for many years now, those who clandestinely control the U.S. government, and the new world order. Now this guy is an award winning documentary film producer and is one of the foremost researchers into what's really going on, and into the new world order. And if anybody was to be given the title of expert, or specialist, of the new world order agenda it would be given to him decisively and hands down, please believe that folks. His name is Alex Jones and he lives and works out of Texas and if you want to learn, and educate, yourself about those who clandestinely control the U.S. government, the new world order, and what's really going on then I strongly suggest that you hit one of his web sites and at the time of this writing he has 3, which are: www.prisonplanet.com, www.prisonplanet.tv and his biggest one www.infowars.com and at these sites you will find a wealth of information on those who clandestinely control the U.S. government, the new world order and on what' really going on . . . and not only that but there's a plethora of books, videos, and other related material. And now that I'm officially bringing this thought to a close I'm going to go ahead and list the books that if you want to learn all about those who clandestinely control the U.S. government, and or the new world order you must get:

The Truth Will Set you Free, by David Icke

Conspirators Hierarchy, the Story of the Committee of 300 by Dr. John Coleman

The Rise of the Fourth Reich, by Jim Marrs

Ruled by Secrecy, by Jim Mars

Barbarians Inside the Gates, by Col. Donn de Gran Pre

Secrets Behind the Societies, by Jon Rapoport

The Biggest Secret, by David Icke

The New World Order, Our Secret Rulers, by Eustace Mullins

Death in the Air Globalism, Terrorism, & Toxic Warfare, by Dr. Leonard G Horowitt

Behold a Pale Horse, by William Cooper

Pawns in the Game, by William Guy Car

The True Story of the Bilderberg Group, by D. Estulin

And like I said before you can get any of these books by calling 1-800-729-4131 or on Amazon, or where ever books are sold. And if your new to these topics I suggest you start with: Rule by Secrecy, by Jim Marrs . . . it's a phenomenal book and you can go from there . . . and on a last note there's a great magazine about freedom that you might want to check out. And this magazine is very informative, and insightful, on current issues of freedom, liberty, rights, and privacy. And this magazine is put out once a month for free by the Foundation for Economic Education which is a nonprofit institution devoted to the fight for freedom, rights, liberty, and privacy . . . and the name of the magazine is Ideas on Liberty. And this institute holds seminars, public lectures, dinners, and a host of other programs in America and around the world advocating the freedom cause. So if you're into freedom, rights, liberty, and privacy, you might want to check them out at 914-591-

Thoughts on Life And the Absolute Power of Thought

7230 or at www.fee.org. Or you can write them at: 30 South Broadway, Irvington on Hudson, NY, 10533 . . .

616. The interest behind the Bush Administration, such as the CFR, the Trilateral Commission, Founded by Zbigniew Brzezinski for David Rockefeller Sr. and the Bilderberg Group have prepared for and are now moving to implement open world dictatorship on the world . . .

> ---Dr. Johannes Keopple, Former
>
> Official of the German Ministry
>
> For Defense, and Senior Advisor
>
> To NATO . . .

Alright in this thought here, I'm going to call this thought the new world order part 2 because the last thought you read was the first new world order thought. But that thought was first written back in 2005, and 2006, and for very strange, and unforeseen, reasons this book has been impeded from making it to the publisher since then until now, but since then until now and I don't even know the word, some very remarkable, profound, No I know the right word execrate developments have took place concerning the furtherance, and implementation, of the new world order. And in this thought here the new world order part 2 I'm going to delineate a few sound bites of these most recent execrate developments. And not only that but these execrate developments that I'm about to delineate here will absolutely, and totally, enrage any true patriot for their blatant, and total, disregard of the U.S. constitution, and the end runs they make around it. And let me remind the people of an all but forgotten U.S. Supreme Court case that said:

The U.S. Constitution is the supreme law of the land and Chief Justice Marshall said that all laws which are repugnant to the constitution are null and void . . . Marbary V. Madison (- (- (1- cranch) 137, 174, 176, (1830) . . . meaning that any law or statute that is not in total congruence with the constitution is null and void . . and these most recent execrate developments concerning the furtherance, and implementation, of the new world order are most definitely repugnant, and incongruent, and in straight violation of the constitution. But as I delineate them I'll let you be the judge. Well there are laws or executive orders that if and when the president declares a state of national emergency these laws will immediately go into effect and when these laws go into effect they will actually, and literally, strip all Americans of their rights, liberties, and property, real and otherwise. Now the recent developments that I'm talking about and are about to delineate here only add to and further enhance the aftermentioned executive orders . . . Now you need to understand these developments that I'm talking about in this thought are so draconian, utterly unbelievable, and execrate that I honestly and truthfully don't know what to say I'm speechless. Again I'll just let you be the judge. Alright in May of 2007 George W. Bush Jr. enacted what I call the George W. Bush Jr. Supremacy Act of 2007 and in that act or acts because there was more than one he George W. Bush Jr. arbitrarily issued presidential or national security decision directive #51 (NSDD) which blatantly states that if he the president declares a state of national emergency for any reason economic, depression, terror attach, anything the U.S. constitution will be suspended and martial law implemented. Now what I just stated is old law and you already know from previous thoughts . . . but it is still a travesty of justice, and of are integrity in government. But what NSDD#51 does and add to the already existing executive orders that already provide for if the president declares a state of national emergency, the constitution can be suspended, and martial law implemented is that it NSDD#51 clearly states that (and by the way this is why I call these enactments the George W. Bush Jr. Supremacy Act of 2007) . . . but anyway NSDD#51 says that once the president declares a state of national emergency, and the constitution is suspended, and martial law implemented and you might want to sit down for this one because you are about to be taken totally aback Congress, and the U.S. Supreme Court, will absolutely have no say at all and if anybody else in any other branch of government tries to protest or contest anything in NSDD#51 they can and will be prosecuted for treason now that's deep . . . and you might just want to check out Homeland Security Decision Directive #20 (HSDD) which just calls, and provides, for more of the same.

Like for example let me give you a sound bite from HSDD#20 which completely supersedes the National Emergency Act which explicitly said that Congress had a say if and when the President declared a state of national emergency. Now that's all the way dead with HSDD#20 Congress has no say at all if and when the president declares a state of national emergency and that's all per HSDD#20 . . . and again this is why I call these most recent enactments the 2007 George W. Bush Jr. Supremacy Act, or acts, whatever you like . . . because he is unilaterally, and arbitrarily, usurping all the power of the U.S. government on to his self. And let me tell you what I utterly just cannot believe and that's why has not Congress of the U.S. Supreme Court, or any other court for that matter challenged George W. Bush Jr. on these clearly unnatural, and unconstitutional enactments . . . but I don't even know why I'm sitting here kidding myself when I already know just like I've been telling y'all all along the U.S. government has long been subverted, and usurped, by those who now clandestinely control it . . . but that is just so hard to believe sometimes but still and yet so very true. And that is why George W. Bush Jr. has not been challenged by anybody, or any branch, in government for them clearly unnatural, and unconstitutional enactments he solely enacted. So if anybody is going to challenge him it's going to be you the people . . . and with that said I sincerely hope that this book causes and engenders a grass roots movement that the world has yet to now I want to speak on something else that you might or might not know about but is most definitely part of the new world order agenda. And that's the North American Free Trade Agreement (NAFTA) super highway a.k.a. the Trans Texas Corridor that is going to be 4 football fields wide. And is going to run all across America and do you know how many homes, businesses, and private property, are going to have to be displaced to make room for this enormous highway? Countless that's right . . . and like I been telling you this is all a script a plan that been a long time in the making because just look at the recently revised Eminent Domain Laws by the U.S. Supreme Court that now give total, and complete, cart-blanche to the government when they decide to invoke Eminent Doman and take your property and do you think that was just a coincidence yeah alright then you're still asleep and need to wake up. Because now when the government invokes Eminent Domain and takes your property hear me, and hear me, well there's absolutely nothing that you can do but take the offer and keep it moving. Meaning take the money and go about your business. But anyway the NAFTA Super Highway was brought together under an agreement known as the security, and property, partnership (SPP) which was a series of conferences that were attended by among others George W. Bush Jr., the Prime Minister of Canada, and the President of Mexico, and check this out, under this reprobate agreement there are provisions where United Nations (UN) laws will under certain conditions supersede U.S. law and let me just say this and I don't know how pivotal this is to you people out there but as of this writing Aug of 2008 the state of North Carolina is now putting the NAFTA or North American Union logo on all of their drivers licenses, and ID cards, and the logo is on the back of the licenses, and ID cards, and most people that I talk to did not even know what it was until it was pointed out to them. And like I said as of this writing I don't know how many states are doing that but for a fact North Carolina is . . . and by the time this book comes out I can almost guarantee you that many more states will be putting the NAFTA, or North American Union logo on their drivers licenses, and ID cards. And let me brief you a little bit on these free trade agreements which is what NAFTA is the North American Free Trade Agreement or Union, then they got the Central American Free Trade Agreement (CAFTA) for all of Latin America, then they got the Asia Pacific Economic Co-operation (APEC) Union which is the free trade area for Asia and Australia. And the same is planned for Africa with the African Union that replaced the African Unity Organization. And we all already know about the European Union that is now a full fledged national government with its own law makers and currency the Euro after it started as a European Free Trade Economic Common Market, or community, and these 5 unions cover virtually the whole industrialized world. See these unions are nothing but a ploy, a ruse, by those who clandestinely control the U.S. government to set the skeleton, or the frame, if you want to say of the new world order and then they're going to cause terror attacks, or some giant calamity, or calamities, or whatever but the point is to bring them all together into one and then have one global union or better said a one world government a.k.a. a new world order. And how they are going to do it is like I just said cause calamities, depressions, terror attacks, and bring each region, or area, down to its knees suspend constitutions, implement martial law and then bingo bring all the unions together into one, and you got a one world government, and the complete takeover of the planet has been accomplished . . . pretty sinister huh but very much true. And you must remember just like I told you in the last thought, the first new world order thought that this new world order is nothing new its been a long, long, time in the making. And the developments that I just delineated in this thought like NSDD #51, and HSDD#20, among others should let you the people know that those who clandestinely control the U.S. government are getting ready to make a move here in America. Meaning cause a calamity, or calamities, or terror attack, or depression, or a complete collapse like I will illustrate to you in a few thoughts. Or maybe all of the above. So they can go head and suspend the constitution, implement martial law, nationalize all the people's businesses, property, real and otherwise, and bring in the secret arms to guard the people here in America because mind you the people will no longer be free, all of their former rights, liberties, and freedoms will now be gone and the people will now be subjects, or to be all the way frank with you prisoners living in and under complete totalitarianism in a total police state . . . and that will be one area, or region, knocked down to its knees . . . and if you don't believe that there getting ready to do something here in America then I strongly suggest that you go on the internet, or go somewhere and procure yourself a copy of the John Warner Defense Appropriation Act which funds and puts inordinate amounts of money aside for marital law and if that don't tell you something then god I really don't know what will . . . and before it slips my mind I just want to mention something else just to let you know that George W. Bush Jr. and gang are absolutely for real about creating a North American union or state out of NAFTA . . . and that's the creation of the Northern American command or Northcom by George W. Bush Jr. in April of 2002. Now Northcom is a military – intelligence agency that has its own troops that are specifically for deployment here in the United States or North America.

Northcom is the military arm of the North American union . . . and if you don't believe me check this out according to the Pentagon Northcom will coordinate Homeland defense for North America and for the first time Mexico, so now Mexico comes under Pentagon command?? What does that tell you?? Well it tells me that they are using gradualism which is one of the oldest tricks in the book. First they get Mexico under Northcom jurisdiction then they wait a little bit and slide Canada under Northcom jurisdiction and then bam you got the whole of North America under Northcom jurisdiction which was the whole point from Jump Street. Because like I just said the North American Command – Northcom is going to be when this North American Union fully materializes its military arm . . . and if you don't think that what I'm saying in this thought is reality then think about this how is it that we are 10 years into supposedly a war on terror and are borders with Mexico, and Canada, are not secure?? And 1/10th of Mexico's population is now living here in America with over 40 consul offices here in America to protect their civil rights . . . and let me just mention something else that I was just informed of recently and that I was totally incredulous to. And I damn sure know that you're going to be incredulous to what I'm about to say too. And mine you that what I'm about to disclose to you comes from people of impeccable character who I've known for a number of years that are highly placed in the U.S. State Dept. and I'm not going to disclose who they are because what was told to me was told in strict confidence and I would never breach that and comprise them or their positions. But I'm going to disclose what they said and let you judge and go research for yourself because like I've said before this book is to inform and that's it and that's all . . . but anyway what they said was that back in the end of 2005 the Bush administration surreptitiously gave the state of Alaska to the Russian government and the reason and all the details are being kept all hush, hush, and when I asked my contacts how could Bush possibly do this without Congress saying nothing, or doing nothing, they simply said just like Bush arbitrarily enacted National Security Decision Directive #51, and Homeland Security Decision Directive #20, that actually, and literally, subverts are whole form of government without nobody in Congress, or the judiciary, or in any other branch of government saying or doing nothing and with that there I could not say nothing else I had no come back for that they were absolutely correct . . . and my contacts went on to say that the new world order and everything for it, to implement it that is, is already in place all there waiting on is the trigger and we already know what that is, that's the declaring a state of national emergency in America. So if my contacts are correct in what they told me and I have absolutely no reason to doubt them then the state of Alaska is now and has been since the end of 2005 de-jure Russian property. And the American people living in Alaska now are only there in a de-facto capacity . . . and I guess that when they implement the new world order then they will tell the people that Alaska belongs to the Russians but hey what will it matter then . . . and let me just go back to martial law for a min because right now as we speak and for like the last 8 years the U.S. government under the direction of those who clandestinely control it has been actively preparing for martial law here in America. And again let me substantiate what I'm saying and I'm going to do that via some developments that took place in 2005. Alright the Bush administration in 2005 opened up in El Salvador the International Law Enforcement Academy (ILEA) to specifically and surreptitiously train thousands of police recruits in martial law tactics such as crowd suppression, mass relocation, and a bunch of other repression, and control, tactics to be used on the people by the police not if but when martial law is declared here in America and it's not surprising that many are calling ILEA the new world order, training school, and or academy because anyone who goes there will be thoroughly indoctrinated in one world, collectivism, martial law, and police state, ideology and some have even said that the recruits that go to ILEA are being covertly brainwashed via drugs . . . I mean just think about it since when would the government care about establishing an international police academy outside the country to train police if they did not have a hidden agenda come on now?? And not just that but what I'm about to disclose to you next should really wake you up and put you on edge about the government preparing and getting ready to declare martial law here in America and this particular development started back in 1996 when the FBI under the direction and control of those who clandestinely control the U.S. government started something known as infragard . . . and now your naturally going to ask what is infragard? And well I'm going to tell you infragard is an FBI operation and basically it's nothing but Hitler's Gestapo all over again where the masses of people are compensated in an assortment of different ways for spying, keeping tabs, and telling, and informing on each other. And the cold thing is that the people the average Joes, and the average Janes, enlisted in this infragard grouping are under the guise of being in alliance with the FBI to flight terrorism but nothing could be further from the truth . . . but like I just said the average Joes, and the average Janes that make up the mass majority of infragard membership have no idea what they are really a part of and how they are being manipulated, and deceived, into spying, keeping tabs, and telling and informing on their countrymen . . . see infragard overtly, and ostensibly, is an organization or grouping ran by the FBI to partner with management heads, supervisors, CEO's, or really who ever that may have something to offer from the private sector and or business world. And as of January 2008 infragard according to their own website www.infragard.net had 23,682 active members scattered throw out the American private business sector and these include everything from agriculture, banking, and finance, the chemical industry, defense, energy, food, the information industry, telecommunications, the media, the entertainment industry, the religious establishment, and academia, and 350 of our nation's Fortune 500 companies have a member or representative in infragard . . . but anyway now here is what's going on just like in any other organization, or grouping, there is within infragard a core elite that knows the truth about infragard what it really is, and what its real aims, and objectives, are because like I said the mass majority of infragard members really believe in their heart that there helping the FBI fight terrorism . . . but they don't know or understand that the government and specifically those that clandestinely control it will do nothing but lie to them . . . and if you're an infragard member with genuine intentions and you've read this book this far I strongly urge you to read on . . . but anyway its already bad enough that the infragard members have been manipulated, and deceived, into keeping active surveillance on their own countrymen for the FBI all with secure communications lines all provided by the FBI for what I call unjustified snitching, and telling . . . no that's the least of it here's where it gets good. Infragard holds meetings and runs training sessions for its members and in those meetings, and training sessions and especially in the training sessions the infragard members are being trained really conditioned, and programmed, into how to act not if but when martial law is declared . . . and check this out and this is part of the infragard charter and that's, that all infragard members will be able to shoot to kill with impunity when a state of national emergency and or martial law is declared . . . and not just that but in those training sessions like I said the infragard members are being trained just like the international law enforcement academy recruits in martial law tactics such as crowed suppression, mass relocation, and other repression and control tactics . . . and the infragard members are being manipulated, tricked, and deceived, into believing that such tactics in such a situation (a state of martial law) is the best thing for the country and the mass of the people just won't or don't understand that the government has their best interest at heart, yeah and I can fly too . . . and just look at the craftiness of this the infragard members are being told not to speak to their friends, family, or to anybody else that is not an infragard member about the training they are receiving concerning martial law . . . because if they do they could be undermining national security so because of that the FBI and the mass majority of infragard members will think that there doing the right thing and deny receiving any such training concerning martial law . . . and if you are an active infragard member then you know the truth . . . and if you know an infragard member confront him or her with this and tell them that there is no need to lie that you know the truth concerning infragard . . . and there was one brave and courageous member of infragard and who did not even mine her name being printed because she said that what infragard was doing was clearly wrong . . . and her name is Christine Moerke who is a business continuity consultant for Alliant Energy in Madison, Wisconsin . . . she said she was an active infragard member and remembered attending infragard meetings, and training sessions, that went into graphic details about what kind of civil patrol functions including engaging in lethal force that infragard members were going to be not called upon but required to perform, and do, once a state of national emergency and or martial law was declared . . . and just so you'll know infragard is relentlessly recruiting members of the clergy, pastors, and preachers, of all denominations, and faiths, and is covertly enlisting them in their cause so don't be surprised if your church is divulging details about you and your life to the FBI . . . and to add insult to injury these infragard recruited clergymen, pastors, and preachers, are preaching and telling their congregations that the government should under any and all circumstances be listened to, trusted, and obeyed, (once I tell you about operation Northwoods at the end of this thought I want to know if you feel the same way) and if a state of national emergency or martial law is declared the people should listen and obey the government and not try to resist because the government only has there the peoples best interest at heart . . . that right there is all bullshit of the first order and if you don't believe nothing else in your life believe that . . . so basically what these infragard recruited clergymen, pastors, and preachers are preaching and telling their congregations is to just voluntarily give up their life, freedom, and all the rights they ever had and to just go head and go to a relocation center better known as a detention camp (prison) and to just without resistance submit to a life of totalitarianism and serfdom. Yea if it was up to me it should be criminal and those clergymen, pastors, and preachers, who are promoting, and pushing, that infragard bullshit about no resistance and just go along with whatever the government says should be prosecuted for treason against their fellow man and thrown in jail for life . . . and its a known fact that the actor Tom cruise is a spokesman for the Church of Scientology and the Church of Scientology is an active card carrying member of infragard . . . and as I begin to wind this thought down let me just say this to all those that have been either knowingly, or unknowingly, it does not matter (you are still guilty) programmed, conditioned, or trained, to act against their own countrymen and help those that clandestinely control the U.S. government usher in their new world order. I'm going to tell you like this and you better hear me, and hear me well, once you done performing your services against your own countrymen and helping them the evil ones reach their reprobate objectives and your thinking that it's all good, and you done did the right thing, and you done served your country they those that clandestinely control the U.S. government are basically just keeping it all the way real with you, are going to turn on you like you never thought and lock your ass up in the same place the relocation centers, detention camps, (prisons) that you helped put all your fellow countrymen in . . . then how are you going to feel?? And as I bring this thought to a close for all of you that still might be in some doubt as to whether the government does nothing but lie and plot against the people I want you to read and check out operation Northwoods which was just recently declassified and mine you this was a real, and true, operation that would have been carried out by the pentagon, the CIA, and the FBI, were it not for president John F. Kennedy who would not go for it and put a stop to it . . . and that's another reason why they killed him . . but anyway Operation Northwoods was a completely contrived up plot by the joint chiefs of staff (the pentagon) the CIA, and the FBI, to trick America and to win public and international support for an invasion of Cuba and the Northwoods documents state and this is verbatim:

> The plan which had the written approval of the chairman and every member of the joint chiefs of staff, called for innocent people to be shot on American streets, for boats carrying refugees fleeing Cuba to be sunk on the high seas, for a wave of violent terrorism to be launched in Washington, D.C., Miami, and elsewhere . . . people would be framed for bombings they did not commit, American airlines would be hijacked and blown up . . . and using phony evidence all of it would be irrefutably blamed on Castro and Cuba. Thus giving Lemnitzer (the chairman of the Joint Chiefs of Staff) and his cabal the excuse, as well as the public and international backing they needed to launch their war and invasion of Cuba.

> Now what you just read is verbatim from the declassified Northwoods documents. The plan was to stir up so much hatred for Cuba in the United States that the people would support an invasion and even demand that this was done . . . the plan included attacks on the now infamous U.S. base at Guantanamo Bay in Cuba. The documents speak of a series of well coordinated incidents in and around Guantanamo to give genuine appearance of being done by hostile Cuban forces . . .

the techniques included but were not limited to starting rumors, landing U.S. personnel, operatives, in Cuban uniforms over the fence to stage the attacks on the base, capturing U.S. personnel, operatives, acting as Cuban saboteurs inside the base, starting riots near the bases main gate, blowing up ammunition inside the base, blowing up aircraft on the base and blaming Castro using propaganda and contrived up evidence, capturing a militia group (of CIA operatives) which storms the base, and blowing up a U.S. vessel in Cuban water and blaming it on Cuban aircraft and issuing false casualty lists to the U.S. mainstream media to whip up public opinion against Cuba . . . and check this out there was even appropriations to stage and conduct mock funerals . . . and the Northwoods documents also call for the use of Cuban look-a-like aircraft flown by U.S. operatives to harass and attack U.S. civil aircraft . . . and it was further planned to shoot down a U.S. air force plane flying in international air space using a properly painted F-86 so that it would like look the Cuban (MIG) aircraft and therefore this would allow the (ICAO) International Civil Aviation Organization in the Western Hemisphere to tell the world's media and the U.S. what happened to the aircraft instead of the U.S. trying to sell the incident . . . and a memorandum dated July 27, 1962 says that operation Northwoods would mean an enormous increase in Cuban and American casualties . . . and check this out the Northwoods operation also called for the shooting down of an American commercial airliner on a flight from the United States to Jamaica, Panama, Guatemala, or Venezuela . . . the destination would be chosen so the route would cross Cuba . . now everything that you just read is very real, and true, and comes from the official now declassified Northwoods Operation Documents that were kept classified and secret for 40 years . . . and if you would like the full and complete scoop on operation Northwoods cause what I just gave you here was nothing but a sound bite then you need to hit operation Northwoods into a search engine and you will get a response replete with hits . . . and as I bring this thought to a total close I just want to leave you with this on your mind so you can fully, and totally understand for those of you that are new to this kind of material what kind of extremely nefarious and malevolent forces have been and are at work with in the U.S. government and that's, that it has long been suspected that the 1964 Gulf of Tonkin incident . . . the spark and or reason that lead to America's long war in Vietnam was largely staged by U.S. officials in order to build up Congressional and public support for American involvement in Vietnam . . . over the years, serious questions have been raised about the alleged attack by North Vietnamese patrol boats on two American destroyers in the Gulf . . . but defenders of the Pentagon have always denied such charges, arguing that senior officials would never engage in such deceit . . . and all that I can say to that is -- Haaaa . . . and for more on what you read in this thought you must go to the following websites: for information on the security prosperity partnership you must go to www.spp.gov , and www.worldnetdaily.com, and for more information you can go to www.ustalknetwork.com, www.divinecosmos.com, www.infowars.com, www.copvcia.com, www.expansions.com, www.fair.org, and for the Northwoods documents go to www.nara.gov, search for Northwoods and you should find descriptions and digital copies added 12-7-1999 scroll down to joint chief of staff central files 1962 & 1963 and click on nail . . . scroll down to digital copies – search . . . put joint chiefs of staff in the first key word box and assassinations records review board in the second and click submit search. You should retrieve 99 hits . . . click display results, click more hits and select view all thumbnails on hit 10 Northwoods www.nara.gov, and for the complete and true story about Vietnam you must go to www.fair.org, and or get the book: The War With In, America's Battle over Vietnam, by Tom Wells . . .

617. Hitler became Chancellor of Germany on January 30, 1933. And on February 28, of that year Hitler invoked Article 48, of the Weimar Constitution that allowed civil liberties to be suspended during a state of national emergency . . .

618. The truth is yes, you do have these stand-by provisions, and plans are here, whereby you could in the name of stopping terrorism evoke the military and arrest Americans and put them in detention camps . . .

--Congressman Henry Gonzales

619. Presidential Executive Orders . . .

Now in this thought here I'm going to show and expose you to how those who clandestinely control the U.S. government have already laid the legal ground work for their execrate, totalitarian, socialistic new world order. Alright, first of all you must know and understand that the President of the United States has the power with little or no oversight at all to write law through Presidential Executive Orders of which myriad Executive Orders/Laws have been written by all Presidents that the masses/average person knows little if anything at all about. Now this is the vehicle that those who clandestinely control the U.S. government have used to avoid virtually all oversight, legislative, judicial, and otherwise of the laws that lay the legal ground work for their execrate new world order. But none the less these laws have been enacted and are therefore legal and active operating law. Now in the next thought when I speak on the coming collapse of all our communication systems, utilities, and supplies and with that will come the crash of our economy. But anyway when that happens like I told you in the previous thought the President will declare a state of national emergency and then based on the exorbitance of that national emergency will suspend the Constitution in the so called interest of America and the public good and/or safety. But just like I told you in the previous thought the Constitution will never again be restored and that will be the beginning of the end for us, for America, because that's when those who clandestinely control the U.S. government will fully and overtly implement their execrate new world order of which like I told you the legal ground work has already been laid through Presidential Executive orders of which I will expose, and reveal, a few. And these Presidential Executive Orders are like I said the legal groundwork for the new world order and they authorize the federal government to legally take over America, and virtually take America away from American people, and completely enslave the American people. Now remember that these Executive Orders are actual, real, laws that are just dormant right now one could say until the time comes for them to be utilized. But like I said none the less these are real and enacted laws. Now a small excerpt of these laws goes as follows:

Executive Order #10995 provides for the government to take over all the communications media;

Executive Order # 10997 provides for the government to take over all of the electric power, petroleum, gas, fuels, and minerals;

Executive Order # 10988 provides for the government to take over all of the food resources, and farms without exception;

Executive Order # 10999 provides for the government to take over all modes of transportation, control of highways, seaports, etc.

Executive Order # 11000 provides for mobilization of all civilians into work bridges under government supervision;

Executive Order # 11001 provides for the government takeover of all health, education, and welfare functions;

Executive Order # 11002 designates the Post Office and Post Master General to operate a National Registration of all persons;

Executive Order # 11003 provides for the government to take over all airports and aircrafts;

Executive Order # 11004 provides for the housing finance authority to relocate all cities, towns, and communities and to designate what areas are to be abandoned, and establish new locations for populations;

Executive Order #11005 provides for the government to take over all railroads, inland waterways, and public storage facilities:

Now check this out all of these laws that I just mentioned were combined into one huge Executive Order (11490) under President Nixon, which allows all of what these Executive Orders state to take place and happen, if the President declares a state of national emergency. And also check this out, if you doubt or feel that these Executive Orders don't exist or are not laws, please feel free to check them out for yourself. And this is also why I gave you the number with each Executive Order. And just so you know, there is a federal agency called the (Federal Emergency Management Agency) FEMA that was created back in 1979 by those who clandestinely control the U.S. government for one purpose and for one purpose only and that's to administer, carry out, and implement, the after mentioned Executive Orders that are the legal groundwork for their execrate new world order. Because in a nutshell it's like this FEMA has the power by Executive Order of the President of the United States to direct "all" other federal agencies to assist in the event that a state of national emergency is declared. So FEMA will be the head directing, and controlling all other federal agencies in the implementation of the after mentioned Executive Orders which will be in effect the overt implementation of the new world order. And also pertaining to this you might want to check out the 1983 defense industrial revitalization and disaster relief act . . .

620. The Coming Collapse

Alright, in this thought here I'm going to give you what might be rightfully called or termed a prediction for the not too distant future. And as you already know from previous thoughts that I do not forecast or make direct predictions for the future, but I feel that it is imperative that I disclose the following to you. Well it's like this in the not too distant future there is going to be massive chaos and this chaos has been planned for the masses by those who clandestinely control the U.S. government . . . and this carefully planned chaos consist of the total breakdown and collapse of all of our communication systems, utilities, and supplies, as we know them. That is going to be precipitated probably by an engineered nuclear or terrorist attack on America just like 9-11, only this attack is going to be of such immense proportion that untold millions are going to die. And with that, there will be turmoil, confusion, and chaos of astronomical proportions here in America. And this is just part of their plan to declare a state of national emergency and then because of this extremely exorbitant national emergency the President is going to deem it necessary and in the best interest of the country and of the people to suspend the Constitution for a time. So that martial law can be declared and the army/military can come in to our cities and towns and maintain public order and safety. But what the people don't know is for one that the constitution is never going to be restored. And for two the army/military that is going to come in is not your regular army/military but a special army/military that has been specially trained for the last 40 some years for this exact purpose. And if you would like to know more about these secret armies please refer to thought #613. But like I said this is all part of their plan and there plan as you already know is to usher in a totalitarian socialistic new world order on us. Now can you just imagine for a minute the chaos, confusion, looting, riots, panic, and turmoil that the complete collapse of all of our communication systems, utilities, and supplies is going to bring? There is going to be no street lights, all telephones are going to be down including all cell phones because they're going to tell you the satellites are down. But in actually the satellites are going to have been shut off. And all gas stations and most markets will be closed. And to make matters even worse there will be myriad storms all over the country. Because the weather modifying technology they have, well it will be utilized during this time to make, strengthen, and steer storms all over the country. And you best believe that this weather modifying technology is real, and the instruments are already in place to make, strengthen, and steer storms all over the country. So please take heed, and prepare for you and your family a complete emergency kid that can sustain you and your family for at least 90 to 120 days. And a must is a portable generator or some kind of generator with enough spare oil and gasoline to last you at least 90 days, and guns, and weapons, storage is a must, very pivotal to you and your survival. And then you want to have enough food for you and your family, such as canned and dehydrated food . . . and don't forget beverages. And most of all you want to have enough water storage and even that will not stay pure without special care. So a camping purifier pump is a good idea and make sure to buy extra filters. And there's nothing wrong with being creative and buying anything else that you think that you might need to protect and sustain you and your family for at least 90 to 120 days. Because what I just gave you here is nothing but a brief list of some of the bare essentials that you will need. And don't forget to update your emergency kits annually. And I'm going to close this thought with saying this the government has in place right now technology capable of jamming all of America's communications systems indefinitely so the days coming ahead are dark and are even going to get darker. And must I remind you of what happened in 2005 in New Orleans with Hurricane Katrina, them people were not helped or aided by the U.S. government because the government could not because of manpower, resources, or finances, help, or aid them! No, no, that's the furthest thing from the truth and if you believe that I must say you really are crazy. But the people in New Orleans were not helped, or aided during the Katrina catastrophe; because that's the way it was ordered and planned by those who clandestinely control the U.S. government. So that right there should let everybody in America know that you must be ready and able to help yourself because the government damn sure isn't going to do it. And as a dude I met named Little Torch from the Young Foundation in Long Beach, CA, used to say that's real talk. But remember one must stay positive no matter what, and one must not lose his or her will to do. Because these are just part of the trials, troubles, and pains manmade and natural coming on earth in these days and it's nothing but a natural cycle that happens every 26,000 years. But above all else if one is to make it through these extremely trying times it is imperative that one get in tune and stay in tune with his or her self. And if you would like to read more about the coming collapse and how those who clandestinely control the U.S. government are going to engineer it, then you must get the following book: One second After by William R. Forstchen or call 1-800-729-4131. And if you would like to learn how to survive the coming collapse then you must get the best survival guide that I ever read, that actually tells, and depicts, what to do in virtually any natural disaster that one can conceive of, topics include but are not limited to survival preparedness, self sufficiency, what to do even after nuclear disaster, how to find and store water, how to select emergency equipment, what food to store and how to store it. And believe me, much, much more, and the book is: The Sense of Survival, by J. Allen South, ISBN# 0-935329-01-3 . . . or go to www.survivalblog.com.

621. Did you know that the U.S. government surreptitiously can, and does, control the world's weather? And that they have been having weather modifying technology since the early 1960's when they were experimenting with it? Well I'm here to tell you that it's now long been perfected, and the U.S. government claims that it's only part of their military arsenal. And only to be used on an enemy, as a last resort tactic or weapon. But that's what they say, but we know better. We know that's a straight lie, because the U.S. government has been completely usurped by those who clandestinely control it. And their main concern right now is getting their new world order implemented. And they will and are going to use any, and all, there means to do so. So you best believe me, that their weather modification technology that they got will be used to that effect. And you the people will not know anything about it. If they have to create prolonged periods of drought, storms or whatever. You best believe me that they will, and the masses of people will not know anything about it, or what's really going on. The people will just think it's mother nature acting up again or something. Because right now as your reading this the U.S. government has weather modification technology so advanced that they can control weather virtually anywhere on the face of the earth for indeterminate periods of time. And I'm talking about able to create, and control, such things as storms, hurricanes, tornados, tsunamis, global warming, melt the polar caps, heat the oceans water, create earthquakes of any magnitude, control and interface with wild life migration patterns and these are only but a few of the things this technology is capable of. The technology is called the High Frequency Active Auroral Research Project . . . HAARP, for short. But if you would like to learn all about it then I suggest you get the following books: Weather Wars, and Unnatural Disasters, by Steven Quayle; and you can get it at (1-800-729-4131); and Angles Don't Play this HAARP, by Nick Begich and Jeane Manning, ISBN# 0-9648812-0. And check this out on a last note the U.S. government just recently brought their weather modification technology out of there super secret covert black operations, and if you don't know what black operations are, well black operations are operations with no congressional, judicial, or legislative oversight and that's

another whole subject there and I could literally write volumes on the government's nefarious surreptitious black operations. But like I just said the government just recently brought their weather modification technology out of there covert black operations and into the open and ostensible with the weather modification operation and research act that was passed into law on March 3, 2005, and is to become effective on October 1, 2005 and the bill # is X517 and what this bill establishes legally is the covert office somewhere deep in the pentagon of weather modification. And again they're saying that weather modification will only be used as a weapon or tactic of last resort on an enemy. But like I said previously we know better we know that the U.S. government has been using weather modification technology for the last 30 to 40 years. There just now for whatever reason or reasons making it overt and legal. And that hurricane Katrina that devastated Louisiana, Alabama, and Mississippi in late August of 2005 I have absolutely no doubt that it was manmade and caused to happen with HAARP or one of the many HAARP like systems under the order and control of those who clandestinely control the U.S. government. Why? Well first of all my sources tell me that Katrina was what they call a shock tester meaning it was an experiment and for various reasons, and one of the main reasons I'm told was to gauge the public's reaction as to whether this catastrophe was manmade or an act of nature. And further those who clandestinely control the U.S. government are trying and endeavoring to create a total and complete negative planet meaning they want the people thinking and putting out negativity by any and all means and as the people become scared, worried, and fearful, that's all negative energy of the first order and that's just what they want. So let's not fall for their tricks people because there full of them, and this is why I've belabored people throughout this book to stay positive, think positive, and to put out positive energy no matter what, because if not like I'm explaining and have explained in great detail then we are all doomed. And just so you know there's going to be many more manmade catastrophes like the 2005 hurricane Katrina in the coming future that's why it is so very pivotal that you the people know that these things are not acts of nature but are manmade concoctions devised to bring about great human suffering, and misery, so to cause enormous wide spread prevalent and palpable negativity. And like I just said having and making the people scared, worried, and fearful is all nothing but negativity. But there is hope and a way that we can turn all this negativity around and that's if we as a nation and a collective, stay positive think positive and incessantly put out positive energy via are thoughts and this is something that everyone and this is the best part of it can do in private and as many people don't know there are few things in the world more powerful than mass concentrated thought and this is in the negative or positive polarities meaning for good or for bad. But anyway now back to the weather modification and this is for those of you that like to research and substantiate what you read there was a great and all inclusive article on weather modification technology in the Boston Globe of July 3, 2005 in section K1 and it even speaks on the weather modification operation and research act that was passed into law on march 3, 2005 and it postulates that the U.S. government has been messing with and tinkering with weather modifying technology since 1951 it's a great article and a first of its kind that I done seen meaning for the exoteric and if you're interested in weather modifying technology I recommend you procure it and read it. And like I said a great book on this is Weather Wars and Unnatural Disasters by Steven Quayle and you can get it by calling 406-586-4848 or 1-800-729-4131 or at www.stevequayle.com and Steven Quayle has been researching and writing on topics like this for the last 35 years and has many other good books on these topics. So if you're seriously interested in this topic then I strongly suggest you go to www.stevequayle.com.

622. In this thought here I just want to say that thought, the power of thought, and consciousness, is just so powerful that it really is ineffable. And if I sat here trying to really, and actually, tell you how powerful, and or how much power there is in thought, and consciousness, I couldn't do it. Because the power of thought, and consciousness, is absolute, and completely ineffable and immeasurable please believe that. Now what I can do is give you a few factual examples of the power of thought, and consciousness, and the examples I'm about to give you have been proven and documented. Such as certain

mystics, and shamans, have been known to exhibit phenomenal powers by the power of thought, and consciousness, alone such as levitation, instantaneous healing, telepathy, telekinesis, remote viewing, remote influencing, bilocation, and de & rematerialization of objects, things, and themselves. Now please believe me I am not overestimating or being pretentious here. I have no reason to be. And let me if I can here use one of Oprah Winfrey's favorite statements, and or lines, and that's a side from everything else what do I know for sure, and I'm going to tell you like this what I know for absolutely sure and that's if I don't know nothing else and that's, that thought, the power of thought, and consciousness, are absolutely and for a certainty and this is without any doubt what so ever real . . . and that thoughts are things. And that people can project and put forth thoughts and thought energy and create anything, and please hear me here, that's anything that's capable of existing in the material physical sphere . . . that's what I absolutely without any doubt in my being know for sure. And people hear, and understand, me I'm not just talking form 2nd, or 3rd, hand accounts, or from anecdotal accounts, no I'm talking from first hand direct personal experience . . . see let tell you one of the main reasons why a lot of people fail to harness the power of thought to create, and or manifest, whatever there trying to create, and or manifest. And that's because if they project thought energy for a day, a week, a month, or even a year, and if what there endeavoring to create does not happen or manifest then they say damn this, this shit don't work . . . but that's the greatest mistake that one could ever make, and that's to lose all faith and give up. Because like I told you previously this is no quick fix it, or overnight scheme. And if that's what you were thinking or had in mind then you had better put this book down and go about your business. Because this is nothing less than a way of life and I don't say that lightly I mean every syllable of that. And I'm going to tell you from direct personal experience that one of the main keys to creating your own individualized reality via your thoughts in incessantness, and perseverance, there isn't no other way about it period . . . you must have the mind frame that you are going to project the thoughts, and thought energy with intense desire and feelings of what your endeavoring to create and that you will incessantly project this thought energy no matter what happens objectively, or overtly, and for however long it takes, if it has to be until the day you die, then so be it. This is your life and this is how you live period. But I do guarantee you this that if you do what I just said in the foregoing faithfully and long enough meaning that you persevere you will most definitely reap a great and most wonderful reward. See you have got to understand that creating your own reality via your thoughts is a skill and its just like anything else it has to be developed meaning it first has to be understood, then learned, then mastered . . . just like the shamans and mystics, who I just told you about who have the ability to make their thoughts manifest instantaneously into the physical, therefore being able to exhibit such extraordinary powers as levitation, telepathy, telekinesis, re & dematerialization, and many others . . . they have not just started last week, last month, or in the last few years creating there realities via their thoughts they have been doing it all most if not all of their lives so they are extremely proficient at it. Look let me tell you a little story and by the way this is a true story a few years back I and some friends were in L.A. in California at one of the modern esoteric schools in that area and while we were there a Tibetan lama was visiting the school and anyway to get to the point and make a long story short the lama actually and in real life levitated for us and I right after he did it went right up to him and asked him how did you do that?? And he seemed kind of surprised at my asking, and he said what do you mean how did I do that?? And I said yeah how did you do that? Bullshit he was going to tell me, and he just said he created a feeling and I said what kind of feeling and he said an intense feeling that's all. And he told me the main key to creating your reality via your thoughts and or making your thoughts manifest is feeling, you must feel it and when I say feel it you must visualize whatever your trying to create in your mind then you must actually feel with all the intensity you possess how it would feel to experience whatever your endeavoring to create via your thoughts. And the more you do this the faster will your thoughts become actual reality. And remember that you're not going to become proficient at creating your reality via your thoughts over night. But like I just told you creating your reality via your thoughts is a skill just like anything else that must be learned and developed then after continued practice will one be able to raise his or her intensity of thought feeling to the point of making his or her thoughts manifest in a reasonable short span of time. And believe me that if you keep at it you will soon be able to raise your intensity of thought feeling high enough to make your thoughts manifest instantaneously i.e. being able to levitate. Let me tell you what I do to raise and stimulate my intensity of thought feeling to high levels I use music and trust me it works excellent for me here's what I do I get a CD or a song that I like or that I can resonate with and I might play the CD or the song for hours at a time but while I'm playing it I'm putting out thought energy and visualizing what I'm endeavoring to create and the music raises, and stimulates, my intensity of thought feeling to phenomenal levels where sometimes when I'm really feeling it I'm all most in a trance like state and I'm going to tell you a few times while engaged in this and mine you want I'm about to impart to you has only happen maybe a dozen times to me and that's that while engaged in this exercise musing going and me vividly projecting thoughts of what I'm endeavoring to create I have reached such high levels of intensity of thought feeling that other people sometimes in adjacent rooms have come over to me and just stared at me and then when I stopped doing what I was doing and looked up at them and I say what's going on?? They say yeah what's going on? Are you all right? And I say yeah I'm all right what's going on? And they say damn you didn't feel it? That feeling? That feeling that was coming from this room? And it was emanating from you. I don't know what it was and I can't even begin to describe it but I felt it at the other end of the house what is it? It just felt like energy, or power it was extremely palpable I've never felt nothing like that, what was that? And I just say it was nothing, nothing, don't worry about it. And they look at me crazy . . . But I damn sure know what it was and like I said this has only happened to me no more then maybe 10 or 15 times. But in those few times is when I was able to raise my intensity of thought feeling to that phenomenal level or if not all the way there it was damn sure something close to that level of intensity of thought feeling that allows mystics and shamans, to levitate and exhibit other extraordinary powers at will just like the lama told me when he levitated that he just created a feeling . . . so yeah I said all that to say that music is a great stimulus to raise your intensity of thought feeling when your projecting your thoughts to create your reality . . . and I'm just going to say this have you ever heard of somebody in immediate grave danger and while there in the midst of that immediate grave danger there able to exhibit phenomenal powers or strength such as lifting cars, or trucks, or other inexplicable powers and then when there done people ask them how did you do that?? How did you lift that car like that? And the person says I don't know I just did it. Well I can tell you how they did it the immediate grave danger was the stimulus and stimulated in them that phenomenal level of intensity of thought feeling that allows mystics, and shamans, to levitate at will, and will alloy anybody else who can attain it the same phenomenal, and or extraordinary, powers . . . (smile) because that's a beautiful, and most wonderful, great thing . . . and before I bring this thought to an end let me convey something else to you that I feel is important that the Tibetan lama told me and that's that the impossible is nothing just like that and I of course asked him what did he mean and he said again that the impossible is nothing. And I said again that I didn't understand and he said that the impossible as I know it and conceive it is nothing and I said why is that? And he said didn't I know that there were powers and energies that supersede what I know and conceive to be impossible by millions of times to say the least. And that those powers and energies were absolutely available to me or to anyone for that matter who knew how to harness them. . . and then I asked him specifically what those powers, and energies, were and he said they were the powers, and energies, that made and hold the universe and everything in it in place they were the powers of thought . . . that was deep and I am not going to lie I was taken totally aback. That's deep just think about that for a min . . . and the lama went on and said yes the impossible is nothing and can easily be overtaken and overcame but not instantaneously as we westerners tend to think about everything that is if something can't be done quick or with haste then its useless or no good. And that's where we westerners go mostly wrong at and I had to concur with him there. But how the impossible is easily took down and overcame he said is through imperturbably intently focused felt thought meaning thought infused with intense desire and feeling. So the key to overcoming the impossible no matter of what degree as long as its capable of existing in the material physical sphere is like I just told you previously is being able to project thought with a phenomenal level of intensity and desire incessantly, and continuously until you reach your end or ends. That's it, that's the secret and for that method and or secret I speak from direct personal experience and that's the truth. I've employed it and please believe me by it I've overcame the impossible more than once . . . the only thing I'm going to tell you is that you must be able to persevere. Because I'm going to tell you and I again I speak from direct personal experience when I was projecting thought some years back to bring about and create some major things in my live and without no exaggeration these endeavors could easily be categorized as the impossible. Believe me there is inevitably going to be times where everything that could go wrong has went wrong, or will go wrong . . . believe that. And great abjection, and despondency, will set in and your having grave doubts about everything what you believe, what your trying to achieve, what you're doing, everything . . . but I'm here to tell you and that's a great benefit because I had no one to tell me that its natural and inevitable to go through them degenerate cycles . . . I mean everything in the universe is tested even gold is tested by fire and you must think why should you be any exception . . . but the thing is not to fail when your tested that's it and that's all. Because like I just said its natural and its inevitable you're going to be tested. And let me tell you why a lot of people fail and give up when there tested and that's because for some reason they think its just them that ever went through whatever their going through. But that's a straight uncut lie and untruth if I ever heard one . . . because like I just told you, you got a real benefit here that I didn't have and that's for somebody to tell you that its not going to be just all play and feel good and no hurt and hard work, bullshit you are going to be tested its both natural and inevitable. So like I been telling you creating your own reality via your thoughts Is a way of life and its nothing short of that. But let me tell you this if you do choose to hold fast to it, it's a most wonderful, wonderful, way of life words really, and actually lack the ability to describe and adequately convey the joy, all the joy, the pure joy, that comes with getting what you really want, and not just that but getting it so exact and right . . . and again I speak from actual experience I know the nirvana, the state of empyrean, the bliss, and all the joy, just indescribable joy of living this way of being able to create your own individualized reality via your thoughts . . . which is just such a beautiful thing, damn you have no idea this has got to be one of God's greatest gifts to us and just writing and thinking about this is starting to just fill me and overwhelm me with the joy my God. And this pen isn't doing me no good, because it can't help me to actually, and adequately, convey to you all the power and joy that can be yours if you choose only to live this way damn and that fucks me up so please let me just stop for a min. Alright I'm back I just had to take a quick break. But anyway before I bring this thought to a final close I want to convey one more thing to you and that is concerning all the programming, and conditioning, because most people have been programmed, and conditioned and therefore have been indoctrinated and brainwashed, all their lives by the educational system, the media, and mainstream society in general. So the majority of people's perception and belief of how reality comes into being and is manifested is grossly distorted to say the least. And when these people hear the word impossible or that something is impossible there whole body, mind, and soul, immediately says oh that cannot happen, but that's nothing but there lifelong programming and conditioning kicking in and you can't fault them for that because that's all they know. But I'm here to tell you that this kind of mainstream society type of programming, and conditioning, must be broken, and I say it again it must be broken before you can successfully begin to create your own reality via your thoughts . . . because let me tell you something you got to believe the impossible is nothing, and can be easily overcame before you can project any meaningful thought energy to that effect . . . do you feel me? Mainstream society has programmed, and conditioned, people to live in pygmy huts (and that's small) potential wise when in all actuality we can be and most definitely are giants potential wise. But people have no idea, and I say again have no idea what power they can possess through thought, and believing . . . but like I told you at the beginning of this thought, the power of thought and consciousness, is completely, and totally immeasurable, and ineffable, believe that . . . and there's really no known limit to it. Because the power of thought is very much able and capable of both overcoming, and surmounting, the impossible as well as creating the impossible for people and if you want to read about that, then you must get the book: Think and grow Rich, by Napoleon Hill. And I'm going to tell you like this it is one of the most inspirational books that I've ever read in my life . . . and that's no lie people . . . but once again and damn, I don't mean to belabor you with this but the programming, and conditioning, of the media, the educational system, and just main stream society as a whole with all of its dogmas, tenets, and beliefs, must be completely and totally repudiated from your belief system before you can successfully begin to create your own reality via your thoughts. And please believe me I cannot say that or stress that enough . . . and just thinking about all the bullshit, lies, trickery, deception, and manipulation, that's put out, and put forth, by the media, the educational system, and just mainstream society in general is starting to make me sick to my motherfucking stomach. And its not just the bullshit lies, trickery, deception, and manipulation, that they put out no, but its how they put it out that's so eternally sinister it's the hidden subliminal, and stratagems, it's the plausible fallacious lies, trickery, deception, and manipulation that they incessantly put out that is so deleterious to the people and the people have absolutely no idea what's being done and or has been done to them but how can they?? And as you read in this book some of the schemes, methods, and trickery, used by those who clandestinely control the U.S. government via the media, the educational system, and just all of the mainstream in general to keep you dumb, stupid, mislead, and basically keep you living in a pygmies hut potential wise. And these methods, schemes, and just basic trickery are so advanced, and highly sophisticated that the average everyday person has never heard of or thought in his or her wildest dreams that people could or would plot, and collude, to such degrees just to keep you the masses of people dumb, stupid, and basically mislead . . . but you better believe it cause its true. And this didn't just start going on or happening, no this surreptitious, control, and manipulation, of the people by those who clandestinely control the U.S. government has been going on for at least and this is at the minimum the last 100 years. That's why I said if you plan on having any real success on creating your own reality via your thoughts then it is imperative that you repudiate yourself from the programming, and conditioning, that the media, the educational system, and mainstream society in general has covertly inculcated in you. And before I actually, and literally, bring this thought to a close I just want to say that remember to effectively create your own reality via your thought you got to be able to focus and hold your concentration for extended periods of time. Just like I told you a few thoughts back that you got to be able to project, and hold, a thought frequency of what your endeavoring to create. And not just that but when your projecting your thought frequency to create whatever your endeavoring to create and your alone, in total solitude, and you got your music going or whatever to stimulate your intensity of thought feeling you don't want to be burdened with the mundane, and the exigencies, of life and you don't want to have things on your mind or things bothering you such as things that didn't go right, or your thinking about past transgressions, or misdeeds, that you might have engaged in or committed. You don't want none of that on your mind and believe me I speak from experience you want your mind free from all negativity, problems, worries, etc. etc. The only thing that you want on your mind is whatever your endeavoring to create via your thoughts . . . and I'm just going to say this and I'm done here if people and I'm not just talking about the people of this state, or that state, or of just America, but I'm talking about if all the people of the world would just adhere and implement the principals outlined in this book humanity as a whole could be exalted beyond their highest conceptions and not just that but the fulfillment of their loftiest dreams would be a reality . . . and for more information on how to create your own reality via your thoughts please go to the following excellent websites at: www.livingthefield.com and www.theintentionexperiment.com . . . and for those interested in the power of music to up lift consciousness then you must get: The Secret Power of Music, by David Tame . . . and after you get done reading that book you will never look at or think the same about music again . . .

623. So today his feet stand grounded in that place which yesterday when contemplating the august nature of the work, his eye could scarcely see . . .

--Isreal Regardie . . .

624. Times they are changing, and people better recognize, understand, and know it . . . and people please understand me I don't say that lightly . . . because the time that we are living in now the 1990s, and the years from 2000 to 2012, and especially the years from 2008 to 2012 are going to be the most pivotal years for humanity in the last 26,000 years please believe that. And just so you understand let me elaborate a little bit on what I'm talking about . . . ok all of creation is governed by cycles, the earth, and the rest of the planets circle or cycle the sun just like the sun cycles the center of the galaxy. And on a smaller level you see the seasons, spring, summer, autumn, and winter, are all nothing but cycles. But on a bigger level there are cycles that govern creation and the consciousness of humanity and these cycles were known and recorded in hieroglyphics, allegories, symbols, and in sacred writings by the ancients like the Sumerians, Egyptians, Hindus, Chinese, the Mayans of Central America, and the native Americans like the Hopi. And according to the ancients and many others every 26,000 years the cycle governing creation and the consciousness of humanity changes or shifts to a new cycle and at the shift or change of the old cycle to the new there is a phenomenal transformation, and uplifting, and rising, of human consciousness that those who clandestinely control the U.S. government know about but are relentlessly trying to suppress right now . . . and that is why I said that right now the 1990s and the years from 2000 to 2012 and especially the years from 2008 to 2012 are the most pivotal years for humanity in the last 26,000 years. And the ancients knew of these great cycles of change and studied them in depth and they all say that the date for the great shift of the cycles is December 21, 2012. And not just that but all the calendars of the ancients like the Egyptians, Mayans, Tibetans, Chinese, and others all end on December 21, 2012. And some of them calendars date back eons like the Egyptian calendar dates back some 39,000 years and the Mayan one dates back some 18,000 years. And the Mayans said that there would be a transition period between the old world and the new as a one version of time was replaced by another. They called this period of time the time of great transformation, and change, and said that it would start in July of 1982 and go on until the great shift on

December 21, 2012. And according to two scientists in the United States Terrance and Dennis McKenna who have extensively studied this great shifting of the cycles they say that the transformation, and change, has been and is showing itself in the speed of technological development, and advancement, that keeps on doubling and picking up pace in smaller, and smaller, time frames and will keep on doubling in even small, and smaller, time frames until the shifting of the cycles on December 21, 2012 . . . and not just that but Terrance and Dennis McKenna say that the years 2008 to 2012 are going to be the most pivotal years for humanity of all . . . now that's deep!! That's profound. I absolutely have no words for that . . . that's ineffable. And why they say that is because they say that the speed of transformation, and change, the speed at which consciousness will be uplifted and raised for all of humanity between the years of 2008 to 2012 will be absolutely phenomenal and not just that but check this out they say that in the 384 days leading right up to December 21, 2012 there will be more transformations, and changes, and uplifting, and raising, of human consciousness then in all the previous 26,000 years. Now I don't know how you're taking this but again that's deep. And if I can say anything to you on that all I can say is that, well this is the best and most wonderful time to be alive in the last 26,000 years. (Smile) And if that don't put a smile on your face then I don't know what will . . . and I'm not done but Terrance and Dennis McKenna go on to say that in the last six days of the 384 days leading up to December 21, 2012 there will be transformations, and changes, and upliftings, and raisings, of human consciousness that will move even faster than in the previous 378 days. And not just that but in the last 2 to 3 days to December 21, 2012 there will be enormous transformations, and changes of all kinds and phenomenal upliftings, and raisings of human consciousness that no one is even able to predict right now . . . and let me just say this everything that Terrance and Dennis McKenna have said here comes from their 30 plus years of scientific research into the great shifting of the cycles. And all this was told and known by the ancients, and mystics, and shamans, from all cultures who have been predicting and saying throughout the ages almost verbatim what Terrance and Dennis McKenna have said here.

So as transformation, and change, are now rapidly accelerating at a pace nothing like has been seen in the last 26,000 years . . . and human consciousness is being raised and uplifted at the same exponential pace people will begin to understand why things are moving so fast, and will continue to pick up pace until the great shifting of the cycles on December 21, 2012. And now if you remember I said a few thoughts back that time was and is now moving faster, and faster, until time will be moving so fast that people will literally be scared shitless . . . and this is also why I said that during this time of great change, and transformation, while everything is moving faster, and faster, people had better be and or get in tune with their selves, and slow down meaning find time for their selves in total solitude for them to think, meditate, and project the thoughts of what they're trying to do and or create in their life . . . and if not people will be in serious peril of getting caught up in the whirlpool of things moving faster, and faster, and will be out of sync with what's going on and then just to give it to you uncut this great and wonderful time that we are living in will be nothing but bad, and detrimental, to them and if they don't watch it there liable to go crazy point blank . . . but it does not have to be like that you can take full and unabridged advantage of this great and wonderful time of transformation, and change, and of raising, and uplifting consciousness for humanity . . . and let me just say this just in case you don't already know and that's that as the raising, and uplifting, of consciousness continues to pick up pace as it is, and will continue to do so until the great shifting of the cycles. Thoughts will begin to manifest in shorter, and shorter, time frames and that right there is just a beautiful and wonderful thing for those of us who know how to project thought to create our own realities. And that right there thoughts beginning to manifest in shorter, and shorter, and time frames is just one of the many auspicious elements of this most pivotal time that we are now living in. So people hear me and hear me well wake up and take full advantage of this most wonderful time that we are now in. And if you need a little help use this book and the principals that it imparts as a guide and you best believe me that you'll be alright . . . see the times that we are now living in are not end times. Its not about to be the end of the world like some so naïve people think its not about to be Armageddon. The times that we are now living in these are the times of great transformation and change, and that is why it seems that things are in all a state of chaos, and discord, because everything is in and going through a state of transition and change right now. But like I said previously and so many others who came eons before me have said and predicted that this time right now is the best time in the last 26,000 years to live and or be alive in. And let me elaborate a little on that. The time that we are now living in has so many advantages and so much potential for people to create via their thoughts whatever they so desire for themselves that for people not to take advantage of this they be utter fools. I mean the ancients and mystics, and shamans, from all cultures around the world and anybody else who knew the truth about life, nature, and the universe has been predicting this time that we are now living in for centuries. And I don't know if you really understand or really feel me on the profoundness of what I'm trying to convey to you here. Let me put it to you this way the basic energies that hold manifested creation in place are now being poured out on all of humanity!! Now do you understand me!! Now you understand the profoundness of what I'm trying to convey to you here . . . the energies that hold manifested creation in place are the most subtle, and powerful, energies that exist in the material physical sphere and they are now at this time being poured out on us humanity to a degree and in measures not known or seen in 26,000 years now that's deep. Sit back, stop reading, and meditate on that for a min. Alright now that your back I hope what you just read gave you an epiphany of the potentials of the time that you're now living in. This is the time of unlimited creation, enlightenment, and personal and spiritual ascension for those who are ready for it and who want it. There has been no better time in 26,000 years then now to be alive in . . . and as a human consciousness and the energies that hold manifested creation in place, quicken and sharpen and increase. Synchronicities will become more, and more, common place and people will experience them more, and more and if you didn't know synchronicities are nothing but thought attracting to it self and manifesting . . . so like I said people this is a great time to be alive and there has not been a time with so much potential for change, creation, uplifting, enlightenment, building, and just doing then this in 26,000 years. So my sincere hope is that you get in tune with yourself and in sync with what is going on and take full advantage of this most wonderful, and great, time that we are now living in. And the raising and uplifting of consciousness that has been going on since like 1982 is synonymous with the spiritual awaking that people have been feeling for the last 15 to 20 years and just like everything else is quickening and picking up momentum by the day. This spiritual awaking that I'm speaking on everybody that has been alive in the last 15 to 20 years and or is alive right now has been feeling it and this is whether they are, or were aware, of it or not . . . and you best believe me that those who clandestinely control the U.S. government are well aware of and absolutely know all about this spiritual awaking aka raising, and uplifting, of consciousness that is now and has been since like 1982 being conveyed on humanity . . . and they those that clandestinely control the U.S. government are now and have been for like the last 20 some odd years been relentlessly trying to thwart and suppress via all their power, resources, tricks, and tactics, this most wonderful spiritual awaking and raising, and uplifting, of human consciousness. But I'm going to tell you something and please understand and hear me. Because of the quickening of everything and the raising, and uplifting, of human consciousness those that clandestinely control the U.S. government have never been at a more vulnerable point then now . . . and they know it. And I'm telling you that if humanity or if the people come together as a collective and project those positive thoughts to remove those that clandestinely control the U.S. government from power we the people will be victorious believe that, if we can get enough people to project the positive thoughts of getting rid of these idiots meaning get enough people to reach a critical mass in the mass consciousness we will be victorious. Because that is just what they are doing right now, and have been doing for years now. And that's relentlessly endeavoring to get the people to think and project negative thoughts of all and any kind so they can reach a negative critical mass in the mass consciousness and therefore create a total and complete negative planet and solidify their position, and power, and control, for who knows how long? Probably another 26,000 years?? So do you understand that the stakes right now for you, your posterity and humanity as a whole are not just high they are immense and trust me that's even an understatement. And let me tell you something else that was disclosed to me by a contact that's highly placed in the intelligence community. And what I'm about to impart should help you to comprehend and understand the seriousness and how adamant those who clandestinely control the U.S. government are to get people to think and or project negative thoughts, and thought energy, so they can reach a negative critical mass in the mass consciousness and therefore they can create a total and complete negative planet. And like I told you solidify their power and control over humanity . . . alright what was disclosed to me by this highly placed intelligence operative was that for like the last 20 or so years those that clandestinely control the U.S. government have had their own highly trained mystics, psychics, intuitives, and sensitives, think and project nothing but highly malevolent, and negative thought and thought energy to North America and virtually the world. And these mystics, psychics, intuitive, and sensitives are like I said highly trained in all orders of the occult and the esoteric, so they know how to project thought and thought energy and they work in shifts so this extremely malevolent and negative thought energy is being projected and disseminated to us 24 hours a day, 7 days, a week nonstop . . . but like I said this just goes to show and illustrate how serious, relentless, and adamant, those who clandestinely control the U.S. government are about creating, and getting a negative critical mass in the mass consciousness. Nah they aren't playing, believe that. Nor should we be playing either about getting a positive critical mass in the mass consciousness and therefore removing and getting rid of those that clandestinely control the U.S. government . . . and as you know in previous thoughts I've disclosed some of the other trickery that those who clandestinely control the U.S. government are now using (via highly sophisticated technology) to get the masses of people to think and project negative thoughts, and thought energy . . . and as I bring this thought to a close I just want to say this, during these times of great transformation, and change, you will see major earth changes and erratic weather patterns as never before. And add to that the extremely advanced weather modifying technology that those who clandestinely control the U.S. government have.

And the earth's geomagnetic field is dropping at an alarming rate and according to published reports of the U.S. geological service will soon reach zero . . . the field is now 50% less powerful then it was 1,500 years ago and the speed of this fall is increasing very quickly . . . and this abatement in the earth's magnetic field is the real reason for global warming not all that bullshit they put out in the mainstream media such as a carbon monoxide, and emissions, and all that other bullshit they blame global warming on . . . that's all bullshit of the first order. Because as the planets magnetic field slows the planet rotates slower, and slower, and that causes the planet to heat up from within . . . and this is not just happening to our planet right now but is happening to all the planets in our solar system at this time. And its nothing but part of the great shifting of the cycles. And before I go I'm going to tell you this there have been for a number of years now some major geophysical changes and events that have been happening and taking place but have been subjected to a well orchestrated media blackout . . . so I'm just going to tell you like old Art Bell on the Coast to Coast Radio Talk Show used to say – you want to go for a ride cause you best believe me in these years from 2008 to 2012 we are in for one hellava, hellava, ride! And for more on this 2012, and the great shifting of the cycles you must get the following books: The Biggest Secret by David Icke and go to chapter twenty . . . or the Galactic Alignment by John Major Jenkins or go to www.divinecosmos.com or www.portal2012.org. And a couple other good books on this are: The Mayan Code by Barbara Hand Clow . . . and the Mayan Calendar and the Transformation of Consciousness by Carl Johan Calleman Ph.D. available at www.amazon.com or by calling 1-800-246-8648 . . .

625. Always remember that one of the most deleterious effects of the news, the mainstream press, and the rest of the outlets of public information is there constant barrage of negativity . . . meaning and please pay attention and read carefully here because this is pivotal. All that they tend to put out or let me be precise about 75% to 80% of what they put out is straight negativity or disempowering in some way, form, or fashion, again meaning they got (and they encourage and look for these stories) nothing but copious disasters, upheavals, tragedies, and

other people in hopeless or destitute situations being promulgated . . . and I mean all these things are true indeed. But please believe me that's not all that's' going on. There's a whole, whole lot more going on in the world that the media and the mainstream press does not bother to speak on. Why because there not suppose to, that's why. The controllers know all too well that if they constantly feed people negativity, hopelessness, and destitute situations via all the outlets of public information (which they all own and control) the pliant and docile masses of people will in no time come to believe that this is all there is to life, and inevitability will come to thinking negative, and hopeless, and destitute thoughts about themselves and their lives which will most definitely become there manifested realities . . . the controllers know this to be true. Now this book is the diametric opposite of what the mainstream in all its facets put out. And please believe me there's a whole lot of positivity in the world and miracles and the miraculous does happen more than you think or are ever told by the mainstream . . . and not just that but there's a whole other world, or order of things that I guarantee you that if you been getting your information from the mainstream outlets of information you know nothing about. And this other order that I speak of is a completely different paradigm from all the things you have been fed, and conditioned, and programmed, to believe all your life via the mainstream . . . such things as the cures for cancer and that's plural because there have been numerous developed in the last 100 years. And free energy machines, anti-gravity propulsion systems, carburetors and fuel systems that get a 100 miles a gallon and this is as far back as the 1930s so this is nothing new. And for more on that high mileage carburetors specifically you got to check out: The Works of George Arlington Moore, published by the Madison Co. But what I'm trying to tell you is that there is a whole other order of things that exist that have been systematically suppressed by orthodox science and medicine and just the mainstream as a whole. That you know nothing about and this book here that your reading and all the books it makes reference to are devoted to awakening you, and enlightening you to this other order of things that have been suppressed. And if you don't believe me about the cancer cures, the free energy machines, the anti-gravity propulsion systems, and all the other phenomenal technologies and inventions that have been suppressed then I strongly suggest that you get the highly informative and detailed book: Suppressed Inventions and Other Discoveries, by: Jonathan Eisen. And if you're into the suppressed cancer cures and all the other stuff I just named then this book is for you. Its 550 pages of highly detailed and sourced information that can be checked out via the internet or public or private records. And remember the more mainstream information you take in the more disempowered you'll become . . .

626. Always remember that consistency is mostly an illusion --- why? Because each passing day brings changes within you – and you must not be afraid to express these evolutions -----

627. Always remember that having an absolutely unshakeable belief, and supreme confidence, makes you fearless, and persistent, allowing you to overcome great obstacles that stop most people in their tracks . . . .

628. Always remember that this book is a systematic yet consistent, although flexible, assault on the specific conditioned reflex that which compels people to look outside themselves. To their leaders, elected representatives, or governments, for direction, help, or strength . . .

629. Always remember that there is no guide superior to pure and uncut reason . . .

630. In modern usage, opportunist is generally a derogatory term that refers to people who will do anything for themselves. They have no core values beyond promoting their own needs . . . they contribute nothing to society, this however is a misreading of the phenomenon and stems from an age-old elitism that wants to see opportunities kept as privileges for a powerful few. Those from the bottom who dare to promote themselves in any way are seen as Machiavellian while those already on the top who practice the same strategies are merely smart and resourceful . . . opportunism is in fact a great art that was studied and practiced by many ancient cultures . . . the greatest ancient Greek hero of them all, Odysseus. Was a supreme

opportunist. The Greeks venerated him as one who had mastered life's shifting circumstances . . . in their value system, rigid, ideological people who cannot adapt. Who miss all opportunities, are the ones who deserve our score – they inhibit progress . . .

--The 50th Law

By 50 Cent and Robert Greene

631. Always remember a monopoly on the means of communication may define a ruling elite more precisely than the celebrated Marxian formula of a monopoly on the means of production . . . since man extends his nervous system through channels of communication like magazines, newspapers, the T.V., and the media as a whole – so, he who controls these mediums controls part of the nervous system of every member of society – because the contents of these mediums become part of the contents of every individuals brain.

632. Always remember that in a busy, dynamic, and fluctuating universe such as ours where no two snowflakes are identical, and no two trees are identical, and no two people are identical, and indeed, even the smallest subatomic particle. We are assured, is not even identical with itself from one microsecond to the next, so therefore meaning that most categorical card-index systems of classifications that people subjectively hold to be true are nothing but self delusions for example he is a doctor, he is a rapper, he is a poet, or he is black, white, or Jewish mean to the categorical classification holders that my experience with him will be just like my experience with other doctors, rappers, poets, blacks, whites, or Jews – which is wrong and therefore negates all individuality.

633. All powers not delegated to the United States by the Constitution, nor prohibited by it to the states, are reserved to the states or to the peoples . . . to take a single step beyond the boundaries thus specially drawn around the powers of congress, is to take possession of a boundless field of power, no longer susceptible to any definition –

--Thomas Jefferson

1743 – 1826

634. Man has the right to live by his own law, to live in the way that he wills to do, to work as he will, to play as he will, to rest as he will, to die when and how he will, he has the right to eat what he will, to drink what he will, to move as he will on the face of the earth . . . man has the right to think what he will, to speak what he will, to write what he will, to draw, paint, carve, etch, mold, build, as he will, to dress as he will – to love and hate as he will – and last but not least man as a divine and sovereign being created by God has a right to kill those who thwart these rights.

--The Equinox: A Journey of

Scientific Illuminism,

1922 . . . Edited by

Aleister Crowley . . . .

635. Always remember that people exist on a spectrum from the most redundant to the most flexible . . . the latter, unless they are thoroughly trained in psychodynamics, are always at a disadvantage to the former in social interactions – the redundant do not change their script. The flexible continually keep changing, trying to find a way of relating constructively – eventually, the flexible ones find the proper gambit, and communication, of a sort, is possible . . . . they are now on the set created by the redundant person, and they act out his or her script, the steady exponential growth of bureaucracy is not due to Parkinson's law alone, the state, by making itself ever more redundant, incorporates more and more people into it's set and forces them to follow it's script.

636. Isn't it ironic that no one ever goes to jail for waging wars, let along advocating them? But the jails are full of people who protest war or peaceful protesters, i.e. the Occupy Movement peaceful protesters who are now in 2011 & 2012 being jailed across America – just think about that for a second –

Thoughts on Life And the Absolute Power of Thought

637. Life is short, break the rules, 4 give quickly, and love truly –

--Pop-Star & Movie Icon

Jennifer Lopez

638. Most people can't handle boredom. That means they can't stay on one thing until they get good at it . . . and they wonder why they aren't got nothing or are unhappy . . .

--Rapper 50 Cent

639. Always remember that deep and meaningful relationships are most definitely a pivotal part of life . . .

640. Always remember what's more important than truth . . . !!! Now no matter how you answered that in the end you will still only have the truth . . . and that's regardless if you know it, believe it, or even understand it. So he who has eyes, let him read and understand.

641. Nor let him despair though he take and make many false steps. For the greatest philosophers have learned most by their mistakes.

--The Metamorphosis of Metals

By: Elranaeus Philaethes

1694 A.D.

642. Always remember that politicians are not chosen for virtue. But for their skill at playing roles . . . their like actors in movies . . .

643. Events are precipitated in the world at a terrifying speed: quarrels, wars, rumors, famines, epidemics, earthquakes, --- everything which even yesterday was impossible today is an accomplished fact –

--Serge Nilus in his book

The Anti-Christ Is At Hand

644. Until archaeological advances beginning in the 19th century, virtually everything we knew about life came from the Bible filtered through the church priesthood . . .

--Jim Marrs

Author of the Best seller:

Ruled By Secrecy

645. If man is the great miracle mentioned by Hermes Trismegistos, then the discovery of his own inner powers will turn him into a god . . .

--Giordano Bruno

646. Always remember that all the success in the world, without somebody to share it with is nothing . . .

647. Always remember that it was once said that life is problems – but just think what would life be without them? Yes boring, very boring. And extremely unedifying and you got to remember that we over here in the west tend to become so embroiled in our problems, worries, & mishaps that we lose all focus of our true and real aims whatever they may be – then our problems, worries, and mishaps instead of being puzzle that we're to figure out totally consume us . . . which is not how it's supposed to be – because your problems, worries, & mishaps are puzzles that are to be figured & worked out by a completely objective mind – and you never want to cease putting out that thought energy of what you would rather be experiencing. Always remember that one of the first and most basic prerequisites to waking up from the state of programming, conditioning, and just plain indoctrination that has been inculcated in us by the media, academia, and the main stream as a whole is, and this may be completely contrary to what you've been taught all your life but is never the less true – and that's to learn how to doubt everything – why? Because everything no matter what it is must be tested before given validity and this is not negative, or wrong, in no kind of way as the mainstream, the

media, and academia would like you to believe it is only using your God given critical reasoning faculties – of which is so sad to say have been put to sleep in the vast majority of the people. And this is why the people are so docile and accept and believe whatever their fucking told by the media, the main stream, and academia as true – wake up people and start using your mind and the reasoning features God gave you – or if not you can continue in your zombie state – but remember the first step to waking up, and to enlightenment, is learning how to doubt everything without exception before giving it validity.

648. Now in this thought let me just say this if you're looking for a quick fix it remedy or scheme to your life and your problems you might as well go head and beat the traffic and put this book down now . . . and that's real talk. Because this book is the diametric opposite to any quick fix remedy or scheme. This book lies down and outlines principals that if sincerely adhered to and made into a way of life can and will bring one great wealth, happiness, joy and abundance. Now the core of these principals are believing and thought projecting meaning that you absolutely in the depths of your heart and soul believe that you can get, achieve, or do, whatever you're endeavoring. Then one must constantly project and put those thoughts out and it must become a burning obsession and a way of life. Now either one of two things are going to happen when you sincerely adhere to this book you are either going to die first and that's going to be that with that or what you are endeavoring to achieve or do is going to come to pass. Only one of the two is going to happen once this becomes a way of life. This is why I said this book is the diametric opposite of a quick fix it remedy or scheme. But I'll say this and I speak from vast personal experience in this way of life of believing and thought projection and that's that I've never known somebody to sincerely believe and to incessantly project those thoughts without due regard to how it was going to happen but just knowing that it was going to happen and not be successful within an average time of 5 years. And that comes from direct empirical and anecdotal data so it's basically unimpugnable. Now when I said that believing and thought projection are a way of life I actually and really mean that that's how you live

your life by sincerely and in the depths of your heart and soul believing in the success of whatever you're trying to achieve or do, and then incessantly projecting the completed successful outcome in thought until it actually comes to pass. Now I must warn you thoughts are tricky but as you're consciously creating your reality via your thoughts you'll learn the ins and outs of consciously creating your reality. And if you're a neophyte at this I say with all the empathy that I'm capable of that when things seem not to go your way and you know that you have sincerely been believing and incessantly putting out that thought energy and you start to honestly believe that all this stuff about creating your own reality via your thoughts is hogwash now listen to me, and please listen to me well I've been there, and still at this stage sometimes end up there. But I'm here to tell you that when you honestly and sincerely in the depths of your soul get to that state and really feel all this create your own reality via your thoughts is bullshit you must express those thoughts and actually project them and I know that seems opposite to what I've been telling you all along but all I know is that it's true when you honestly and sincerely hit the aftermentioned stage of dejection you must sincerely express and project those thoughts and after a while I absolutely guarantee that you'll see changes in whatever you're endeavoring that will make you change back to that good positive mode. Now what I just exposed is some of the Arcanum of thought manifestation and projection and I exposed it so when the neophyte hits that dejection stage he or she will not get discouraged they'll know to just go head and express and project those dejected feelings.

649. Did you know that the mental activities and thoughts of most people are scattered like spray though out the day. And that's not good. Because the true thinker realizes that his mind is capable of fatigue. And while this fatigue may not be apparent in the grosser activities it precludes the possibility of exactness in fine thinking. But back to people's thoughts and mental energies being scattered like spray throughout the day. I'm just going to say this the mental faculties, and energies, (thoughts when properly focused can and will give expression to potentials never dreamed of).

650. Did you know that it's been said that the faculty of sustained focused concentrated thought is the least developed faculty of the American people.

651. Remember the lawmakers don't control the people, but the ones who control the money which is those who clandestinely control the lawmakers and the people alike. Just like M.A. Rothschild said: "Give me control over a nation's currency, and I care not who make its laws."

--Mayer Amschel Rothschild

1743 – 1812

652. Well as this being one of the last thoughts in this book, and I sincerely and truly hope that you enjoyed it. And that is has awakened and enlightened you in many more ways than one. And if this book has had a profound and positive impact on you and your life, then please pass it on and share it with a friend. And if not then again please disregard everything that you read. But if this book has had a positive impact on your life than I want to disclose a radio program that comes on all across America and whether you believe it or not is the number one rated late night talk show in the world. And it comes on over 500 stations not only nationwide but worldwide. And I don't care what city or locality you're in. In America this radio program that I'm talking about is syndicated in your area somewhere on the AM-dial at 10:00 pm Pacific Time. Now the radio program that I'm talking about is called Coast to Coast AM and if you would like to know what stations it comes on in your area then all you go to do is go to www.coasttocoastam.com. And please believe me if this radio program was not worth mentioning I would not be mentioning it. But it Coast to Coast is most definitely worth mentioning and if you liked and enjoyed the topics in this book then Coast to Coast is the place for you. Believe me you'll love it. All the topics that I spoke on in this book they speak on them every night live for 4 hours from 10:00 to 2:00 am 7 days a week, uncut no bullshit straight live talk. Like I said there not the number one rated late night talk show in the world for nothing.

Folks get up on it. This is real. Like I said if you liked and or enjoyed the topics in this book, then you'll absolutely love Coast To Coast please believe that. And if for whatever reason or reasons you don't have a computer or access to one then all you got to do is at 10:00 pm Pacific Time turn your radio on and carefully scan your AM dial and I guarantee that you'll find Coast to Coast.

Sources and Additional Help

1. www.infowars.com all about those who clandestinely control the U.S. government

2. www.radioliberty.com all about real and uncut news . . .

3. www.nomorefakenews.com all about real and uncut news . . .

4. www.spychips.com all about RF receivers

5. www.defruadingamerica.com all about the CIA and government corruption

6. www.davidicke.com all about those who clandestinely control the U.S. government

7. www.nohoax.com all about books on these subjects

8. www.911inplanesite.com the truth about 911

9. www.willthomsonline.net about how cell phones can cause cancer

10. www.starfire.com talking about time shifts

11. www.projectpegasus.net talking about teleportation

12. www.divinecosmos.com talking about 2012

13. www.expansions.com talking about the Rothschilds and all kinds of good shit

14. www.theintentionexperiment.com talking about thoughts

15. www.livingthefield.com talking about thoughts

16. www.stevequaly.com all about weather modification and other related topics

17. www.flouridealert.org how fluoride in our drinking water is killing us

18. www.ghostcop.com is a renown spiritual median who does personal readings

19. www.naturalnews.com the best website you'll ever go to for your health, food, and the truth about FDA

20. www.republicfortheunitedstates.org the sovereignty of America website

21. www.joshuapwarren.com a paranormal investigator who sells 3rd genrtsyion goggles that allow you to see into the supernatural realms

22. www.whowhatwhy.com a governmental corruption website

23. www.myheartbook.com if your into rejuvenating your body, your heart, your limbs, or other organs with stem cells then you need to hit this site

24. www.visionquest.com all about thoughts and consciousness

25. www.worldhealthnation.com if you got cancer or are dealing with cancer close to home you might want to hit this site

26. www.henrygrovers.com is a video of the coming collapse

27. www.earthfiles.com is all about aliens, ET's, and real life high strangeness

28. www.illumniatiplayingcard.com is a picture of America as the controllers plan

29. www.jimmarrs.com is about those who clandestinely control the U.S. government

30. www.responsibletechnology.org all about genetically modified food

31. www.celllevelhealing.com all about naturals energy healing

32. www.modernmiltia.com for anyone who believes that the constitution is the supreme law of the land…and would not mind defending it, then this site is for you.

CPSIA information can be obtained at www.ICGtesting.com
Printed in the USA
LVOW06s1526281215

468117LV00012B/1249/P